# EMF
# PRACTICAL GUIDE

The Simple Science of Protecting Yourself, Healing Chronic Inflammation, and Living a Naturally Healthy Life in our Toxic Electromagnetic World.

Lloyd Burrell

**EMF Practical Guide:** The Simple Science of Protecting Yourself, Healing Chronic Inflammation, and Living a Naturally Healthy Life in our Toxic Electromagnetic World.



ISBN (Web): 978-29-57080-51-9
ISBN (Paperback): 978-29-57080-52-6
ISBN (E-Book): 978-29-57080-50-2

Published By:
ElectricSense
132 Avenue de Rochefort
17200 Royan
France

https://www.electricsense.com

All the stories and testimonials in this guide are real but the names of certain individuals have been changed to respect their anonymity.

Technology changes quickly, so I've put together a resource guide on my website for book buyers that will stay updated which you can find here:

www.electricsense.com/bookbonus

The statements made in this guide have not been evaluated by the United States Food and Drug Administration. This guide is not intended to diagnose, treat, cure, or prevent any disease. Affiliate disclosure: if you visit some of the websites in this guide and its bonuses and purchase recommended products, we may receive monetary compensation via an affiliate commission. We only recommend products we believe in.



The ideas, procedures, and suggestions contained in this book are not intended to replace a one-on-one relationship with a qualified healthcare professional and are not intended as medical advice. Always consult a knowledgeable medical professional about your symptoms. The author encourages you to make your own health care decisions based upon your research and in partnership with a qualified health care professional.

While every care has been taken to ensure the accuracy of the information contained on these pages, neither the author nor the publisher is responsible for any errors or omissions. The Internet addresses shown in this guide were accurate at the time of publication; neither the author nor the publisher is responsible for errors, or for changes that occur after publication. Neither the author nor publisher has any control and does not assume any responsibility for author or third-party websites or their content.

# Praise For EMF Practical Guide

This book is so important, it will provide you with much of the practical information that you will need to protect yourself and your family from the progressively increasing EMF exposures that all of us will have once 5G and satellite internet is fully implemented. Lloyd does an excellent job of reviewing this important topic in simple easy to understand language and I am grateful for his contribution to helping us all understand the extent of this issue.

**Dr. Joseph Mercola, Founder of Mercola.com**

This book offers the full range of current thinking on EMF dangers and protections. Alongside the latest devices and approaches to EMF reduction, Burrell offers a comprehensive list of protective strategies from nature herself, how we can become better protected from within, a rare contribution to the frenzied debate around EMFs. Worthy of special note: his inclusion of water as an important feature in buffering and balancing EMF impacts.

**Gina Bria, Founder and Head of Hydration Foundation**

Lloyd Burrell does a wonderful job in presenting everything you need to know about the shadow side of the wireless world. His practical solutions and insights will benefit every man, woman, and child on the planet in our increasingly EMF ridden world. THIS is the resource the whole planet needs today.

**Ann Louise Gittleman, PhD, CNS**

If I had to choose just one book to recommend as a primer on the health effects of EMF (from house wiring, appliances, etc.) and microwaves (from mobile phones, WiFi, etc.) exposure on health, then it would be this one. An interesting, concerning and yet very helpful guide on how and why to protect yourself and the people you love.

**Alasdair Philips, Director of Powerwatch UK**

EMF Practical Guide offers a refreshingly balanced and accurate perspective on EMFs – what they are, and what you can do about it. Lloyd's new book is practical, concise, and yet easy to read and use. I highly recommend this book to anyone who is concerned about electromagnetic fields and their health.

**Michael R Neuert, MA, BSME, EMF Engineering Consultant, www.EMFCenter.com**

Everyone needs to read this book to gain knowledge on how to protect yourself during a time of high environmental toxicity. This is full of information on how to change your life, gain your power and health during a challenging time. I highly recommend you read this if you are suffering from EMF sensitivity or want to avoid it.

**Emma Jones Phillips, Naturopath and Founder of the School of Naturopathic Nutrition**

Lloyd's work has directly impacted my own life. His work is thoroughly grounded in science and his determination to help others to navigate this EMF soup we have created for ourselves deserves the highest respect and admiration. I highly recommend this book.

**Garrett L. Smith NMD CSCS BS**

The EMF Practical Guide by Lloyd Burrell is a very readable, comprehensive and completing summary of what are the known and suspected effects of electromagnetic fields on humans, animals and nature. This Guide provides a wealth of information not only on the hazards, but also on how to measure EMFs and how to take steps to reduce exposure and protect your health.

**David O. Carpenter, M.D. Director, Institute for Health and the Environment, University at Albany**

Lloyd Burrell has written a comprehensive guide for those who are electrically sensitive and non-sensitive alike to learn how to navigate this complex and often misunderstood topic. Lloyd has put a tremendous amount of knowledge into an easy to read and well-organized book where you can easily access tips on how to cope with EMFs. This is a welcome resource on a complicated subject.

**Oram Miller, BBEC, EMRS, Director of Learning and Development for the Building Biology Institute (BBI), CreateHealthyHomes.com**

Lloyd has interviewed everyone on the who-is-who list of electromagnetic fields and health. His new book is full of eye-openers and practical tips to protect yourself, with a 5G chapter as a bonus. It's your chance to learn a lot about the asbestos of the 21st century, from someone who has personally experienced it.

**Jan-Rutger Schrader, PhD**

The clarity of Lloyd Burrell's book is obvious to anyone in the field, and the pieces of advice are easy to follow, and simple to adopt to any given situation. To spend money on his book is to spend money on your immediate health and well-being. I definitely recommend it, and I tell you: you will not be sorry.

**Olle Johansson, PhD, Associate Professor Karolinska Institute (retired)**

The EMF Practical Guide is a tour de force! This well-researched, and well-communicated, guide offers just what the public needs to learn about how to live more safety in a wireless world (until we come to our senses and return to hard wired telecommunications). Comprehensive, accessible, substantive. Highly recommend.

**Camilla Rees, MBA, Award Winning Health and Environmental Activist on the Biological and Health Effects of Electromagnetic Fields and Senior Policy Advisor, National Institute for Science, Law, and Public Policy**

Lloyd has shown that becoming ES you do not have to become a victim. He has provided a wonderful outlet through his work to show that ES sufferers can provide a critical service to the world that is still waiting to know if microwave technology is safe.

Providing peer reviewed science, personal experience and the dovetailing of the two shows a powerful testimony to the dangers of microwaves and the coverup that industry, and governments, who have a conflict of interest, do not want the population to know. Read this book, take action and you can prolong the lives of your family in good health.

**Brian Stein CBE, Chairman of the Radiation Research Trust and Trustee for the Charity ElectroSensitivity UK**

Lloyd Burrell has crafted a cutting-edge survival guide for a wireless world. Thoroughly researched and easy to digest, he brings clarity to the many issues associated with manmade electromagnetic fields (EMFs). Follow this book and you will benefit from his own expertise as well as the knowledge of over 200 specialists. The EMF Practical Guide is an essential read for anyone serious about being truly healthy in the 21st Century.

**Dr. Ian Tennant, Author of Restoring Balance**

Rarely has there been a book so comprehensive in scope, and yet so understandable and practical. This book is a home run for anyone who is ready to take control of their exposure to harmful electromagnetic radiation. Lloyd provides many "nearly free and easy" solutions which are measurable and verifiable.

**Bill Cadwallader, Certified Electromagnetic Radiation Specialist**

# Contents

# Acknowledgements

THE SEED OF THE IDEA to write this book came from my website visitors, customers and subscribers, who for years have been asking me to write an actual book. So thank you all for your persistent reminders.

My friend, coach and mentor, Terry Dean, who's guiding mantra throughout has been "keep it simple, Lloyd." Thank you, Terry, for helping me do just that.

Thank you also to the 150+ EMF consultants, Building Biologists, medical doctors, naturopaths, scientists, researchers, authors and truth seekers I have had the pleasure of interviewing on my podcast and at the EMF Health Summit, who provided much of the raw material laid out on these pages.

Special thanks to Dr Joseph Mercola, Oram Miller, Jan-Rutger Schrader PhD, Michael Neuert, Alasdair Philips, Walter McGinnis, David Getoff, Gaetan Chevalier PhD and Gina Bria, who generously provided precious input in their various areas of technical expertise.

Particular thanks to my wife and family for their tolerance and patience through this writing marathon, for whom I've had little time. I promise now to be more reasonable. Lastly, thanks to my daughter Tabatha, for stepping in at the last minute and helping me with the final edits. You are my knight in shining armor.

# Foreword

FOR MANY DECADES IN THE mid-twentieth century, cigarette smoking was common practice. People smoked at home, work and school, while eating at restaurants, driving in cars, and flying on planes. A pack of cigarettes was proudly displayed in most men's shirt pockets and lay nestled women's purses.

Fast forward to the present. Smoking is outlawed in nearly all public spaces and tobacco use has greatly declined. But cigarettes were such a mainstay of daily life and communal culture throughout the world that it was difficult to imagine things any other way.

We know now that the tobacco industry became aware of the disastrous health effects of smoking in the 1950s, yet it hid the accumulating evidence from the public, whom it relied on to buy its products. For decades, the public was blatantly lied to about the safety of cigarettes. It wasn't until a few brave whistleblowers brought the hidden research and manipulative industry tactics to light that our government began taking steps to reduce dependence on tobacco products. But hundreds of millions of lives worldwide were likely prematurely lost in those intervening years.

As the calendar turned over to the twenty-first century, something began replacing all those packs of cigarettes in shirt pockets and purses: cell phones. In the two decades since the turn of the millennium, these communication devices that were once a novelty have become an inescapable part of modern life.

Sadly, smoking and cell phones have more in common than their popularity. They also share the fact that they are each an enormous threat to individual and public health. The danger of cell phones doesn't come from the cell phones themselves, but from the electromagnetic fields (otherwise known as EMFs) your cell phone—and other electronic devices that communicate wirelessly—use to function.

EMFs are invisible to your eyes and exist in a spectrum of frequencies that include radio and TV waves, microwaves, visible light, ultraviolet light, X-rays, and radioactive elements. Some sources of EMFs are natural, such as sunlight, while others are man-made—such as the energy used to cook foods by microwave ovens.

These EMFs have demonstrable negative physiological effects, but very few people fully grasp this. We have been lulled into a false sense of security by an industry that is going to great lengths to keep us in the dark, just like in the early days of smoking.

And our government appears endlessly willing—even eager—to allow technology companies to do pretty much whatever they want, including spending mountains of money to dissuade legislators from passing laws that would regulate an industry that is making it harder and harder to understand what the dangers are, much less avoid them.

I understand that the information in this book may be disheartening. After all, cell phones and Wi-Fi offer incredibly useful conveniences. And they are ubiquitous: few of us are ever more than a few feet from our cell phones at any given time—even during sleep. We spend most of our working hours an arm's distance away from a computer that is connected wirelessly to the Internet. We live in homes, neighborhoods, and cities that are in direct and constant contact with these fields through electrical wiring, microwave ovens, cell phone towers, and Wi-Fi.

The wireless industry and the government agencies that are supposed to regulate this industry want you to believe that the science is settled and wireless exposures are safe. Unfortunately, this message is not reality. EMF damage can manifest in myriad ways that include many conditions that are occurring in ever-increasing amounts, such as decreased sperm counts, impaired sleep, anxiety, depression, Alzheimer's disease, and cancer.

That is why this book is so important; it will provide you with much of the practical information that you will need to protect yourself and your family from the progressively increasing EMF exposures that all of us will have once 5G and satellite internet is fully implemented.

Lloyd does an excellent job of reviewing this important topic in simple, easy to understand language and I am grateful for his contribution to helping us all understand the extent of this issue. I have also written a book called EMF'D. If you would like to access my free bonus chapter on how to remediate the damage, you can get it by going to EMF.mercola.com.

**—Dr. Joseph Mercola, Founder of Mercola.com**

# Introduction

If you'd have said to me one day, Lloyd you are going to write a book about electromagnetic fields, I'd probably have laughed in your face. Electromagnetic what?

This is how most people react, because EMFs are the elephant in the room that hardly anybody is talking about. My life changed the day I experienced "a close encounter" with my cell phone. It literally was like flicking a switch. One day I suddenly started experiencing debilitating symptoms around my cell phone and then, bit by bit, around a whole load of devices found in most homes which, frankly, made my life hell. Within a matter of weeks, that is where I found myself, in a living hell. Despite following my doctor's best advice, consulting numerous specialists and spending a small fortune on "quick fixes", for nearly three years my health continued to deteriorate.

If only I'd known what I was dealing with and had a roadmap for dealing with "EMFs." Well, that's what this book is, an insider's guide to dealing with EMFs.

The first thing is to understand the nature of the beast, which you'll discover in Chapter 2. The terminology might seem confusing at first, but these basics will prepare you for the practical EMF protection tips, which are the main thrust of this guide.

Another reason EMFs are so confusing is because there is so much misinformation and disinformation out there. Yes, there are people circulating incorrect information to keep you in the dark about these dangers. In fact, there is an entire industry doing this, often with the connivance of our governments.

Sounds like a conspiracy theory? Yes, it does. But it's more of a question of sheer greed, to the extent that corporations are determined to make profits regardless of the cost to human health. In Chapter 3, I lay out the evidence and shatter the big EMF myths.

In Chapters 4 and 5 you'll see even more evidence, this time of the scientific kind, of the multitude of ways that EMFs can zap you and eat away at your health and well-being EVEN THOUGH YOU CAN'T FEEL IT.

I can't stress this enough. EMFs silently, surreptitiously zap you. There is a good deal of evidence, reviewed in Chapter 5, to suggest that EMFs are behind the slew of previously unknown chronic diseases and disorders which have burgeoned in a 25-year period.

Life and our universe are about frequency, in more ways than you can begin to imagine. Owning an EMF meter will enable you to measure these frequencies so you can then take action to protect yourself. You'll find this in Chapter 6.

Chapters 7 and 8 are devoted to practical ways of dealing with wireless exposures, which have proliferated in the last two decades. Chapters 9 and 10 explore the other side of the EMF coin, wired exposures. These are often overlooked and yet, in some cases, their impact can be more devastating than wireless.

Chapter 11 goes deep into what constitutes the foundation of a healthy life, your sleep. Everybody knows the importance of sleep, but few people understand to what extent nighttime EMF exposures can upset the delicate balance between health and dis-ease, and how to correct this balance.

Whilst many people are eager for 5G, the latest generation of cellular technology, there is a growing sentiment amongst EMF activists and EMF sensitives that 5G means we are doomed. In Chapter 12, you'll discover why this is not the case, and what you can do to safeguard your health on an individual and collective level.

Chapters 13, 14 and 15 include simple safety tips for computers, laptops, and Bluetooth devices, along with some practical solutions for dealing with cell tower radiation and smart meter radiation.

My credo is "natural solutions for living a healthy life in our electromagnetic world," so I couldn't write a book about EMFs without talking about earthing. Yes, earthing is controversial, but it's a subject that is poorly understood. Chapter 16 demystifies earthing and explains how and when to earth, but also when not to earth.

In Chapters 17 and 18, the spotlight is on women and children because there are particular concerns and unique solutions for these groups. In Chapters 19 and 20, you'll discover advanced solutions to EMFs and natural solutions to EMFs and other toxins.

EMFs are omnipresent and they represent a clear and present danger to your health and the health of your children. That should be abundantly clear as you read these pages. This guide offers an easy way to wise up and start taking action today to safeguard you and your family's health.

# Chapter 1

# Close Encounters With A Cell Phone

It's Autumn 1989. My French girlfriend (soon to be wife) and I were students and renting a studio in Muswell Hill, North London.

One day our landlord visited us. He was standing in our living room/bedroom when the big black leather pouch on his belt started to ring. He opened it up and took out a brick-like telephone, pulled out the aerial and started having a conversation.

I was impressed. This was my first encounter with a cell phone.

In 1998 we were living in France. I'd set up a small business, renting holiday accommodation to the Brits. Business was booming so I invested in my first cell phone. I transferred the incoming calls on my office line to the cell phone so I could take calls from customers without being tied to the office.

My cell phone made my life a LOT easier. I could be outside doing plumbing or electrical work but still answer any calls that came in. I could get so much more done in a day. I was seduced!

From February to May, during the run-up to the summer season, I used my cell phone for about two hours a day. Over the summer months, because I had to be in the office for arrivals and departures, I used it very little. The rest of the year, I was an occasional user.

**My yearly cell phone use would be considered light by today's standards.**

One sunny but cold day in February 2002 I was working outside. I remember as if it were yesterday, I was laying on my back doing some piping work under one of the rentals when my cell phone rang. I scrambled out and raced to retrieve my phone from my jacket pocket before the ringing stopped. I pressed talk and put the phone next to my ear to answer the call. That's when it all started.

I began to feel light-headed and slightly dizzy. By the end of the short conversation, I felt slightly confused and dazed.

A few minutes later the phone rang again. As I was speaking, I noticed my ear my phone was against started to feel warm from the outside in. This burning sensation then spread to the whole side of my face where I was holding my cell phone.

After a few calls, the unpleasant feeling had turned into a searing pain on the side of my head. The longer I spoke, the worse it got until the pain was so intense it was excruciating.

This was beyond weird. I'd never experienced a pain like this before. The only thing I knew for sure was that it was my cell phone that was causing it because the symptoms came on as soon as I answered a call.

Not being one to let aches and pains stand in my way, over the next few days I just carried on as before, thinking "this will pass." Little did I realize my life was about to change forever.

### Day-long blinding headaches became the norm.

These weren't normal headaches I was experiencing. It felt as though my head was being held in a vice. Other symptoms were quick to follow, like abnormal tiredness. A short cell phone conversation would leave me massively fatigued. Almost like I was drugged. It felt like the life force had been sucked out of me. No matter how many hours I slept, I woke up feeling tired and I was constantly fatigued.

Dark circles appeared under my eyes and I had acquired a peculiar permanent metallic taste in my mouth. My thinking was muddled, and I was developing a kind of brain fog. Or was it just the fatigue?

Nevertheless, good little soldier that I was, I carried on as if nothing was wrong. Or tried to.

### But every time my cell phone rang and I put it to my ear it hurt, dang, it hurt.

Very quickly the pain from just a brief cell phone conversation became so intense that I had to stop using it completely.

I had to take action. I had to sort this thing out NOW. My livelihood depended on it. My whole life depended on it. How could I live, how could I function without my cell phone? How could I live without my computer? These were the kind of thoughts I was having.

Because, yes, now I was reacting to my computer as well, which was fully wired! And not just my computer. Within a few days, a long list of other previously innocuous electrical devices—my TV, the radio in my car, even my regular corded landline telephone—started to have the same effect on me.

**This was like my worst nightmare come true.**

Unfortunately, it gets worse. I began to develop multiple inexplicable symptoms. It was as if my body was trying to tell me something.

After a few days, I reluctantly went to see my doctor. He gave me a thorough check-up, prodded, poked and gave me a prescription to get some blood tests done. But the results came back clear. He could find nothing wrong with me except that my blood pressure was slightly high. He said it was stress, that I should take some time off work and it would go away.

I took his advice and we went away for a week with the kids. It was great. No phone, no computer, I was symptom-free all week long. I felt fine. Then Monday morning came around and I went back to work. A few minutes after getting into the office, my cell phone rang and—bam—there it was again. The pain hadn't gone away at all. It was just lying low.

I went back to see my doc again and again. He sent me for scans, tests, and I saw a long list of specialists; otolaryngologist (ear, nose and throat doctor), gastroenterologist, psychologist, physiotherapist, osteopath, acupuncturist, homeopath. They all drew a blank.

**One neurologist I went to see, after explaining everything I was going through and laying myself bare, promptly dismissed me, falling just short of calling me a barefaced liar!**

As far as the doctors were concerned, my illness just did not exist. And yet all the time my condition was deteriorating. It seemed as though there was no way out.

Below were my symptoms when using or near a cell phone.

| Immediate Symptoms | |
|---|---|
| Hot ear—a burning sensation around my ear | Searing pain in the ear when using the cell phone |
| Dizziness | Feeling as though my head was being held in a vice |
| Confusion | Hot head |
| Altered spatial awareness | Prickly, tingling skin on the side of my face |

| Prolonged Symptoms | |
|---|---|
| Overwhelming and constant fatigue that wasn't alleviated by any amount of rest | Tightness/stiffness in muscles |
| Extreme sensitivity to light | Metallic taste in the mouth |
| Constant headaches | Dark circles under the eyes |
| A burning sensation all over my body | Deterioration of eyesight |
| Prickly, tingling skin on my body | Continual cramps in feet and legs |
| Stomach pains, gas, loose stool | Anxiety and irritability |
| High blood pressure | Feelings of hopelessness and despair |
| A stiff neck | Pain in the back of the ear |
| Joint pain, initially in the shoulders and spreading to the elbows | Unexplained muscular aches and pains |

My developing symptoms meant that my world was getting smaller because the only thing that seemed to work was avoiding all the things that were affecting me. Which was a lot.

I found myself increasingly being confined to the four walls of my home. Not that I felt particularly well at home, but at least I could control the situation. It made me feel safe.

Life was getting complicated. Queuing to pay at the supermarket, having a meal at a restaurant, visiting friends and family, doing just normal everyday things, my symptoms would rear their' ugly heads and I would just have to drop whatever I was doing and try to get away from whatever was bothering me.

**Bottom line: the growing use of wireless everywhere coupled with my growing sensitivity made any form of social interaction difficult.**

**My symptoms progressively meant that I was unable to:**

- Use a cell phone or to be around people using a cell phone; consequently, I was out of the loop communication-wise
- Spend time in an environment with Wi-Fi activated; any kind of socializing became challenging
- Spend time in an environment with cordless phones
- Be around a TV when it was switched on; spending time with my family became difficult
- Play with my children on wireless game consoles
- Stay in hotels or friends' homes with Wi-Fi and cordless phones; traveling became difficult
- Use the computer for any length of time; my business was affected
- Use a corded landline at my most sensitive time, making it very difficult to work at all
- Go into supermarkets and similar shops and spend time around super-market checkouts, making it difficult to shop and spend time in towns
- Go into electrical shops selling computers, TVs, and appliances.

**In terms of cars and transport, I was progressively unable to:**

- Be in a car with a cell phone switched on, making it difficult to travel with other people
- Use the car radio because of the speakers, often irritating or inconve-niencing other passengers

- Travel in a car with Bluetooth activated, making travel in modern cars no longer an option
- Travel in a car with GPS; this one caused difficulty navigating and much arguing!
- Do long-distance travel, due to the scanners on airport security and the EMFs in planes.

My escalating sensitivity and the symptoms this caused affected not only my quality of life, but the lives of the people around me.

**The more time went by, the more desperate I became. I needed answers. But I could find no books on this, the medical establishment couldn't help me, and using the Internet was a catch-22 situation.**

The severity of my symptoms varied from day to day. Sometimes, after spending just a few minutes in front of my computer, my symptoms would kick in, "hot head," tingling/prickly skin, "hot body," to the point where I could no longer concentrate and would give up. The worst was when I used my computer in the evening, or if the previous night I'd not slept well or had a few glasses of wine or beer.

What little research I was able to do suggested that what I was experiencing was related to something called "electromagnetic fields," a term that was vaguely familiar from my physics class at school. But reading about science just intimidated me and left me feeling frustrated.

What made me feel better was buying stuff. There were devices out there that promised to make my cell phone safe, to make EMFs safe, and I was buying them. Pendants, chips, diodes, home harmonizers, neutralizers, resonators.

The packaging would usually talk about neutralizing or harmonizing the EMFs. Each time I ordered, I felt a glimmer of hope that this time I'd found what I needed to solve all my problems. Occasionally, what I bought did give me some respite, but the symptoms always came back.

It seemed as though I was becoming more sensitive. I could tell if someone around me had their cell phone switched on. When friends came to visit, I would ask them to switch their phones off, sometimes they would say they had, but somehow the cell phone was still switched on. I would know.

Mentally, I was not in a good place. I was running out of options. My health was deteriorating and I felt powerless to do anything about it. I was putting a brave face on things and trying to carry on as best I could, but this "disease" was destroying my life.

For nearly three years I lived in a perpetual state of doubt, fear, and denial. Pretending I was okay was the only way I could cope. What had become abundantly clear was that I was on my own. No one could help me. And my biggest fear was that this thing was just going to get worse until I could no longer function, no longer work, no longer spend time with my family and friends. By pretending I was okay and that the symptoms were "all in my head," at least I could get through the day.

**I thought I was going crazy.**

Then one day I happened to read an article in my newspaper about a UK chief executive who could not use cell phones or a computer because of the pain it caused him. He couldn't use modern cars, electrified trains or take long-distance flights. At night, he had to switch off the electricity just so that he could sleep.[1]

I wasn't going crazy! I wasn't the only person in the world suffering from this condition! The relief was huge.

And finally, I had a name for what I was experiencing. The newspaper article used the term "electromagnetic hypersensitivity" to explain the collection of symptoms I was experiencing.

Having a serious-sounding medical term I could trot out to people, even if I was self-diagnosed, was a big comfort. Because keeping up the pretense to myself and others that I was okay was really tough. Part of the reason I did this was pride, not wanting to show weakness. But the other reason was that in some ways I felt I didn't have any choice. I couldn't give them a nice doctors' diagnosis, because I didn't have one.

It took me nearly ten years to recover my health, but today I no longer experience debilitating symptoms around EMFs. I'm able to use my computer all day every day if I want to. I can go out, shop, use buses and other forms of public transport, socialize with friends and travel. One of the things I missed most was not being able to travel long distances. I now take two to three international flights a year and can happily spend time in hotels with Wi-Fi and stay in urban areas with high levels of EMFs.

---

1 https://www.telegraph.co.uk/news/uknews/1481862/I-have-to-switch-the-mains-off-to-get-to-sleep.html

I'm truly able to live the life I choose.

**The crowning glory came the day when I was told by a medical doctor that I was healed of electrical hypersensitivity.**

Now, at this point in our story you might be thinking, "Poor Lloyd. That does sound like an awful thing that happened to him, but I can't possibly see how any of this relates to me". Wrong. On both counts.

It did seem like a terrible, awful thing at the time. In fact, at one point I seriously thought I wasn't going to live to see my children grow up. But from the realization that I was not going crazy, that I was not on my own, sprang a glimmer of hope and a strong determination that I was going to overcome this thing and be healthy again.

In time, my victim mentality was replaced by one of deep gratitude. I felt grateful and blessed to be in the position of knowing just how dangerous EMFs are and acquired a deep sense of knowing that I was going to recover my health.

**Everything that I have learned from this experience has shaped my life for the better.**

On that day in 2002 when I first *felt* the symptoms, I was lucky. I instantly knew it was my cell phone. But how many others are suffering and have no idea that EMFs are causing their ill health? Some people never put two and two together, and if they do it's only after years of functional impairment, huge expense and misdiagnosis.

Are you or someone you love going down this path of functional impairment, expense and misdiagnosis? Could EMFs be behind what you are experiencing? One thing I am absolutely certain of is that EMFs affect EVERYONE. I will talk about the science in detail later...

**This guide is the fruit of my experience in dealing with EMFs.**

Here's a simple and effective way to find out if any symptoms you may currently be experiencing are related to EMF exposures. Leave your cell phone at home and go away for a couple of days to a remote location for a little camping holiday. You're trying to get away from EMFs so ideally you want a campground without Wi-Fi. Also try to avoid being close to a cell tower (don't fret it if you can't avoid this). I know it sounds simple but countless people have shared with me how they accidentally did this (sometimes they just slept over at friends) and realized the EMFs in their home were causing the problems.

What you need to take away from this chapter:

- I developed a debilitating reaction to my cell phone and other EMF devices within a few days
- I developed this reaction without any warning
- I had never used my cell phone intensively and I had only been using it for four years when my symptoms started
- The medical establishment was unable to help me
- Ultimately, this experience has been a very positive one for me
- EMFs affect everyone
- How a short camping holiday can help you get clear if EMFs are causing/ contributing to any symptoms you are currently experiencing.

It took me nearly ten years to recover my health. But if I'd known back then what I know now, what's laid out in this guide, I could have slashed my recovery time.

Before outlining what you need to do to get EMF protection, I want to get clear on what EMFs are.

Chapter 2

# What Are EMFs?

IMAGINE A LANDSCAPE WITH A mountain. When it rains, water flows down the mountain, creating a stream. This stream meets other streams to create a river which runs through the hills below the mountain.

When the river flows, this can be compared to electrons (or electricity) flowing through a wire to light a bulb. The presence of the electrons in the wire with or without movement of those electrons creates an electric field. When those electrons move, this creates a second field, called a magnetic field. Imagine a landslide occurs, which blocks the river and create a natural dam. For a time, the river no longer flows and the water is stationary, being held back by the dam.

When the river ceases to flow, it's as if the light bulb has been switched off. Without electrical current flowing there are no magnetic fields but there is still an electric field in the wires. This electric field is there at the light switch, ready to light the bulb. It is a potential or pressure, a similar pressure to the water that is being held back by the dam.

With the dam, there is a danger that if the pressure becomes too great, the dam bursts. The danger with our electricity in the wire to the bulb is two-fold. Firstly, just being within a few feet of the wire when the light is switched on means you expose yourself to an electric field. The second issue occurs if something (wiring errors, for instance) causes the magnetic fields to extend out into the room.

Keep this river analogy in mind as I talk about EMFs. What does EMF mean?

Here are some definitions:

> ***A field (as around a working computer or a transmitting high-voltage power line) that is made up of associated electric and magnetic components, that results from the motion of an electric charge, and that possesses a definite amount of electromagnetic energy.***[2]

2 https://www.merriam-webster.com/medical/electromagnetic%20field

***Electromagnetic fields are invisible forces that surround us.***

—*Martin Blank, PhD*[3]

***Electric and magnetic fields are really just abstractions that scientists have made up to try to understand electricity's and magnetism's action at a distance. A field is represented by lines of force, another abstraction, to indicate its direction and shape.***

—*Robert O. Becker, MD*[4]

So far so good, yes? Some people use the term EMF to mean electromagnetic frequencies. Electricians, for instance, often use the acronym EMF to talk about magnetic fields. Which is strange, because if anyone should know about EMFs, you'd think an electrician would know. But very few do. More about this later.

And some people prefer to use the term EMR, defined below. Here are some more acronyms:

| | | | |
|---|---|---|---|
| EMF | **E**lectro**m**agnetic **F**ields | EMR | **E**lectro**m**agnetic **R**adiation |
| RFR | **R**adio**f**requency **R**adiation | MW | **M**icro**w**ave Radiation |

Some experts and authors use RFR for radiofrequency radiation and MW to mean medium wave or the medium frequency radio band in radio broadcasting.

This is all very confusing, I know. Throughout this guide, just know that when I say EMF, I mean electromagnetic field.

EMFs are invisible forces that surround us. You can't see, hear, touch, taste or smell the—most people can't, anyway. I also like to think of an EMF as a region of space where electric and magnetic forces interact, because they are always both there to a greater or lesser extent. But that then begs the question, what are electric and magnetic forces?

**An EMF contains both electric and magnetic forces of energy.**

Hard-line physicists would argue that a force is not the same as a field. They are right, but for our purposes it's not worth splitting hairs on that.

3 Martin Blank, 2015. *Overpowered: What Science Tells Us About The Dangers of Cell Phones and other WIFI Age Devices.*
4 Robert O. Becker, 1985. *The Body Electric: Electromagnetism and the Foundation of Life.*

Electric and magnetic forces or fields can be described as follows:

- **Electric Field:** This field is the "potential difference", known as voltage, between two places. The field becomes stronger at higher voltages or as you get closer to a source, such as a lamp cord. An electric field exists even if there is no electric current flowing through it.
- **Magnetic Field:** This field is created through the natural flow of electrons along a metallic path, known as electrical current. As the current becomes stronger, the magnetic field grows stronger and extends further from the source, such as the electric wire powering your TV.

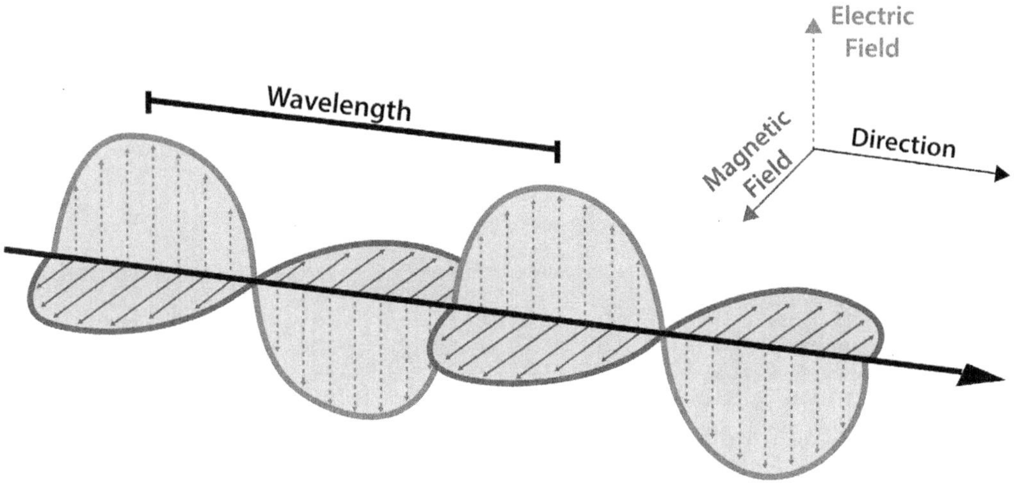


In the diagram above,[5] you see the electric field, shown vertically, and its corresponding magnetic field, shown horizontally, at right angles to it. This means that whenever you have one type of field, there is the other type of field at ninety degrees to it.[6]

A lot of people, when they hear the word EMFs, think it's some modern thing invented by a mad scientist. Not true.

Natural (non-man-made) EMFs have been around forever.

5 Strictly speaking you would only see this relationship, with electric and magnetic fields on electrical wiring, in outer space. This is because, due to the length of the wave, we are always in the "near field". This is confusing, I know, but just bear with me on this.

6 However, as Building Biologist Oram Miller explains, "you can have one type of field present in a room without the other if you are within what engineers call the 'near field' where magnetic and electric fields are not coupled with each other and can be independent. What this means on a practical basis is you can measure a low magnetic field, in a bedroom for instance, but still have a high, and unhealthy electric field."

***The play of electricity across the galaxy, the magnetic rhythms of the planets, the eleven-year cycle of sunspots, the fluctuations in the solar wind, thunder and lightning upon this earth, biological currents within our bodies—the one depends upon all the others.***

—*ARTHUR FIRSTENBURG*[7]

The most common natural magnetic field is that of the earth, also known as the geomagnetic field because it's a magnetic field that extends from the interior of the earth out into space.

This natural magnetic field is believed to be generated deep down in the earth's core and is caused by the Earth's spin, which also causes swirling whirlpools. This flow of molten iron generates electric currents, which in turn produce magnetic fields.

It's thought that birds and other animals, like dolphins and sharks, use the magnetic field of the earth to navigate.

**This natural geomagnetic field is MOSTLY a direct current, or DC, magnetic field and is very weak compared to the much stronger alternating current, or AC, magnetic fields found in many homes.**

A good example of an electric field in nature is lightning. A lightning strike is caused when the voltage on a storm cloud is high enough to make an electrostatic discharge to the Earth (or, in some cases, from the Earth up to a cloud).

Have you ever received a "shock" when touching the metal handle of a car door or walking in stocking feet on a carpet? That's the discharge of a direct current electric field, too.

**Electromagnetic fields, whether man-made or natural, surround us at all times.**

So, electricity was never invented, it was discovered.

7 Arthur Firstenburg, 2017. *The Invisible Rainbow: A History of Electricity and Life.*

Then, bit by bit, we learned to harness this energy to conduct it via wires into our homes and places of work to power heating and cooling systems, lighting, appliances, and electronic devices.

| Electric Field | Magnetic Field |
|---|---|
| Created by differences in voltage. | Created when electrical current flows or when magnet's are moved (e.g. magnetized car tyre EMFs). |
| Higher voltage = stronger electric field. | Greater current = stronger magnetic field. |
| Field strength decreases as distance increases. | Field strength decreases as distance increases. |
| Field strength is diminished by building materials and can be shielded. | Field strength is not diminished by building materials. Shielding is difficult. |
| Field strength is the same (regardless of the power being consumed). | Field strength varies according to power consumption. |
| Field exists even when an electric current does not flow. | No current flow = no AC magnetic field. |

## Advanced EMF Information

The following is some advanced information provided by Building Biologist Oram Miller.[8] This may help you better understand how magnetic fields are created on electrical wiring, but you don't have to read this to understand the dangers.

Whenever you have an electric current running along the hot and neutral conductors in a circuit or lamp cord, you have a magnetic field around conductor called a "flux field." The hot wire takes current from the source, meaning the breaker panel, to the load, which can be a light bulb, motor, or electronic device. As the current travels along the hot wire, it causes a magnetic field that passes through any and all building materials as it emits into any room.

The current then travels through the load (light bulb, motor, etc.) and back on the neutral wire, which it must do in order to complete the circuit. The light bulb

8 Oram Miller is the founder of http://createhealthyhomes.com/

does not light if the current does not make it back to the breaker panel. When that current travels back to the source on the neutral wire of the cord or circuit, it, too, causes a magnetic field.

That means that the magnetic field around the neutral wire is turning in the opposite direction of the magnetic field around the hot wire. If you put the center of those two fields together, which happens in all modern wiring and lamp cords, *and* the size of those two current loads are equal, then those two magnetic fields superimpose upon each other and cancel *almost* completely.

**This cancellation is why you don't have magnetic fields throughout your home when current flows on circuits and lamp cords.**[9]

What happens if the hot and neutral wires are separated, such as in old-fashioned "knob and tube" wiring from the 1920s and 30s? You will end up having magnetic fields coming out of your walls when you turn on loads. The solution is to replace the knob and tube wiring with modern wiring.

What then happens if the wires are together, as they are in all modern wiring since the 1930s and 40s, but the amount of current returning on the neutral wire is less (or more) than the current going out to the load on the hot wire? This happens when wiring errors are present, which is common in a large percentage of homes, particularly in North America, and less so in parts of Europe and Australia.

When there is less current on the neutral wire, the magnetic field around the neutral is smaller than the magnetic field around the hot wire (and going in the opposite direction). Therefore, cancellation is not complete. Some magnetic field is left over on the hot wire that is not cancelled by the smaller field around the neutral. That remaining magnetic field extends into the room whenever you turn on the overhead light or whatever load is on that circuit. This is caused by a neutral-to-neutral or neutral-to-ground wiring error. Fortunately, these wiring errors can be traced and fixed by an electrician, once they are shown what to look for. Electrical code inspectors in North America, however, usually do not look for these particular types of wiring errors, even though the code book says to avoid them.

Don't worry if you don't understand this, I will go into all this in detail in the upcoming chapters.

9 You have (almost) full cancellation when wiring errors are not present. More about this in Chapter 9.

## Wavelength And Frequency

When we talk about EMFs, we usually talk about them in terms of their frequency and wavelength. But, what does frequency and wavelength mean?

I'm sure you've seen images of electrical waves before, in a book or in physics class at school. Well, imagine EMFs as a series of very regular waves that travel at the speed of light. "Frequency" describes the number of complete waves that go by a fixed point per second, or oscillations per second. "Wavelength" describes the distance between one wave and the next. Wavelength and frequency are inseparably intertwined.

The higher the frequency (number of oscillations per second), the shorter the wavelength (distance between the waves). The longer the wavelength, the lower the frequency. We use something called the EMF spectrum to show this inverse relationship.

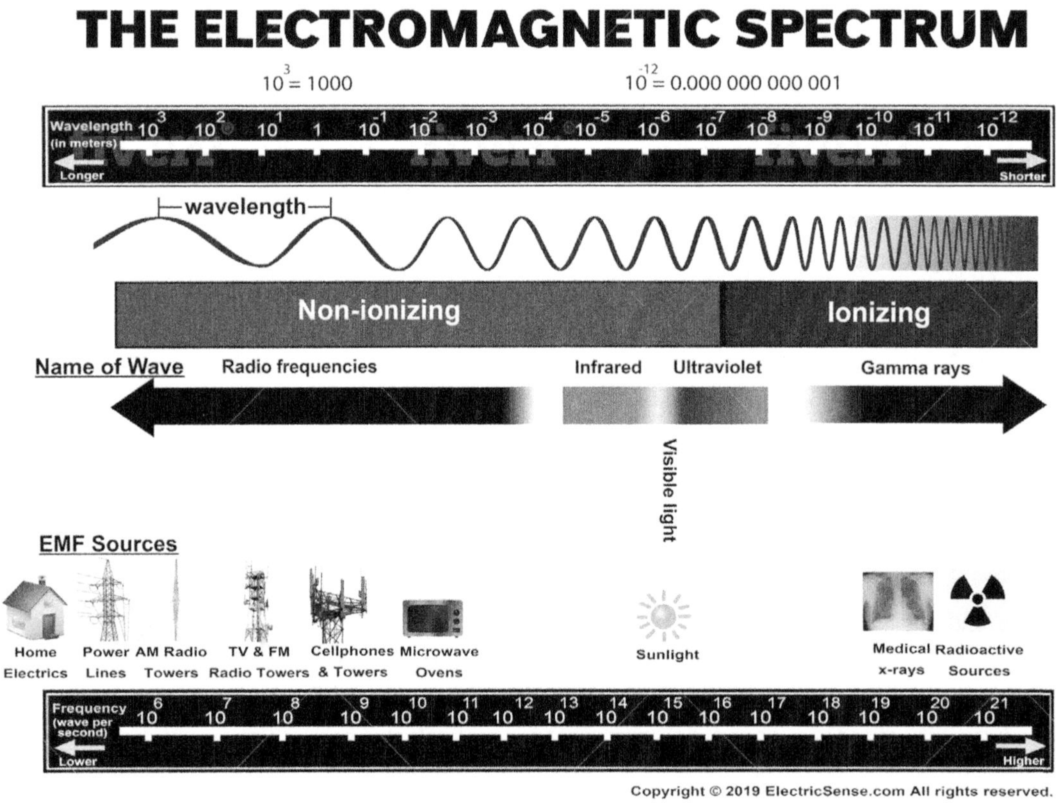

There's a lot to be said about the EMF spectrum. Look at the scales at the top and bottom of the diagram. Notice how:

1. The top scale measures the wavelength. If we move to the left, we go towards a longer wavelength and if we move to the right, the wavelength is shorter.

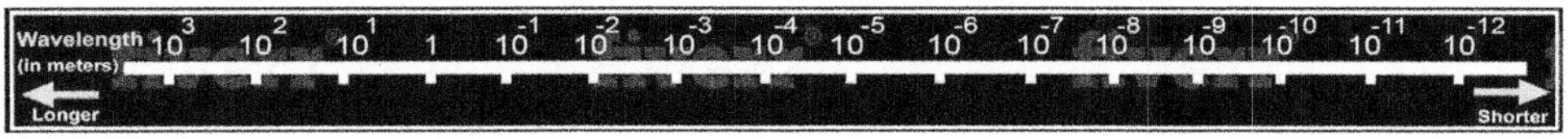


2. But look what happens to frequency as we do this: the bottom scale[10] measures frequency. If we move to the left, we go towards a lower frequency and if we move to the right, the frequency is higher.

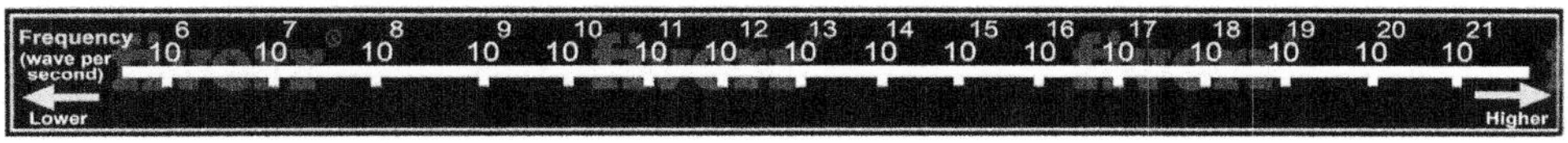


3. Under "name of wave", radio frequencies and microwaves sit towards the left-hand side (so we know they are lower frequency and longer wavelength) while gamma rays and X-rays sit on the right of the diagram (so we know they are higher frequency and shorter wavelength).

Are you getting the idea? This EMF spectrum gives us a LOT of information.

## Basic Frequency Definitions

Let me give you some basic frequency definitions, particularly as I'm going to talk about radio frequencies, or RF:

| | |
|---|---|
| **1 hertz (Hz)** | 1 cycle per second |
| **1 megahertz (MHz)** | 1 million cycles per second (1,000,000 Hz or $10^6$) |
| **1 gigahertz (GHz)** | 1 billion cycles per second (1,000,000,000 Hz or $10^9$) |

10 This diagram is not 100% accurate. The frequency scale is non-linear, so the points on the scale should not be equally spaced.

Now look back at our EMF spectrum diagram to see what this means. An EMF with a frequency of 1 GHz ($10^9$ on the bottom scale), which is in the RF band (which cell phones and Wi-Fi use) has a wavelength of 300 millimeters (the corresponding point on the top scale). That is to say, a little less than a foot. That puts the magnetic and electric fields of RF waves within a human scale.

## Non-Ionizing And Ionizing Radiation: What's The Big Deal?

Let's look at our EMF spectrum diagram again to understand non-ionizing radiation and ionizing radiation. You can see radio frequencies and microwaves, and even electric and magnetic fields, fit into this *non-ionizing* category, while things like medical X-rays and radioactive sources fall into the category of *ionizing* radiation.

What does ionizing and non-ionizing actually mean? Is this a big deal? Yes, kind of. Ionizing/non-ionizing lies at the heart of all the controversy about EMFs. Everyone agrees that ionizing radiation is dangerous. On the one hand, industry, governments, and even the World Health Organization say non-ionizing radiation is dangerous *only* when there are thermal effects (heating of tissues). On the other hand, independent scientists, Building Biologists, and a growing number of health professionals (and me) say non-ionizing radiation is dangerous at levels *wayyyyyy* below those at which tissue heats.

Who's right? All will become clear, but first let me explain what some of these terms mean.

Let's look at the atom. All matter is made from atoms: you, me, everything. These atoms are made up of three types of particles with different charges—*protons*, *neutrons*, and *electrons*—which orbit around a nucleus. It looks a bit like a solar system.

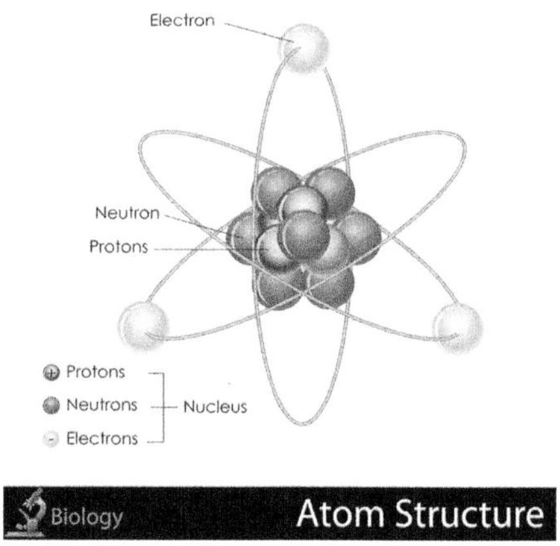


Protons carry a positive charge and electrons a negative charge (neutrons are neutral). These charges cause an electric field which forces the particles to move—the same kinds of charges (both positive and negative) repel, while unlike charges (one positive and one negative) attract. This movement causes a magnetic field.[11]

11 Katie Singer 2014. *An Electronic Silent Spring.*

Some EMFs have so much energy that they can cause electrons to shift orbits in atoms, which creates unpaired electrons. When one of these bonds between electrons is broken, an uneven number of electrons remain. This is called a "free radical". And this is said to ionize atoms.

**Ionizing radiation causes chemical reactions that cause damage to our biological systems.**

I'm sure you've heard somewhere about free radicals and how dangerous they are. Not quite true. Free radicals in themselves are not dangerous. It's when there are too many of them that they are believed to cause chemical reactions, which can lead to premature aging and a variety of serious diseases, including cancer.

**High energy EMFs that have sufficient energy to knock an electron free from its orbit are called ionizing radiation.**

EMFs at lower energy levels, however, cannot break molecular bonds and ionize atoms, so they create non-ionizing radiation. Examples of non-ionizing radiation are electromagnetic fields with a long wavelength and low frequency, including microwaves, household electricity, and radiofrequency fields.

When I interviewed Martin Blank PhD[12] a few years ago on this question, this is what he said:

> ***There have been a number of physicists who correctly state what physicists know that non-ionizing radiation cannot and doesn't have enough energy to knock electrons out of chemicals... but the fact of the matter is that that's irrelevant in biology.***

In other words, the distinction between ionizing and non-ionizing radiation in so far as it relates to our bodies and living things generally, is irrelevant. Professor Blank went on to say:

12 Dr. Blank was special lecturer in the *Department of Physiology and Cellular Biophysics* at *Columbia University* at the time, the interview is in the EMF Experts Solutions Club.

> *A few milligauss* [of magnetic field energy] *can affect a reaction that moves ions that weigh much more than electrons. And it can also affect the flow of sodium and potassium that are very much heavier than an electron. So, you may not move an electron, but the whole system is rigged so that these ions can be affected in the motion.*

Units of measurement, like Gauss and Tesla, are what's used when we measure magnetic fields. A milligauss is one-thousandth of a Gauss. As you will learn in the upcoming chapters, most of us are regularly exposed to non-ionizing magnetic field levels which far exceed a few milligauss, so our bodies are being constantly impacted in a potentially harmful way.

**Non-ionizing radiation can cause nearly identical biological damage and disease as ionizing radiation—it just does it in a different way.**

Anyway, let's not get ahead of ourselves. Just try and keep the EMF spectrum in mind as you read this guide, it will help you understand things better. NASA has a very good five-minute video introduction to the EMF spectrum, see:

http://www.electricsense.com/bookbonus.

## What About Cell Phones And Wireless?

So far, we've talked about magnetic fields and electric fields, but you're probably wondering where cell phones and wireless fit into all of this.

We know they fit into this because we can see them at the upper end of our EMF spectrum diagram. But here's something I want you to understand; whenever you see the word wireless, what that really means is radio frequency radiation. In fact, what that typically means is radio frequency microwave radiation.

**Wireless = Radio Frequency Microwave Radiation.**

In England, before TV and the Internet, people used to sit around and listen to the radio to get their news and to hear music. We used to call these old radios "the wireless". Nowadays, radios are mainly found in cars. These radios are only receiving a wireless signal and don't *emit* waves. But, virtually every other kind of wireless

device does emit waves because they both receive *and* transmit. These include cell phones, cordless phones, cell towers, Wi-Fi, and Bluetooth devices.
It also most likely includes:[13]

- Baby monitors
- Virtual reality headsets
- Game consoles
- Cars with Bluetooth, Wi-Fi and radar
- Activity trackers/watches and wearables (Fitbits and similar)
- Home central heating system[14] thermostat and central lighting control units
- Anything smart.

When you use any wireless device, or anyone around you uses a wireless device, that means you are being zapped by radio frequency microwave radiation.

By the way, that last category, anything smart, is huge and keeps getting bigger.

## Why Smart Is Not Smart

You've probably noticed the word smart popping up on appliances you've bought recently. It can be anything from a lawn mower to a dishwasher to a toothbrush.

All these objects are part of a brave new world called the Internet of Things (IoT). What this means is that by virtue of a smart grid, objects will be able to communicate with each other and supposedly make life easier for you. Your refrigerator will be able to order more milk from the store when you're running low and get it delivered by drone. Your washing machine will order more detergent when it needs it. Your toothbrush will be able to order more toothpaste.

I explore all of this in detail in Chapter 12. But know this: "smart" really means "wireless" and wireless means radio frequency microwave radiation.

13 This depends on the device.
14 Also beware of electrical radiant floor heating systems, which can emit high magnetic and electric fields. Water-based plastic piping installations are generally safer.

## Is All This Stuff Safe?

No, it is NOT. That's why I wrote this guide. Remember what I shared with you in Chapter 1, about how I suddenly developed a reaction to my cell phone and other electronic devices?

That's how I KNEW that these technologies were harming me. But even though every single day the effects were so glaringly, unbearably obvious, for nearly three years I pretty much ignored them.

I did consult different doctors and specialists, but the message I received loud and clear was that cell phones and all the other things I was reacting to were safe and what I was feeling I wasn't really feeling, it was all in my mind.

I chose to accept the status quo. Are you accepting the status quo?

For years, we've been told that cell phones are safe and that all these other wireless devices are safe. But they are not safe. I will explain to you exactly why that is. To do that we need to look at the EMF science.

I know we got a bit technical, so here's a summary of what you need to retain from this chapter:

- The word "EMF" means "electromagnetic field" (in this guide)
- Pressure or voltage creates electric fields
- The flow of current creates magnetic fields
- All sources of EMF can be situated on a spectrum
- The EMF spectrum shows the relationship in terms of frequency and wavelength—between these different kinds of EMF
- Saying an EMF has a certain frequency is an important property of how we describe it
- High energy EMFs—that have sufficient energy to knock an electron free from its orbit—are called ionizing radiation
- Ionizing radiation—from things like medical X-rays and radioactive sources — are widely accepted to be dangerous
- Non-ionizing radiation, as used by cell phones etc., are only considered dangerous by many experts if there is a heating effect—despite much evidence to the contrary
- The distinction between ionizing and non-ionizing radiation, in so far as it relates to our bodies, is irrelevant
- Non-ionizing radiation causes nearly identical biological damage and disease as ionizing radiation—it just does it in a different way.

If you're new to this, this all might seem a lot to grasp. But understanding these fundamentals will allow you to understand how EMFs can impact your life and how to protect yourself and your family.

If at this point you're already on-board with the dangers of EMFs, then you might want to skip straight to Chapter 6. But if you want to learn more about how and why these technologies are dangerous, then read on.

Chapter 3

# Shattering The EMF Myths

Knowledge is power, so they say. The argument goes that the more knowledge you gain, the more powerful you become.

That's not quite true. But knowledge is definitely one of the most important elements of self-empowerment. **And that's what I want to do, empower you to take action to protect yourself from EMFs.** I want to do that by helping you understand some of the EMF science, then I'll share with you the many practical ways I've found to protect myself from EMFs. But first, how about we shatter some EMF myths?

**EMF Myth #1: There is no evidence.** There are no studies to show that EMFs are dangerous. The whole thing is a conspiracy theory like UFOs. Believing that EMFs from cell phones and other stuff could actually harm you is complete and utter bull****.

**Myth Buster #1: Thousands of independent studies show that EMFs are extremely hazardous to human health.** I'm going to share some of them with you.

**EMF Myth #2: If EMFs were really dangerous, we would have been given some kind of official warning to say so.** There are no official warnings.

**Myth Buster #2: We have repeatedly been given official warnings.** Even the World Health Organization has officially declared that radio frequency radiation—of the type transmitted between cell towers and cell phones—is a "possible" human carcinogen.[15]

**EMF Myth #3: If EMFs were really dangerous, I would feel it.** I can't feel anything when I use my cell phone, therefore I know I'm okay.

**Myth Buster #3: Wrong. The science shows that EMFs impact our biology at levels below those that most people can feel or that cause immediate symptoms.** Some people do get symptoms like I did, but this is a minority—most people can't feel the damage being done until they get a full-blown disease and even then they don't always realize that EMFs are the cause.

15 https://www.iarc.fr/wp-content/uploads/2018/07/pr208_E.pdf

Let's look a bit more closely at these myths, I don't want you to think I'm making stuff up!

## Myth Buster #1: Overwhelming Evidence

I'm sure you've heard or read somewhere, "there is no evidence that EMFs are dangerous."

Let me set the record straight here and now—there is a TON of evidence. The most comprehensive listing I know of is that of emf-portal.org,[16] which has a database of over 29,000 studies and it's growing daily.

There are those that say we need more studies. Here's what Olle Johansson, former professor at the Karolinska Institute, Department of Neuroscience, in Sweden who has been studying EMFs since the 1980s has to say:

> ***The number of papers is overwhelming and, from an honest point of view as a scientist, of course I want to do science and study more and more, but from a political point of view and a public health point of view maybe there's no need, really, because we know so much about the downsides of wireless communication and frequent magnetic fields and so on.***[17]

Let's look at cell phone radiation for a moment, because this is where we have the most science. In 2016, a $30 million +10-year US federal study conducted by experienced scientists published its findings—considered by many as the world's largest, most well-designed study of its type on cell phone radiation. Do you know what they found?

> ***After extensive reviews, the consensus is that there was a carcinogenic effect.***
>
> *—DR RONALD MELNICK, NTP STUDY LEAD SCIENTIST.*[18]

In fact, they found that the link between cell phone radiation and cancer was so clear that they decided that other studies, called peer review, needed to be done just to be sure they hadn't made a mistake.

16 https://www.emf-portal.org/en
17 Prof. Olle Johansson - EMF Health Summit interview
18 https://microwavenews.com/news-center/ntp-cancer-results

The other studies were published in 2018, and guess what they concluded?

*"Clear evidence of cancer" from cell phone radiation.*[19]

## Cell Phone Radiation Causes Cancer

Prior to that the biggest study on cell phone radiation was the $25 million Interphone study, a multinational case-control study set up by the International Agency for Research on Cancer (IARC), a division of the World Health Organization.

According to EMF researcher Prof. Magda Havas the study was set up in such a way as to minimize finding any adverse effects.

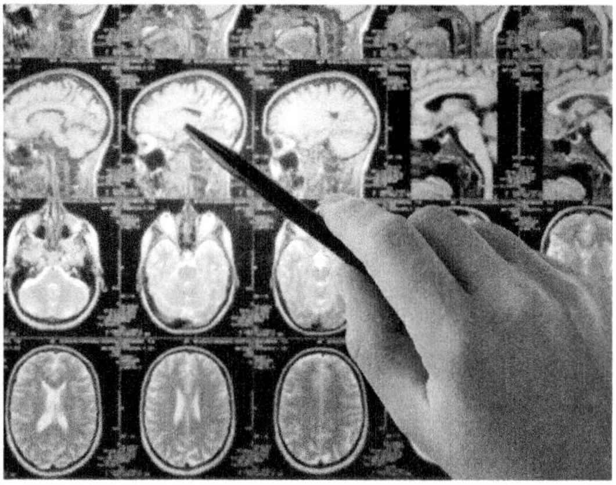

Despite this, they found that regular use of a cell phone can significantly increase the risk of glioma—a particularly deadly type of tumor that starts in the brain or spine—by 40% with 1640 hours of use. Most people survive only one to three years after diagnosis of a glioma.[20]

I know 1640 hours might sound a lot, but it equates to using a cell phone for just 30 minutes per day over ten years.

**Using your cell phone for just 30 minutes a day can increase your risk of getting a brain tumor by 40%.**

Gliomas now represent 80% of all malignant brain tumors.[21] The studies performed by the Hardell Research Group in Sweden are widely regarded as being amongst the best. A recent study published by Prof. Hardell's team found "a consistent pattern of increased risk for glioma and acoustic neuroma associated with the use of cell phones".[22]

By the way, these are not one-off findings, they are consistent with their earlier studies.[23]

19 http://bit.ly/USNationalToxicologyProgram
20 https://magdahavas.com/lessons-from-the-interphone-study/
21 http://bit.ly/SmartMeterNews
22 https://www.pathophysiologyjournal.com/article/S0928-4680%2812%2900110-1/abstract
23 https://www.ncbi.nlm.nih.gov/pubmed/18425337

A recent French study also found evidence of an increased risk of glioma and temporal lobe tumors.[24] A study in the UK on 790,000 middle-aged women found that women who used their cell phones for ten or more years were two-and-a-half times more likely to develop an acoustic neuroma—their risk of acoustic neuroma increased with the number of years they used cell phones.[25]

I'm going to talk in depth about how EMFs impact our kids in Chapter 17 but, according to a 2016 report funded by the American Brain Tumor Association (ABTA), malignant brain tumors are now the most common cause of cancer-related deaths in adolescents and young adults aged 15–39 and the most common cancer occurring among 15–19 year old's.[26]

The 50-page report used data from the Central Brain Tumor Registry of the United States (CBTRUS)—this was the first in-depth statistical analysis of brain and central nervous system tumors in adolescents and young adults.

I've only cited *some* of the most important studies on the cell phone radiation cancer question, which I think you will agree is already quite compelling. But let's explore this a bit more.

## Tumors on Same Side of Head as Cell Phone

One of the most alarming trends is that people are getting tumors on the same side of the head as they use their cell phone. A research paper that reviewed 11 studies found a link between prolonged cell phone usage and the development of an ipsilateral—same side of the head as cell phone use—brain tumor.[27]

The $25 million Interphone Study also found that tumors were more likely to occur on the side of the head most used for calling.[28]

Someone recently posted this comment on my Facebook page:

> ***My realtor back in 91 had a brother that was also a realtor he ended up with brain cancer on the same side of where he held his cell phone. I rarely use my phone to talk on because it gets so hot and I get an ear ache if I hold the phone near my ear.***

---

24 https://oem.bmj.com/content/71/7/514
25 https://www.saferemr.com/2013/05/cell-phone-use-acoustic-neuroma-and.html
26 https://www.sciencedaily.com/releases/2016/02/160224132910.htm
27 https://www.ncbi.nlm.nih.gov/pubmed/19328536
28 https://www.emfacts.com/2010/05/1252-bioinitiative-press-release-on-the-interphone-results/

Besides brain tumors, independent studies have also found that cell phone radiation impacts other important organs and tissues in and around your head.

## Cell Phone Radiation Damages Your Glands

Your thyroid gland is a butterfly-shaped gland in your neck, just below your Adam's apple. Just think for a minute how most people use a cell phone... If you use your cell phone against your ear, you're exposing your thyroid to high levels of cell phone radiation.

An Israeli study that collected human thyroid cells from healthy patients and then subjected them to the type of radiation produced by cell phones found evidence of changes in thyroid cells.[29]

The study authors noted that the rise in thyroid cancer cases in Israel over a decade correlated with the rise in the use of cellphones.

In a 2016 study,[30] the Hardell research team found that in recent years there has been a substantial increase in patients diagnosed with thyroid cancer in Sweden as well as in other Nordic countries. They concluded that this increase coincides with the growing use of smartphones.

A 2019 Iranian study that reviewed 161 research papers also found that cell phone radiation affects the thyroid gland follicles and the volume of cells in the gland.[31]

An Israeli study looking at 460 cases of parotid gland tumors—the parotid is the salivary gland near the cheek where many people hold their cell phone—found an association between cell phone use and parotid gland tumors.[32]

Another Israeli study analyzed deaths as recorded on the National Cancer Registry over a 36-year period. The study found that the total number of parotid gland cancers in Israel had increased four-fold from 1970 to 2006, whereas other major salivary gland cancers remained stable.[33]

There's just one more piece of research I want to share with you here—the cell phone industry's own research.

29 https://www.saferemr.com/2014/07/is-mobile-phone-use-contributing-to.html
30 https://www.stralskyddsstiftelsen.se/2016/10/doctors-confirm-thyroid-cancer-is-increasing-rapidly-in-sweden/
31 https://www.ncbi.nlm.nih.gov/pubmed/31062236
32 https://academic.oup.com/aje/article/167/4/457/233171
33 https://journals.lww.com/epidem/Fulltext/2011/01000/Risk_of_Parotid_Malignant_Tumors_in_Israel.25.aspx

## Cell Phone Industry's Own Research Shows Cell Phones Cause Brain Tumors

The cat was let out of the bag when David Reynard went on CNN's *Larry King Live* on 23 January 1993.[34] Before that, nobody really had an inkling that cell phones might be dangerous.

In August 1988, David Reynard had bought his wife Susan a cell phone. Seven months later, a medical scan revealed a tumor in Susan's brain. She claimed that the tumor was a result of being bombarded by radiation from her cell phone.

In April 1992, Susan filed a lawsuit against the cell phone manufacturer, the network provider, and the retail store that sold the phone. Sadly, a month later, Susan died of brain cancer.

Motorola shares took an instant dive on the stock market. The cell phone industry started to panic. So that same year, they commissioned a $28 million study, the Wireless Technology Research (WTR) program, to confirm the safety of cell phones.

Unfortunately, after seven years of research it became clear the WTR's findings did not align with the industry's objectives and the research project was promptly shut down. But not before the project's lead researcher could voice his concerns.

> ***The big picture is disturbingly clear. There is a definite risk that the radiation plume that emanates from a cell phone antenna can cause cancer and other health problems.***[35]
>
> —*Dr. George Carlo, former head of the industry-sponsored WTR program.*

This is a quick overview of the cell phone radiation debacle. There is also significant evidence linking other EMF exposures from electric fields, magnetic fields and dirty electricity to a long list of serious diseases including cancer—which I'm going to share with you. But for the moment let's carry on debunking the myths.

34 http://journal.media-culture.org.au/0106/cell.php
35 As reported by Jason Bawden-Smith in his book *In the Dark*

## Myth Buster #2: We Have Repeatedly Been Given Official Warnings

Who, globally, is responsible for protecting us from dangerous chemicals and diseases and that kind of thing? It's the WHO! The United Nations' World Health Organization (WHO) agency.

In 2011, the International Agency for Research on Cancer, part of the WHO, issued a press release[36] classifying cell phone radiation as a Type-2B carcinogen. What does that mean? Quite a lot actually.

It means that, at last, it had been officially recognized and acknowledged that cell phone radiation could cause cancer. Putting it in the same category as the pesticide DDT, lead and gasoline exhaust fumes.

But not just cell phone radiation. The Class 2B classification includes wireless radiation in the 30 kHz to 300 GHz frequency range, so that includes radiation from things like Wi-Fi modems and routers, baby monitors, tablets, cell towers, radar, Bluetooth, etc.[37]

This official recognition is important because people pay attention to the WHO. I remember when the WHO published their press release. It did get everyone talking about cell phone radiation, but did the WHO go far enough? Is cell phone radiation just a "possible" carcinogen?

**Many WHO IARC scientists who are WHO advisors and served on the 2011 WHO IARC working group now state that additional scientific evidence indicates that wireless radiation should be re-classified either as a "probable human carcinogen" or a "known human carcinogen".[38]**

A growing number of scientists are saying the WHO classification is wrong and these exposures should be classified as a probable cancer agent—including scientists that were behind the original WHO press release.

Former employee of the World Health Organization and brain tumor survivor, Olga Sheean, comments:

36 https://www.iarc.fr/wp-content/uploads/2018/07/pr208_E.pdf
37 https://ehtrust.org/science/whoiarc-position-on-wireless-and-health/
38 https://ehtrust.org/science/whoiarc-position-on-wireless-and-health/

***Despite the rules about avoiding conflicts of interest and not receiving funding from outside sources, WHO had been receiving laundered money from the wireless telecoms industry for decades.***[39]

But the fact that the WHO, whatever the shenanigans and financial pressure, even went so far as to suggest a link between cancer and cell phone radiation in their 2011 publication, speaks volumes.

## Other Official Warnings

If EMFs are really as dangerous as I'm suggesting, then obviously the government would warn you, right? In fact, not only would they warn you, they would pass laws to protect you. Laws have been passed in different countries.

In 2015, the French National Assembly passed a law banning Wi-Fi in nursery schools[40] and in 2017 banned cell phones from schools for children from first to ninth grade.[41]

Similar laws have since been passed in the UK, Israel, Canada and Australia, though globally not that many—there is a good reason for this, which I will come to.[42]

Also, there have been official warnings in different countries.

In India, the Ministry of Telecommunications published a guide for reducing cell phone exposures. In Israel, a policy of preventive caution has been adopted. In both Sweden and Cyprus, a similar guide has been published.

In the UK, following the publication of the Stewart Report in 2000, the government issued a leaflet advising that children under 16 should only use cell phones for essential purposes.[43]

Toronto Public Health in Canada has issued a fact sheet with precautions for cell phone use. In Finland, a similar fact sheet was published by the radiation authority while in Germany one was published by the Academy of Pediatrics.

In 2017, The California Department of Public Health—the state department responsible for public health in California—published safety warnings and guidelines

39 Olga Sheean, 2018. *EMF Off: A Call to Consciousness in our Misguidedly Microwaved World.*
40 http://bit.ly/betweenrockandhardplace
41 http://bit.ly/TheGuardian_France_ban_mobile_phones_schools_September
42 https://typicalstudent.org/hot/lists/5-countries-banned-mobiles-gadgets-schools
43 Lyn McLean, 2015. *The Force: Living Safely in a World of Electromagnetic Pollution.*

about cell phones, acknowledging that "there are concerns among some public health professionals".[44]

In 2019 in Italy, an education and awareness campaign was launched and in Denmark a review was published.

In May 2011, The Council of Europe—Europe's leading human rights organization—published a report calling for a lowering of EMF exposure limits.

## Doctors and Scientists Have Been Warning Us Too

If governments have been lax about issuing official warnings, over the last 20 years doctors and scientists have been actively sounding the alarm.[45] Here are just some examples of the notices we've been given.

**1997** **Boston Physicians' and Scientists' Petition:** called for halt of ground-level cellular communication transmissions in Boston.

**1998** **Vienna EMF Resolution, Austria**: called for data to be made available to users to allow them to manage the reduction in EMF-exposure.

**2000** **Stewart Report, UK**: called for increased protection from cell phone towers.

**2002** **Salzburg Resolution, Austria**: called for emissions from cell towers to be lowered well below ICNIRP guidelines.

**Freiburg Appeal, Germany**: physicians requested tougher guidelines for radio frequency exposures.

**Catania Resolution, Italy**: called for preventive strategies based on the precautionary principle.

**2005** **Irish Doctors' Environmental Association, Ireland**: doctors recognized electrohypersensitivity (EHS) is increasing and request advice from government on how to treat it.

**Helsinki Appeal, Finland**: pronounced the ICNIRP standards as obsolete, called for new safety standards.

**2006** **Benevento Resolution, Italy**: called for governments to adopt EMF safety guidelines that reflect the Precautionary Principle.

**2007** **BioInitiative Report, USA**: called for EMF safety guidelines to be revised.

44 https://www.cdph.ca.gov/Programs/OPA/Pages/NR17-086.aspx#.WjLdvS2zLZA.twitter
45 http://bit.ly/magdahavas

**2008** **Russian National Committee on Non-Ionizing Radiation Protection, Moscow**: called for measures to protect children.

**Venice Resolution, Italy**: scientists recognized the biological effects at non-thermal levels and called for new standards.

**University of Pittsburgh Cancer Institute**: called for children only to use cell phones in emergencies and gave recommendations on safe cell phone use.

**2009** **Porto Alegre Resolution, Brazil**: called for precautionary practices with regard to wireless.

**2010** **Seletun Statement, Norway:** called for strong preventative action for children and new biologically-based public exposure standards.

**2012** **American Academy of Environmental Medicine**: called for a moratorium on "smart meter".

**International Doctors' Appeal 2012:** follow up on 2002 appeal.

**Vienna College of Physicians:** issued recommendations for using a cell phone more safely.

**2013** **Potenza Picena Resolution:** called for the precautionary principle to be adopted.

**2014** **Open letter by British medical doctors**: called for health agencies and the public to reduce exposure to radiofrequency microwave radiation.

**The Baby Safe Project**: called for pregnant women to limit their exposures to wireless radiation.

**Canadian Scientists**: called for protection from radiofrequency radiation exposure.

**2015** **International EMF Scientist Appeal**: 200 scientists called for children and pregnant women to be protected and safety standards to be strengthened.

**2017** **Scientists warn of potential serious health effects of 5G**: 180 scientists and doctors from 35 countries called for a moratorium on 5G roll out.

If there aren't laws, then surely there must be some sort of safety standards in place to protect us, right?

## The Safety Standards

Most countries all over the world, including the US, have based their regulations on one or a combination of these guidelines:

- The International Commission on Non-Ionizing Radiation Protection (ICNIRP) guidelines
- The Institute of Electrical and Electronics Engineers (IEEE) guidelines
- The American National Standards Institute (ANSI) guidelines.

Sorry to be the bearer of bad tidings, but these guidelines do virtually nothing to protect us.

**Currently, there are no national or international "standards" for safe levels of the radiation emitted by wireless or microwave devices. Instead, the US government adopted "guidelines" developed by the industry, based on decades-old research.**[46]

Firstly, a guideline does not equal a standard. It might sound as though I'm splitting hairs, but this is important. It's your health that's on the line here!

As the Environmental Health Trust points out, guidelines have a much lower certainty than a "standard". One of the main reasons we have no EMF government safety standards is that in the early 1980s, when cell phones were first introduced into the US market, they were exempted from pre-market safety testing.

**In fact, no "safe exposure level" has been scientifically determined for children or pregnant women—so when you read that a device "meets government standards," it doesn't, because there are no safety standards.**

Hundreds of organizations, including other governmental agencies such as the Environmental Protection Agency[47] and the US Government Accountability Office,[48] have been issuing warnings saying that the guidelines don't protect us.

Secondly, in the US, the last time the guidelines were updated was in 1996.[49]

46 https://ehtrust.org/policy/fcc-safety-standards/
47 http://bit.ly/USEnvironmentalProtectionAgency
48 https://www.gao.gov/products/GAO-12-771
49 https://transition.fcc.gov/Bureaus/Engineering_Technology/Orders/1996/fcc96326.pdf

Remember 1996? I do. It was a time that only a select few owned a cell phone (I didn't get mine until 1998) and for those that did, it probably looked something like this →

We are talking over 20 years ago. Nobody had heard of Google, Facebook or Instagram, and iPhone's didn't even exist. It was a world where Wi-Fi and wireless devices weren't everywhere. Exposure guidelines created in the 1990s might have been okay in the 1990s, but what place do they have in today's world? And what place will they have in a world where 5G and the Internet of Things (IOT) will raise the level of electrosmog we are all exposed to unprecedented levels?

Thirdly, let's just look at ICNIRP, IEEE and ANSI. These are the agencies that established the guidelines from which the national guidelines are based. Who are the IEEE? They are a bunch of engineers. Do you think engineers are qualified to make decisions about your health?

Who are ANSI? They are an industry and military organization. Are the industry and military qualified to make decisions about your health? Who runs ICNIRP? The WHO. Remember what I said about the WHO?

## Myth Buster #3: No Symptoms ≠ No Effect

To argue that because you can't feel anything when you use your cell phone, or your Bluetooth headset, or your Wi-Fi must mean that there are no effects is a bit silly really. Are you expecting to feel an electric shock? Come on, seriously?

My symptoms were clear cut. It went from an unpleasant sensation to being painful very quickly. A lot of people, it seems, can feel something when they use their cell phone, a warming sensation, tingling, perhaps, but they choose to ignore it. Then if they get some other symptoms—headaches, difficulty sleeping, tinnitus—they don't make the connection between their symptoms and their cell phone.

Think about air pollution, for instance. People that live in cities are breathing in the particles in the air into their lungs. Eventually, they might get a cough that might develop into a respiratory infection or worse, but it's not because they have no immediate symptoms that there is no effect.

EMFs are the same. Just because you can't feel immediate symptoms, does not mean that there is no effect. The truth is EMFs impact our bodies in very subtle ways. So subtle that most of us can't feel anything.

## You May Not Be Able To Feel EMFs, But Your Cells Can

Cells are the basic building blocks of all living things, you, me, plants, animals, or as Bruce Lipton explains:

> ***As a cell biologist, I can tell you that you are in truth a cooperative community of approximately fifty trillion single-celled citizens.***[50]

Your skin, bones, teeth, hair, liver, heart, all your organs are all made up of a collection of cells. The quality of these cells and the quality of this interaction determines your state of health and well-being. Makes sense, right?

So, what determines the quality of your cells and the quality of this interaction?

There are three things that cells need to survive:

- **OXYGEN**, used to create adenosine triphosphate (ATP), which serves as a source of energy.
- **WATER**, used as a medium for chemical reactions and for the diffusion and osmosis of substances.
- The ability to eliminate its own **WASTE**, otherwise known as detoxification.

We know cells use oxygen to create ATP, which is the fuel for the cell. There is a mechanism inside the cell membrane that pumps the potassium into the cell and the sodium out of the cell. It's called the sodium-potassium ATPase, because it takes ATP as the fuel and uses it to create this ionic movement. What Dr Martin Blank found was that this fundamental process was affected by very, very weak EMFs. That's to say the level of EMFs found in most homes.

50 Bruce Lipton, 2005. *The Biology of Belief: Unleashing the Power of Consciousness, Matter & Miracles.*

He also found that the ATP is directly affected by EMFs. He studied cytochrome oxidase, which is an enzyme that's present in the mitochondria, which is the powerhouse inside cells that makes ATP. That, too, was affected, according to his research.

> ***So, you see at the very foundation of the cell chemistry, the background that's necessary for various things to function inside the cell, you can have an influence at a very, very low level, very low energy [EMFs] in fact it's so low that people don't generally worry about this.***
>
> *—Martin Blank, PhD, EMF Experts Solutions Club interview.*

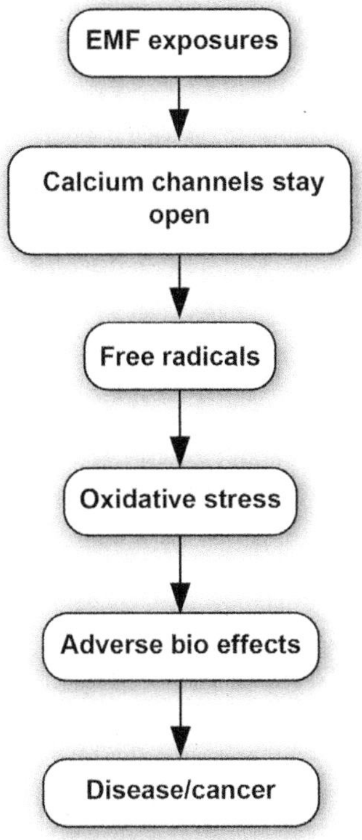


Perhaps more importantly, thanks to Nobel Prize winning research,[52] we've known for over 20 years that cells communicate with each other through electromagnetic signals, which conduct information throughout the body translating into biochemical and physiological processes.

> ***Our cells communicate using electromagnetic frequencies. Our brain emits a constant stream of frequencies and our DNA delivers instructions, using frequency waves. Without them we couldn't exist for more than a second.***[53]

We are truly electromagnetic beings.

## Principal Mechanism Of Harm

For the last ten years or so Martin Pall, from Washington State University, has been studying the voltage gated calcium channels (VGCCs)—which, as the name suggests, are like little gates or doors that let calcium in and out of your cells.

What Dr. Pall found was that very low level EMF exposures (including those from cell phones and electrical appliances commonly found in most homes) can cause

52 https://www.nobelprize.org/prizes/medicine/1994/press-release/
53 From the documentary *Resonance Beings of Frequency* http://bit.ly/ElectricSense-DangersWirelessFrequencies

your cells' calcium channels to stay open, which increases the release of superoxide and nitric oxide (NO). That in turn results in the formation of peroxynitrite (ONOO), which then cascades into other free radicals such as carbonyl—free radicals that can penetrate the nucleus and cause harm.

**This combination of free radical damage and oxidative stress in turn leads to a long list of adverse biological effects and diseases, including cancer.**

Sounds complicated? It is a bit.

That's why I've made the nice diagram, above, to simplify it.

At the moment this NO/ONOO cycle,[54] as it's called, is seen by many experts as being the principal mechanism of harm—that's to say it's the best explanation we have of how EMFs cause disease. What makes this theory even more convincing is that when people are given calcium blockers, the EMF damage is radically reduced[55]—see Chapter 20 for more on this.

## EMFs Damage DNA

How tall you are, the color of your eyes, your bodily functions; all this information (and more) is contained in your deoxyribonucleic acid, in other words, your DNA.

Storing information is your DNA's most important job. The information acts as a blueprint, so your body can keep making different types of proteins, but also determines which systems to turn on and off, so you can continue being you.[56]

The problem is, low level EMFs from cell phones and many other devices commonly found in our homes can penetrate the defense mechanisms of the cells in your body and damage your DNA.[57] This DNA damage is how cancers are believed to form.

> ***When you break a piece of DNA, you've broken the code. It's not like when you get a cut and the skin heals.***
>
> —*MARTIN BLANK, PHD.*[58]

54 https://www.youtube.com/watch?v=6A7r1gemjto
55 https://www.ncbi.nlm.nih.gov/pubmed/23802593
56 https://www.theepochtimes.com/do-cell-phones-and-Wi-Fi-fields-harm-our-body_2155494.html
57 http://mreengenharia.com.br/pathfisology/Pathophysiology-2009_M_Blank.pdf
58 https://www.theepochtimes.com/do-cell-phones-and-Wi-Fi-fields-harm-our-body_2155494.html

More recent studies also show that mitochondrial damage caused by the NO/ONOO cycle can lead to DNA damage.[59] This mitochondrial damage is no small detail either; other research suggests mitochondrial dysfunction could be behind most metabolic and degenerative diseases.[60]

> ***Increased peroxynitrite production from cell phone exposure will damage your mitochondria, and your brain is the most mitochondrial-dense organ in your body.***
>
> —*DR JOSEPH MERCOLA.*[61]

There are other ways that EMFs harm us at a biological level. I will talk about these later. But for now, I want you to understand from the DNA perspective alone just how potentially lethal these exposures can be.

## Doubt Is Our Product

If you're surprised by what I've shared so far, you're probably wondering: "Why is this information not out there? How come everybody thinks that EMFs are safe?"

There are several reasons. One of them is that the science is being manipulated. Industry-funded studies are significantly less likely to show health effects of EMFs compared to independent studies.

**Industry-funded studies found a health effect in 28% of the studies and the independently funded studies found an effect 67% of the time.**[62]

But the truth is nobody much reads the studies. The cell phone industry is doing what Big Pharma and Big Tobacco have done so well before them—creating doubt.

> ***Industry doesn't have to win the scientific argument about safety; it only has to keep the argument going.***
>
> —*BILL CADWALLADER, CERTIFIED ELECTROMAGNETIC RADIATION SPECIALIST*[63]

59 https://articles.mercola.com/sites/articles/archive/2017/09/03/electromagnetic-fields-harmful-effects.aspx
60 https://www.jci.org/articles/view/61398
61 https://articles.mercola.com/sites/articles/archive/2019/03/28/alzheimers-death-rate-doubled.aspx?
62 http://phiremedical.org/research-issues/
63 Bill Cadwallader, 2018. *Exposed: The Electronic Sickening of America – Includes Dangers of 5G and Smart Devices.*.

There are lots of ways they can do this, including:

1. Pay off or discredit scientists who produce research that might damage their interests.[64]
2. Pay for studies which support their case.
3. Feed public propaganda,[65] get people addicted to their product.[66] Exert undue influence on the FCC, up to the point where many believe it has become a "captured agency" and unable to fulfill its role in protecting the public.[67]
4. Ensure that important studies that come to alarming conclusions are downplayed by the media, as was the case for the recent NTP study.[68] Cutting-off funding where research produces evidence which might threaten industry profits—even the military is guilty of this.[69]

## The Dirty Little Secret

What's very clear is that if you expose yourself to EMFs at *very* low power levels, this *will* cause adverse biological effects, which *can* eventually give you cancer or another serious disease. Low level EMFs of every sort, radio frequency radiation, electric fields, magnetic fields, dirty electricity all can do this. I will talk about this in the upcoming chapters. This has been known for a long time and yet, not just industry, but even the military has gone to considerable lengths to stop the information from getting out.

Back in the 1950s, research conducted by ophthalmologist Milton Zaret on radar operators found that radio frequency microwave radiation exposures (similar to what your cell phone uses) were causing cataracts. His employers, the military, mounted a campaign to discredit his work and eventually withdrew his funding. He continued to be active in the EMF arena for some time afterwards, as a commentator and expert, but he was unable to continue his research.[70]

Similarly, in the 1960s, pioneering researcher Dr. Allan Frey had been investigating how radio frequency microwave radiation affects hearing. He discovered

64 http://www.washington.edu/alumni/columns/march05/wakeupcall01.html
65 http://bit.ly/ehtrust
66 Lloyd Morgan, EMF Experts Solutions Club interview.
67 https://ethics.harvard.edu/files/center-for-ethics/files/capturedagency_alster.pdf
68 Dr. Joseph Mercola, *EMF'D.*
69 https://www.gq.com/story/warning-cell-phone-radiation
70 https://microwavenews.com/news-center/milton-zaret-early-prophet-microwave-hazards-dies-91

that RF radiation can cause ringing in the ears, what some people call tinnitus. But it was in the 1970s when he published a paper showing that EMFs can damage our blood-brain-barrier (a very important means of protection for the brain) that he was told by the military to either shut up or risk losing his funding.[71]

**What the industry and governments want you to believe is that EMFs from cell phones and other household devices don't have enough power to harm you.**

If you ask an electrical engineer, who only knows what he's been taught in engineering school, to explain to you what determines how dangerous an EMF exposure is he will probably say the two most important factors are:

1. The power
2. The duration of exposure (how long you are exposed).

If you're only exposed to EMFs for a few seconds, then it's obviously much less of an issue than if you are exposed for days, weeks, months or years. Nobody's arguing about the importance of duration of exposure. But there is controversy about power.

With high power radiation, or ionizing radiation, as with x-rays and gamma rays, there IS a heating effect because there is SO much power. This is blatantly obvious.

But the research shows this is not only about the heating effect, and it's not about the power—it's about the complexity of the radiation. I will talk about this more in Chapter 8.

**The dirty little secret is that it's not just about the power it's about the complexity of the radiation.**

Cell phones and other wireless and wired devices affect us in subtle but profound ways. The words of a song come to mind—Killing Me Softly—I will develop on this in the next chapter.

Here's a summary of what you need to take away from this chapter:

71 https://www.gq.com/story/warning-cell-phone-radiation

- Thousands of studies demonstrate clearly that EMFs are extremely hazardous to your health
- You may not be able to feel EMFs but your cells can
- We are electromagnetic beings—our cells communicate using EMFs
- We've repeatedly been given official warnings—even the WHO has talked of a possible cancer link
- Just 30 minutes of cell phone use a day can increase your chances of getting a brain tumor by 40%
- Multiple studies point to an increased risk of getting a brain tumor on the same side of your head as your cell phone
- There are no standards for safe levels of radiation emitted by cell phones and other wireless devices
- EMFs harm us by causing excess calcium to leak into our cells, which sets off a chain reaction that causes disease
- Few people really know or care about the dangers of EMFs because the cell phone industry is doing what Big Pharma and Big Tobacco have done so well before them—creating doubt
- The dirty little secret is that it's not just about the power, it's about the complexity of the radiation.

## Chapter 4

# Killing Me Softly

HERE IS A LIST OF common EMF symptoms.[72]

| Skin problems | Sensitivity to light and eye problems |
|---|---|
| Tiredness and weakness | Heart problems and high blood pressure |
| Headaches and migraines | Pain in joints and muscles |
| Dizziness | Concentration difficulties |
| Nausea and general poor health | Memory disorders |
| Endocrine reactions | Respiratory and lung disorders |
| Stomach and intestinal disorders | Numbness |
| Influenza and throat problems | Sleep disorders |
| Hearing problems and tinnitus | Tremors, cramps, anxiety, depression |
| Coma, asthma, allergies, speech difficulties, irritability | Haziness, confusion, fainting |

The first clue that I got that I was being zapped by cell phone was in my head. At first it was like a weird spatial awareness, a kind of dizziness and then the headaches kicked in after that. Headaches and migraines are high on the list of reported complaints.

72 http://www.electricsense.com/wp-content/uploads/2012/08/blackonwhite-complete-book.pdf

## EMFs Zap Your Head

It's fairly obvious when you think about it. Your cell phone emits radio frequency microwave radiation and there we all are (most people), putting this EMF emitting device right next to this big squishy thing full of water, your brain.

Notice how I keep talking about "microwave" radio frequency radiation from your cell phone? There's a reason for that. The radiation that your cell phone emits is on a very similar frequency (depending on where you live in the world) to that of a microwave oven.

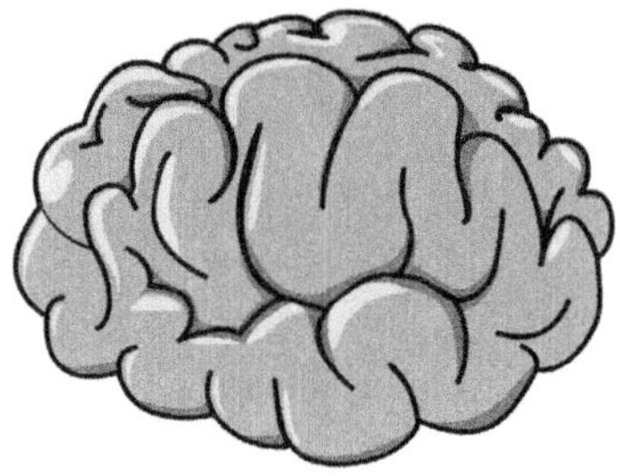

Microwave ovens work by causing molecules that have two opposing poles to spin rapidly. Because of their polarity, molecules like water will constantly align themselves with a magnetic field they're subjected to.[73]

The microwave radiation emitted by your cell phone can have a similar effect on your brain; it excites the molecules. Of course, some people don't feel it, some get headaches, some get other symptoms like nausea, dizziness and fatigue.

## EMFs Zap Your Blood Brain Barrier

Your brain is this rather squishy thing made up of about 75% water. That means it's quite fragile, and is why we are all equipped with a nice thick skull to protect the brain from bangs and knocks. But your brain also has another form of protection called the blood brain barrier (BBB), which is just as important as your skull, perhaps even more so.

**Like many parts of the body, this barrier develops as we mature and does not exist at birth. This so-called barrier is understood to protect the brain from taking in the wrong things.**

The BBB has 2 roles:

1. Preventing toxins from getting into your brain
2. Allowing your brain to get the essential nutrients it needs to function.

73 https://www.scientificamerican.com/article/bring-science-homes-soap-microwave/

Pioneering research done back in the 1970s by Dr. Allan Frey found that cell phone radiation type exposures can damage this BBB.

> ***It is important to note that Frey's research revealed this damage with very short-term exposure, suggesting that abnormal changes begin almost immediately.***
>
> —*Martin Blank, PhD.*[74]

These findings have been confirmed many times over by other researchers.[75]

## Could Your Cell Phone Be Causing Your Headaches?

A 2017 study,[76] which reviewed 2699 previous studies going back to 1990, found a dose-response relationship between the risk of having a headache and duration of cell calls and frequency. The study concluded that cell phone use is "significantly associated with headaches".

**What that means in plain English is the more time you spend on your cell phone, the higher your risk of getting a headache.**

We don't exactly know why cell phone radiation causes headaches; one argument is because it causes inflammation in the meninges,[77] the membranes that surround the brain. Earlier research came up with similar findings.

Here are a few other studies worth mentioning:

- A 2016 Korean study found cell phone call duration to be the main determinant of the severity of headaches.[78]
- A major Danish study[79] of 52,000 pregnant women had similar findings. When their children reached the age of seven, the mothers completed a questionnaire regarding their child's health. The study found that children with cell phone exposure had higher odds of headache-related symptoms than children with no exposure.

74 Martin Blank, 2015. *Overpowered: What Science Tells Us About The Dangers of Cell Phones and other WIFI Age Devices.*
75 https://www.ncbi.nlm.nih.gov/pubmed/8012056
76 https://www.nature.com/articles/s41598-017-12802-9
77 https://microwavenews.com/sites/default/files/sites/default/files/backissues/n-d01issue.pdf
78 https://www.ncbi.nlm.nih.gov/pubmed/27788568
79 https://www.ncbi.nlm.nih.gov/pubmed/23750182

- A 2003 study[80] commissioned by three Dutch ministries on cell towers found that cell phone radiation can cause headaches and nausea. It also found a link with other symptoms such as dizziness, fatigue, weakness, and muscle pain—despite the fact that the study used a lower dose of radiation than that of cell phones.

## EMFs Zap Your Ears

If you put a cell phone next to your ear to talk, do you really think that at some point it's not going to affect your ears and your hearing?

**The temperature of your ear lobes increases by approximately 1°C when a cell phone is used next to your ear for 20 minutes.[81]**

It's been known for decades that exposing yourself to cell phone type radiation can cause "microwave hearing",[82] being able to hear noises that others can't, ear pain, deafness and tinnitus.

Jackie, who contacted me via my website to tell me about how EMFs affect her, discovered that 2+ years of constant ear pain was the result of using her DECT cordless phone.

> *On top of the headaches and ear pain, there's ear itching, ringing, tingling, numbness, and a constant plugged feeling (as if I had just flown on an airplane or swam in deep water). Once I stopped using a DECT phone, my symptoms began to clear. It's been about ten weeks now and the ringing/tinnitus has subsided (maybe a three now vs. a nine-to-ten previously), my ears don't itch, all tingling has cleared and the plugged feeling is nearly gone.*[83]

Tinnitus, or ringing in the ears, always seemed to me like a disease that only the elderly get. Not true; you can get tinnitus at any age, and now it seems exposure to different kinds of EMFs play a role.

80 http://milieugezondheid.be/dossiers/gsm/TNO_rapport_Nederland_sept_2003.pdf
81 Reply to ASSOCHAM comments on Prof Girish Kumar's presentation at the ASSOCHAM EMF Workshop 7th Feb 2012, New Delhi.
82 https://en.wikipedia.org/wiki/Microwave_auditory_effect
83 Taken from blog comments on ElectricSense.com.

Literally hundreds of people have complained to me about tinnitus or ringing in the ears on ElectricSense.com:

> *I have recently developed tinnitus. After much trial and error in trying to determine what sets this off, I think it has something to do with electronic sensitivity. I can have no problems but go into the Apple store and the buzzing begins. When I was recently away from home for two short periods of time, I had no buzzing. When I return the buzzing began.*
>
> *I have not been aware that I am especially EHS, although I suffer from chronic insomnia (eight years now). I seem to have developed tinnitus—it started three days ago. I was in a government building—employees with iPads, lots of people with cell phones—and I started to hear a high-pitched noise—acute, but then it ended. Sometimes I have been in the supermarket and have heard the same, but I didn't hear ringing in my ears after that.*
>
> *My electro-hypersensitivity started back in 2009 when they installed the smart meters. The tinnitus woke me up out of a dead sleep. The sound is only part of it. If you have amalgam (silver/mercury) fillings, like I do, you can pick up electrical sounds that change pitch when you move your mouth or chew. So annoying and tormenting that it makes you wanna pull your eyeballs out and throw them at a wall.*

In a ten-year study on patients with electro-hypersensitivity or multiple chemical sensitivity, Prof. Dominique Belpomme, one of the leading authorities on EMFs and health in France, found that although headaches were the most common symptom, ear pain, tinnitus and hearing disorders were very common too.

## Clinical Symptom Occurrence in EHS Patients[84]

| | |
|---|---|
| Ear pains (otalgia) | 70% |
| Ringing/buzzing in the ears (tinnitus) | 50% |
| Hearing disorder (hyperacusis) | 40% |

84 Taken from a presentation given by Professor Belpomme https://www.youtube.com/watch?v=5xdqxeiKHnY

Prof. Girish Kumar, when I interviewed him on this question, talked about the rising number of teenagers whose hearing is being damaged through cell phone use:

> ***ENT specialists have very categorically said they are getting very large number of patients who are developing one side ear problems and these are partial hearing loss, even to full hearing loss, as well as ear tumors... teenagers are their largest customers because they talk for hours and hours.***[85]

Some possible explanations[86] as to why EMFs cause tinnitus:

1. Dr. Paul Heroux argues that tinnitus is largely due to a lack of ATP in the hair cells of the auditory system. He believes, "it's potentially a real connection".
2. Dr. Martin Pall believes tinnitus, when it's localized in the cochlea of the inner ear, may be produced by the NO/ONOO cycle.[87]

## EMFs Zap Your Eye's

In my case, I quickly realized continuing to use my cell phone was not an option. So, I went back to working in my office more, where I could take calls on my landline and work on my computer.

Within a few days, I developed an acute sensitivity to light. This was a weird feeling. The first time I noticed it, that morning I'd been sitting at my desk working on my laptop (wired, of course!). About lunch time, I went outside to get some air or something and I remember the light suddenly felt so intense it was nearly blinding me—and it wasn't even sunny.

My only symptom relating to my eyes was light sensitivity, but other people have reported to me similar issues and worse.[88]

> ***My own eye problems started after people started using wireless technology in the flats where I live. I had an operation for cataracts a year ago, but have been told by my optician that I still have some condition related to the cataracts.***

85 Extract from EMF Experts Solutions Club interview.
86 Source: EMF Experts Solutions Club interviews.
87 The mechanism I talked about in Chapter 3.
88 ElectricSense.com

Another reader comments:

> ***My thoughts regarding cell tower radiation and related... I recently went for an eye exam for new prescription for glasses and the examiner said that it looked as though some cataracts were starting; could this be radiation caused? Seems very reasonable to me since I live a healthy lifestyle, not doing dumb things, but being bombarded by some "dumb" source(s) of radiation!***

In the 1950s, ophthalmologist Milton Zaret studied eye damage in radar workers and found cataracts in areas of the eye not prone to cataracts.[89] Radar uses similar frequencies to cell phones and some radar systems use even higher frequencies.

Research carried out by King's College London found that every hour a day playing computer games raises the risk of short-sightedness by three per cent, leading to "digital myopia".[90] When I asked Prof. Girish Kumar of IIT Bombay, India about 5G he commented, "it will affect your eyes greatly. All the facial things will be affected much more."

More about 5G in Chapter 12.

## EMFs Can Make You Fat And Diabetic

Sounds crazy, I know. But let's look at the facts. According to researchers from the Centers for Disease Control and Prevention (CDC), the number of American adults with obesity has increased significantly over the past decade. In the years between 2007–2008 and 2015–2016 the rates of obesity rose from 33.7% to 39.6%.[91]

Even more alarming are the stats for childhood obesity, its prevalence having tripled over the last three decades. According to one study, approximately 17% of US children and adolescents are now obese.[92]

What do the studies say?

A 2011 study found that 50 minutes of cell phone type radiation causes increased brain glucose metabolism in the part of the brain closest to the antenna.[93]

89 B. Blake Levitt, 2007. *Electromagnetic Fields, A Consumer's Guide To The Issues And How To Protect Ourselves.*
90 http://bit.ly/independent-uk-smartphone-children
91 https://www.cancer.org/latest-news/obesity-rates-continue-to-rise-among-adults-in-the-us.html
92 https://www.ncbi.nlm.nih.gov/pmc/articles/PMC6262374/
93 https://www.ncbi.nlm.nih.gov/pmc/articles/PMC3184892/

Research done by Prof. Magda Havas from Trent University in Canada has shown that dirty electricity (a form of EMF pollution found on home wiring, see Chapter 10) can cause blood sugar to spike or fall and give rise to a form of diabetes.[94]

A 1994 study found that magnetic fields at levels commonly found in many homes caused increased blood glucose levels.[95]

In another study, it was found that maternal exposure to magnetic fields during pregnancy, "may be a new and previously unknown factor contributing to the worldwide epidemic of childhood obesity/overweight."[96] This study also found a direct correlation between EMF exposures during pregnancy directly and obesity at 12 years old.

Elizabeth Plourde, PhD, comments:

> ***If we alter our fat metabolism pathways with this radiation, these poor kids could probably eat lettuces their whole lives and still be obese. So we're actually altering how we metabolize food with this radiation.***[97]

What does all this mean? EMF expert James Lech believes EMFs to be "**the strongest contributor for causing obesity and diabetes**" in the world, among the other mitochondrial diseases.[98]

Interestingly, live blood research work by Prof. Magda Havas has also shown that just using a computer for 70 minutes can cause your blood to go into Rouleaux Formation[99]—commonly found in cancer patients. Dr. Ross Andersen, who has conducted over 7000 live blood tests, has observed the Rouleaux Formation in people's blood who have been exposed to cell tower radiation and similar frequencies and also oxidative damage to blood. He believes this oxidative damage to be a very strong indicator of significant long-term electromagnetic exposure.

## EMFs Can Ruin Your Sex Life

When a guy finds it difficult getting an erection or keeping a firm enough erection to have sex, or if it interferes with other sexual activity, that's what's called an erectile dysfunction.

94 https://magdahavas.com/diabetes-and-electrosensitivity/
95 T. A. Litovitz et al. 1994. Effect of 60Hz magnetic fields on blood glucose levels of diabetic humans and its inhibition by EM noise.16th Annu. Meeting Bioelectromagn. Soc.; June 12–17; Copenhagen, Denmark. P. 128.
96 https://www.nature.com/articles/srep00540
97 EMF Experts Solutions Club.
98 EMF Experts Solutions Club.
99 Rouleaux formation is a term used to describe when red blood cells stick together like stacked coins.

Typically, the older you get, the more this is a problem. Makes sense. A recent UK survey found that about half of men in their 30s struggled to get or maintain an erection.

Could EMFs be behind this too?

**Men with erectile dysfunction are 2.6 times more likely to have mobile phones in the front pocket of their trousers.[100]**

There's been limited research done on erectile dysfunction, so it's a bit early to draw any conclusions. But the research done on how cell phone radiation impacts male fertility is a lot clearer.

**Male fertility is dropping across the globe.** Around 14% of couples in high-and-middle-income countries have difficulty conceiving and male infertility is involved approximately 50% of the time. Numerous countries are reporting unexplained declines in semen quality.

**Multiple review studies have repeatedly found that cell phone radiation damages sperm and impacts male fertility in a variety of ways.**

Studies show that cell phone radiation exposures can cause:

- Reduced sperm count.[101]
- Reduced sperm motility (ability to move).[102]
- Reduced sperm morphology (irregular shape).[103]
- Harm to sperm quality generally.[104]
- Reduced levels of testosterone (needed to make sperm).[105]

100 Abstracts of the World Meeting on Sexual Medicine. Chicago, Illinois, USA. August 26–30, 2012. The Journal of Sexual Medicine [Internet]. Elsevier; 2012 [cited 2018 Feb 28]. P. 183–302. doi: 10.1111/j.1743-6109.2012.02863.x

101 Agarwal A, et al. 2008. Effect of cell phone usage on semen analysis in men attending infertility clinic: an observational study. Fertil Steril. 89: P. 124–128. doi: 10.1016/j.fertnstert.2007.01.166

102 https://www.ncbi.nlm.nih.gov/pubmed/27601711

103 https://www.ncbi.nlm.nih.gov/pubmed/20236367

104 https://www.ncbi.nlm.nih.gov/pubmed/16087567

105 http://www.ncbi.nlm.nih.gov/pubmed/20714683

Also, several studies[106] have found that cell phone radiation can cause oxidative damage in cells. Oxidative stress is widely regarded as a contributor to virtually every major chronic disease, including cancer, Alzheimer's, heart disease and diabetes.

Guys, what's the sense in eating healthy and working out if you keep your cell phone next to your balls? Cell phone radiation can oxidize the cells inside your testicles, which can also lead to low testosterone levels.

**Cell phone radiation can literally fry your balls.**

There are hundreds of studies[107] on the various ways EMFs impact male fertility—the science is very strong.

**On the basis of these studies, my advice is simple: guys DO NOT carry your cell phone in your trouser pocket.[108]**

And yet for me the even bigger concern is how EMFs impact female fertility—see Chapter 16.

## EMFs Zap Your Heart

When you think of your heart, what do you think of? A big pump which circulates blood through your body? All that's true. But there's wayyyyyyy more to it than that.

Your heart is an *electrical* pump. Which means it has its own electrical activity and creates its own EMFs.[109] The electrical activity can be measured with an electrocardiogram (ECG) and the magnetic activity with a magnetometer. So, it's really not that hard to believe that EMFs from cell phones and other electrical devices in your life could be zapping your heart. These readers' comments speak for themselves:[110]

***I react with an irregular heartbeat and sometimes palpitations... the same thing happens when I am in line at the grocery store or in the post office. All***

106 Yakymenko I, et al. 2014. Low intensity radiofrequency radiation: a new oxidant for living cells. Oxid Antioxid Med Sci [Internet]. 3: 1–3. doi: 10.5455/oams.240314.ed.002. and La Vignera S, et al. Effects of the Exposure to Mobile Phones on Male Reproduction: A Review of the Literature. J Androl [Internet]. 2012; 33: 350–6. doi: 10.2164/jandrol.111.014373

107 https://www.emfresearch.com/emfs-male-fertility/

108 https://www.ncbi.nlm.nih.gov/pubmed/24927498

109 https://www.drpawluk.com/blog/electromagnetic-fields-and-the-heart/

110 Comments on ElectricSense.com

*of a sudden my heart skips and becomes arrhythmic. When I turn around there has been up to now always someone with a cell phone.*

*The five years driving the Tesla roadster as my everyday car and then driving the Tesla Model S P85+ for 6 months affected my heart... the few terrible months after I had purchased the Model S (and driven it as my everyday car) my heart would start beating irregularly.*

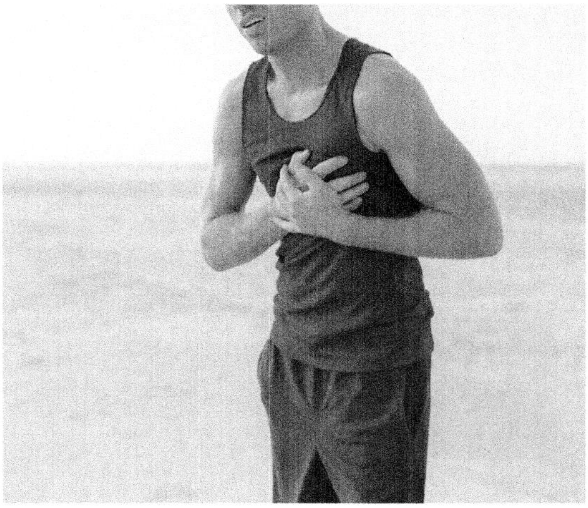

In 1980, heart attacks in young athletes in the US were extremely rare with only nine recorded cases. In 1996, there were 64 cases of fatal cardiac arrest, a 700% increase. Why the sudden spike? According to an association of German doctors, these heart attacks, and many other diseases which young people were succumbing to, were caused by EMFs.

In Germany, three thousand physicians signed an appeal to call for a moratorium on cell tower installations.[111]

**The year that cell phones first went on sale in the US, there was a doubling of heart attacks among young American athletes.[112]**

Prof. Magda Havas did a real-time monitoring study exposing people to pulsed microwave radiation from a cordless telephone. She found that some people developed a rapid or irregular heartbeat.[113]

In Canada, children who attend schools with Wi-Fi were complaining of a racing heart while in school. Two of these children were given heart monitors to wear and the symptoms of one young girl were so bad she'd been scheduled for heart surgery. Realizing the Wi-Fi was causing the problem, her parents removed the Wi-Fi from their home, postponed the operation and her symptoms did not return.[114]

111 Arthur Firstenberg 2017. *The Invisible Rainbow: A History of Electricity and Life.*
112 Arthur Firstenberg 2017. *The Invisible Rainbow: A History of Electricity and Life.*
113 https://magdahavas.com/pick-of-the-week-24-microwave-radiation-affects-the-heart/
114 https://magdahavas.com/pick-of-the-week-24-microwave-radiation-affects-the-heart/

In an animal study,[115] rabbits that were placed in close proximity to a Wi-Fi antenna for one hour were found to have an increased heart rate (+22%) and increased arterial blood pressure (+14%).[116]

Other studies have linked EMF exposures to:

- Heart failure[117]
- High blood pressure[118]
- Heart rate variability changes.

A word about heart rate (HR) variability, because it's an important indicator of health. A 2010 study[119] found "immediate and dramatic changes in both heart rate and HR variability" in people exposed to microwave radiation from cordless phone—at levels well below federal guidelines.

Samuel Milham, an MD and an epidemiologist, analyzed US death records from electrified rural areas and non-electrified rural areas in the early part of the 1900s. He hypothesizes that cardiovascular disease seems to be "strongly related to the level of residential electrification". He wrote a book about it, called *Dirty Electricity*, which includes some very solid statistics. More about Dr. Milham's work later on.

## EMFs Zap Our Furry Friends

How EMFs impact birds:

- Cell phone radiation causes increased mortality in chicken embryos.[120]
- 40% of nests of white storks within 200 meters of cell phone towers were found to have no chicks in a study in Spain.[121]
- In the UK, the population of house sparrows fell 75% between 1994 and 2002, which coincides with the roll out of the cell phone network.[122]

How EMFs impact bees:

- In a German study, a cordless phone was turned on next to eight beehives and the results were compared with eight similar beehives without any

115 https://www.ncbi.nlm.nih.gov/pubmed/26356390/
116 https://www.defendershield.com/top-3-areas-body-most-vulnerable-emf
117 https://www.ncbi.nlm.nih.gov/pmc/articles/PMC3856065/
118 https://www.ncbi.nlm.nih.gov/pubmed/10212373
119 http://bit.ly/Ramazziniinstitute
120 http://bit.ly/alliedacademies
121 https://www.tandfonline.com/doi/abs/10.1080/15368370500205472
122 Arthur Firstenberg, 2017. *The Invisible Rainbow: A History of Electricity and Life.*

cordless phone exposures. Only 7% of the bees returned to the radiated hives compared to 39% in the non-radiated hives.[123]

- An Indian study exposed beehives to 30 minutes of cell phone radiation for three months. The population of the exposed hive was reduced by over 70%.

Bees have their own natural EMF-based guidance system. Man-made EMFs alter their internal navigation, making it so that they can't find their way back to the hive. Some experts predict the honeybee could be extinct by 2035. It seems insects are also very sensitive to EMFs. A 2013 study on ants found that a cell phone in standby mode placed under an ant nest caused the ants to leave their nest immediately. Exposing them to a Wi-Fi router had a similar effect.[124] Frogs don't appear to like cell phone radiation either. In a Spanish study, frogs that were exposed to a cell tower 140 meters away had a mortality rate 21 times higher compared to those placed in an EMF-shielded environment.[125]

Plants are affected by EMFs too. Studies show:

- Cell phone radiation reduces growth in mung bean and wheat seedlings.[126]
- Radio frequency radiation causes death of cells or tissues in aspen seedlings[127]

There haven't been too many studies on how EMFs affect plants, but according to Dr. Andrew Goldsworthy, "Trees are now dying mysteriously from a variety of diseases in urban areas all over Europe and are also showing abnormal photoperiodic responses... all of these can be explained as being a result of weak radio-frequency radiation from mobile phones, their base stations, Wi-Fi and similar sources."[128]

So, EMFs zap us in so many different ways and can cause so many different symptoms, which makes diagnosis or identification of the root cause of your symptoms incredibly difficult. Meaning if you go to your doctor with headaches, tinnitus or heart palpitations, it's extremely unlikely he or she will say, "Oh, it's EMFs that are causing this." A lot of doctors are still saying EMFs don't impact our health and when EMF hyper-sensitive people go to see these doctors they say that it's all in the mind. But how can it be if it's affecting plants and animals? I guess it must be all in their minds too...

123 Martin Blank, 2015. *Overpowered: What Science Tells Us About The Dangers of Cell Phones and other WIFI Age Devices.*
124 Katie Singer 2014. *An Electronic Silent Spring.*
125 https://www.ncbi.nlm.nih.gov/pubmed/20560769
126 http://maxwellsci.com/print/ajas/v4-149-152.pdf
127 https://www.hindawi.com/journals/ijfr/2010/836278/
128 http://www.puls-schlag.org/download/Goldsworthy-2011-02-18.pdf

***We have grass, we have tomato plants, we have flowers, we have bushes, and we have trees that are constantly being hammered by EMFs that are in the order of quintillion times higher [that's a one with 18 zeros after it] than natural background levels.***

*—PROF. OLLE JOHANSSON, EMF HEALTH SUMMIT INTERVIEW*

What you need to retain from this chapter:

- Cell phone radiation damages your blood brain barrier
- The more you use your cell phone the higher the risk of getting a headache
- EMFs can cause ringing in the ears, ear pains and other hearing disorders
- EMFs can cause major eye damage including cataracts
- EMFs increase blood and brain glucose levels and may be a strong contributor to obesity and diabetes
- EMFs can cause erectile dysfunction and ruin your sex life
- EMFs can zap your heart and cause heart attacks
- EMFs are zapping all living things, including plants and animals.

Chapter 5

# Can EMFs Give You Cancer And Other Diseases?

CAN EMFS REALLY GIVE YOU cancer? Actually, the question is more like, "Can my cell phone give me cancer?" For people that are awakened to the dangers of EMFs, that's probably the number one concern.

Unfortunately, most people are completely shut-off about this. Because once you realize your cell phone, or any other of your electrical appliances, could be causing so many problems for you and your family, it's pretty scary.

## Cell Phone Radiation and Cancer

I laid out some of the evidence linking cell phones and cancer in Chapter 3 and I also explained some of the reasons people are so misinformed about all this. Here are some other things you need to know:

1. **Latency (or lag)**, the time it takes between exposure to a carcinogenic agent and cancers to appear, is well known in cancer epidemiology. To put this in the words of researcher Dr. Martin Blank "cancers do not form overnight". In almost all cases, cancerous tumors take many years to form and metastasize. Which suggests we may be sitting on a cancer time bomb.
2. **Flawed Research,** not all of the research points to a link between cell phone radiation and cancer. But then that's hardly surprising given the lengths some researchers go to skew the results. Researcher Lloyd Morgan has laid bare the phenomenon of study bias, as the chart below shows.[129] [130]

129 http://www.mreengenharia.com.br/pathfisology/Pathophysiology_2009_L_Morgan.pdf
130 Data compiled by Dr. Henry Lai, University of Washington.

# Cell Phone Radiation Research - Funding Bias

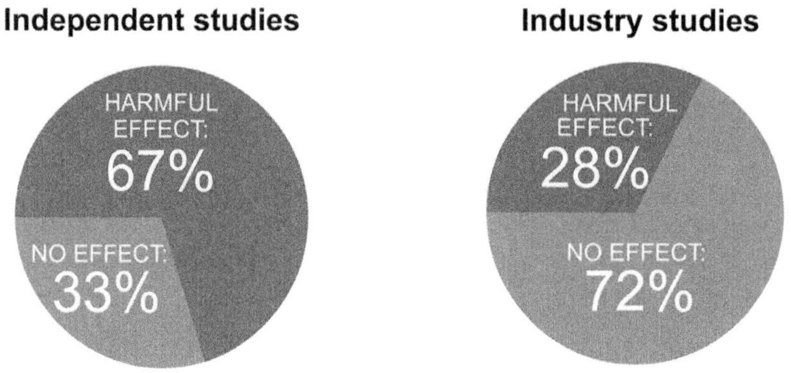


Data Compiled by Dr. Henry Lai, University of Washington

Researchers paid to do industry studies seem to have no end of imaginative ways of engineering their study to give the result they want, or are paid to achieve: [131]

- insufficient latency time
- incorrect definition of "regular" cell phone users
- cell phones radiating higher power levels in rural areas not investigated
- exposure to other transmitting sources not considered
- exclusion of brain tumor cases due to death or illness
- etc.

**The Increase in Disease (1990-2015)**

| Disease | Increase |
|---|---|
| Chronic fatigue | 11,027% |
| Bipolar | 10,833% |
| Fibromyalgia | 7,727% |
| Autism | 2,094% |
| Coeliac disease | 1,111% |
| ADHD | 819% |
| Hypothyroidism | 720% |
| Osteoarthritis | 449% |
| Sleep apnoea | 430% |
| Diabetes mellitus | 305% |
| Alzheimer's | 299% |
| Depression | 280% |

But perhaps there is another important question to ask: why are we focusing on cancer when perhaps the danger lies elsewhere?

131 http://www.mreengenharia.com.br/pathfisology/Pathophysiology_2009_L_Morgan.pdf

As this table[132] shows, in a single generation there has been a dramatic increase in diseases and disorders, many of which were previously unknown.

The increase in these modern diseases is mind-blowing. Richard Lear, the author of the report from which the table comes, points the finger of suspicion at peroxynitrite. But he failed to make the connection between peroxynitrite and EMFs. Researcher Dr. Martin Pall, however, did.

Remember our diagram from Chapter 3? Here it is again:

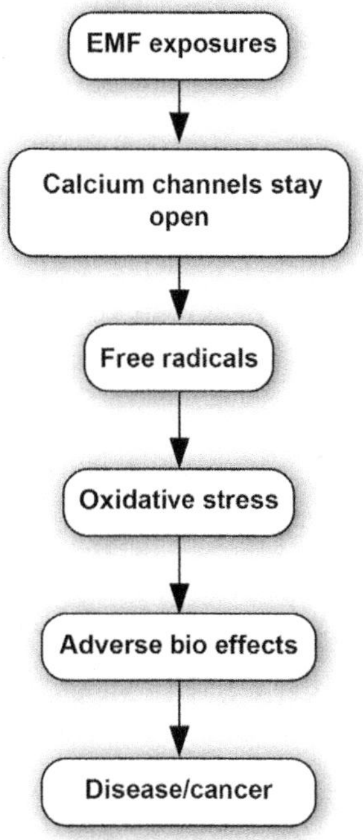


We know that these calcium channels (VGCCs) are incredibly sensitive to EMFs—seven million times more sensitive than other parts of the cell, according to Dr Pall. We also know that there are parts of our body where there is a concentration of these VGCCs, like our nervous tissue, brain and heart.[133] This means we are particularly vulnerable to EMFs in these parts of the body.

**Jason Bawden-Smith argues that EMFs, via activation of the calcium channels and the ensuing cellular damage and production of peroxynitrite, are behind the sudden rise in the chronic diseases listed above.[134]**

Sounds a bit far fetched? Well, let's look at what evidence there is.

## EMFs and Chronic Fatigue

Dr. Ross Andersen shared with me the story of an 11-year-old girl suffering from chronic fatigue that he was treating and who wasn't responding to his treatment. Then it occurred to him that he should measure the EMFs in her home. He discovered that the magnetic field in her bedroom was off the scale—she was sleeping against the outside wall on the second floor, where the electricals came into the house. She was living with her parents in an old farmhouse and she could actually hear the

132 Richard Lear, *The Root Cause in the Dramatic Rise of Chronic Disease* as reported by Jason Bawden-Smith 2016. *In The Dark.*

133 https://www.youtube.com/watch?v=klFvgBtFgQk

134 Jason Bawden-Smith 2016. *In The Dark.*

electricity crackling in the night. She was also sitting at the dining room table to do her homework for two or three hours every evening, which was situated next to the electrical columns that ran to the fuse box in the basement. On Dr. Andersen's advice, she was moved to another bedroom and she also started doing her homework in another room. The next day, she was feeling better and within three weeks, she was completely over her fibromyalgia chronic fatigue, without treatment.

Dr. Pall's NO/ONOO research also suggests that EMF exposures can cause chronic fatigue. Other studies[135] have come to a similar conclusion.

Studies have shown that all these different types of EMF exposure can cause fatigue:

- Cell tower radiation[136] powerline frequencies from electrical wiring[137] and Chronic Fatigue Syndrome (CFS)—is prolonged exposure to environmental level powerline frequency electromagnetic fields a co-factor to consider in treatment?
- Dirty electricity on electrical wiring.[138]
- Cell phone radiation.[139]

A physician in Kobe performed a study on CFS and noticed that about 80% of his CFS patients were frequent users of cell phones, personal computers, TV, games and other IT devices. He concluded that "reduced cerebral blood flow may possibly result from the influence of electromagnetic waves from IT equipment."[140]

## Fibromyalgia

Could EMFs explain the +7000% increase in fibromyalgia cases in our table?

Let's just get clear about what fibromyalgia is. The symptoms include:

- Chronic muscle pain, muscle spasms, or tightness
- Moderate or severe fatigue and decreased energy
- Insomnia or waking up feeling just as tired as when you went to sleep
- Stiffness upon waking or after staying in one position for too long

135 https://www.ncbi.nlm.nih.gov/pmc/articles/PMC6025786/
136 https://www.emf-portal.org/en/article/13498
137 https://www.vws.org/documents/Cell-Project-Documents/OberfeldSpanishstudy.pdf
138 http://www.emfandhealth.com/HavasStetzerWHODirtyElectricityStudies.pdf
139 http://bit.ly/emr-reduction-using-the-mobile
140 https://www.emfacts.com/2007/03/667study-suggests-reduced-cerebral-blood-flow-from-cellphones-etc/

- Difficulty remembering, concentrating, and performing simple mental tasks ("fibro fog")
- Abdominal pain, bloating, nausea, and constipation alternating with diarrhea (irritable bowel syndrome)
- Tension or migraine headaches
- Jaw and facial tenderness
- Sensitivity to one or more of the following: odors, noise, bright lights, medications, certain foods, and cold
- Feeling anxious or depressed
- Numbness or tingling in the face, arms, hands, legs, or feet
- Increase in urinary urgency or frequency (irritable bladder)
- Reduced tolerance for exercise and muscle pain after exercise
- A feeling of swelling (without actual swelling) in the hands and feet.

Look closely at this list. Notice anything? Top marks if you noticed that most of the symptoms listed for fibromyalgia are practically the exact same symptoms that people with EHS are reporting.[141]

I can't mention fibromyalgia without mentioning chronic fatigue syndrome (CFS). What's the difference between the two? As Dr. Bill Rawls points out, the symptoms are very similar but people with fibromyalgia identify more with pain and those with chronic fatigue identify more with a lack of energy or oppressive fatigue.[142]

But what really interests us is not the label we stick on this collection of symptoms but what the root cause is. Could the root cause of these three illnesses, fibromyalgia, CFS and EHS, be EMFs?

What I can say for sure is that with EHS, the role of EMFs is quite clear but with fibromyalgia and CFS it's often ignored.

## EMFs and Autism

In the 1980s, well before cell phone use had become widespread, autism rates in the US were reported at 1 in 10,000.[143] In the nineties, that figure dropped to 1 in 2,500. The most recent data published by the CDC puts that figure at 1 in 59.[144]

141 https://swissharmony.com/fibromyalgia-emf-connected/
142 https://rawlsmd.com/health-articles/fibromyalgia-chronic-fatigue-syndrome-different
143 https://autismsciencefoundation.org/what-is-autism/how-common-is-autism/
144 https://www.cdc.gov/mmwr/volumes/67/ss/ss6706a1.htm

Autism was once thought to be a permanent genetic condition, but that's looking less and less likely since a recent Stanford study on identical twins concluded that genetics alone could only account for less than half of the condition.[145] However, the role of EMFs seems to be clearer.

Here's what independent researchers working in this field have been saying:

> ***You have an epidemic of autism that's increasing worldwide and by definition, an exposure has to be proportional to the increase of the epidemic. Well, I don't know of any other kind of exposure other than microwave radiation that has been growing proportional to the autism epidemic.***
>
> *—Lloyd Morgan, EMF Experts Solutions Club interview.*

> ***The huge increase in autism that has paralleled the huge increase in the electromagnetic energy that's presently increasing in our environment.***
>
> *—Dr. Martin Blank, EMF Experts Solutions Club interview.*

> ***I think there's a very strong case that can be made that the autism epidemic, and I'm not talking about all cases of autism, but this huge increase in the autism incidents occurred over much of the world, that the epidemic is caused largely by microwave EMF exposures.***
>
> *—Dr Martin Pall, EMF Experts Solutions Club interview.*

What all three of these researchers have in common is that they are not prone to making bold statements unless there's some solid science to back it up.

What does the science say? There are currently about a half dozen studies linking prenatal EMFs to autism.

A 2013 paper has argued that autism is the result of a state of overload that comes from many factors affecting the whole body and not just the brain. These environmental factors are composed of medical risks, chemical toxins, lifestyle and EMFs.[146]

Various mechanisms are involved but cellular inflammation through excess calcium—Dr. Pall's work—would appear to be central.

Another important point I need to mention is the link between prenatal exposure to EMFs, particularly wireless and autism. A 2007 study found a clear correlation

145 http://www.clearlightventures.com/blog/2015/9/11/the-emerging-link-between-wireless-and-autism
146 ClearLight Autism One 2018 Booklet v9-spreads.pdf

between EMFs and autism[147] and Dr. Dietrich Klinghardt has stated that he can predict the risks a pregnant mother faces of having an autistic child just by measuring the levels of EMFs in her bedroom.

## EMFs and Alzheimer's

If I say to you, "neurodegenerative condition" what do you think of? Alzheimer's, Parkinson's, perhaps Huntington's diseases? But that's only the tip of the iceberg. There are now literally hundreds of these neurodegenerative conditions—many of which were unheard of before cell phones came on to the scene.[148]

Alzheimer's is the most common neurodegenerative condition[149] and the most severe form of dementia.

The rate of death from dementia has more than doubled in the last two decades—which ties in closely with the massive roll-out of wireless technologies.[150]

Not surprisingly, research is clearly linking EMFs to Alzheimer's disease specifically, and neurodegenerative conditions more generally. Could EMFs explain the 299% increase in Alzheimer's disease in our table above?

There are currently about a dozen studies which link cell phone radiation exposures to Alzheimer's disease.[151] Almost all epidemiological studies (study of diseases in populations) done so far on EMFs and the risk of Alzheimer's and ALS show an increased risk.[152]

Magnetic field exposures are also strongly linked to Alzheimer's. A 2009 study found long-term occupational exposure to magnetic fields could increase the risk of Alzheimer's disease.[153]

A Swiss study on magnetic fields found that people living within 50 meters of high-voltage powerlines were more likely to develop Alzheimer's compared to people living 600 meters away—this risk was found to increase significantly over time.[154]

> ***Beyond leukemia, the illness most closely linked with electromagnetic fields is Alzheimer's disease.***
>
> —LYN MCCLEAN, *THE FORCE: LIVING SAFELY IN A WORLD OF ELECTROMAGNETIC POLLUTION.*

---

147 http://www.avaate.org/IMG/pdf/EMR-Autism-ACNEM-final.pdf
148 https://www.researchgate.net/publication/329773981_Electromagnetic_Fields_and_Neurodegenerative_Diseases
149 https://www.healtheuropa.eu/eu-neurodegenerative-diseases/87348/
150 https://articles.mercola.com/sites/articles/archive/2019/03/28/alzheimers-death-rate-doubled.aspx?
151 http://bit.ly/emf-portal
152 http://bit.ly/33s1dF9
153 http://bit.ly/researchgate-Alzheimer
154 http://bit.ly/researchgate-Neurodegenerative_Diseases

Prof. Belpomme also believes Alzheimer's and EMFs are intimately linked,[155] and that EHS is the first stage of pre-Alzheimer's disorder.[156] This makes a lot of sense when you think about what neurons are and how they operate. Here's what Wikipedia says:

> ***A neuron... also known as a nerve cell, is an electrically excitable cell that communicates with other cells via specialized connections.***[157]

Given that our neurons are electrically excitable, is it so difficult to believe that they are being affected by the sea of EMFs we are now bathed in and are causing Alzheimer's and other neurodegenerative conditions?

## Depression

Could EMFs impact your mood and make you feel depressed? You're darn right they can. It's not an immediate "slap you in the face" effect. It's way more subtle and long term; nevertheless, the psychological effects of EMFs are very real.

The Russian's did a lot of research on the effects of radio frequency microwave radiation on the human body after the Second World War. They found it could cause depression, headaches, nausea and a string of other symptoms which they called "microwave sickness".[158]

Over 50 years ago, after doing its own research, the United States Defense Intelligence Agency was already warning its personnel of the risk from low-level microwaves, including illnesses, flu-like depression, and suicidal tendencies, not to mention cancer.[159]

Recent studies are saying the same thing:

- A 2016 study found that cell phone type EMFs produced widespread neuropsychiatric effects including depression[160]
- A 2002 study on people who lived at different distances from a cell phone tower found that the closer people lived to the cell tower, the more they experienced depression, fatigue and similar symptoms.[161]

155 Dr. Belpomme has questioned and clinically examined more than 1,000 electro-hypersensitivity (EHS) self-reported persons. He says, "These are real sick people who are in a Pre-Alzheimer's state." He says the most conclusive scientific proof of biological effect are animal studies and biological tests in EHS persons which indicate a Pre-Alzheimer's state. For more information, see: http://electromagnetichealth.org/electromagnetic-health-blog/electrosensitivity-a-pre-alzheimers-state/
156 https://www.electricsense.com/13826/treating-emf-impact/
157 https://en.wikipedia.org/wiki/Neuron
158 Dave Stetzer, EMF Experts Solutions Club interview.
159 Amended Declaration of Barrie Trower
160 https://www.ncbi.nlm.nih.gov/pubmed/26300312
161 https://www.ncbi.nlm.nih.gov/pubmed/12168254

- A 2015 study on patients with EHS found tendencies toward depression with suicidal "ideation" in 20–40% of cases.[162]
- A 2009 research paper that compared suicide rates with electrification in the US in 1940 found a very strong correlation between these deaths and electrification.
- About a dozen earlier studies have found a correlation between depression and EMFs.

Medical practitioners and researchers are also connecting the dots on this:

> ***The truth is that people have not been told the truth that their depression, that their insomnia, that their chronic illness is directly linked to [EMFs].***
>
> *—Dr. Dietrich Klinghardt, EMF Health Summit interview.*

> ***Understand that EMFs, especially if you're suffering from an inflammatory-based issue or a depression, low mood, hormonal, it's a big thing to look at.***
>
> *—Dr. Stephen Cabral, EMF Health Summit interview.*

> ***Another thing that blew my mind away is suicide and depression. That's clearly a very strong EMF disease.***
>
> *—Dr. Samuel Milham, EMF Experts Solutions Club interview.*

> ***Depression causes more mobile phone addiction and the mobile phone addiction causes more depression.***
>
> *—Prof. Trevor Marshall, commenting on a Korean study.*

How can EMFs cause depression? Oh no, not the NO/ONOO cycle again? Well, yes, because another aspect of this cycle is the release of chemical messengers in the brain—neurotransmitters—which upset mood regulation.[163] Other studies have found that EMFs deplete other important neurotransmitters like serotonin and dopamine, again, which impacts your mood.[164]

162 https://www.youtube.com/watch?v=5xdqxeiKHnY
163 https://www.youtube.com/watch?v=klFvgBtFgQk
164 https://www.ncbi.nlm.nih.gov/pubmed/23852905

## The Tip Of The Iceberg

There is a ton of science linking EMF exposure to different diseases, as (I hope) you're beginning to understand. I've only skimmed the surface here. The point is when we go to the doctors and they give us a diagnosis of chronic fatigue, insomnia, cancer or whatever it might be, these are the extreme cases. It's only the tip of the iceberg.

**The biggest part of the iceberg is made up of people that have "adverse biological effects" to EMF exposures but they have no clear symptoms around EMFs.**

So you might get symptoms, but not necessarily of the kind I experienced. My symptoms were clear. Cell phone next to the ear equals symptoms; no cell phone equals no symptoms. It's a bit like a slow burning fuse. The bomb is going to go off, but not straight away. In the jargon, these are called "adverse biological effects".

Here's a quick recap of the main adverse bio effects linked to EMFs. Remember, we're not talking diseases here, nor are we talking about symptoms. We're talking about what's going on "under the hood":

- DNA single and double strand breaks
- Disruption of cell metabolism
- Increased blood brain barrier permeability
- Disruption to brain glucose metabolism
- Generation of stress proteins
- Mitochondria (little power houses in your cells) damage

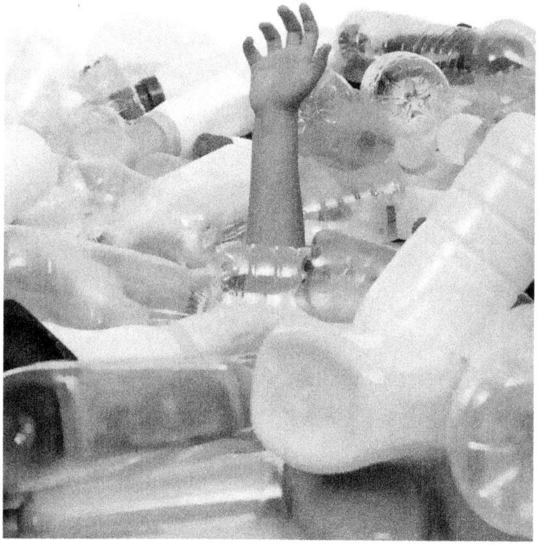

Most of the above can only be observed under a microscope, so this might not make much sense to you. But these adverse bio effects are crucial to understanding how EMFs truly impact us. Think of it like this →

The common thread appears to be the NO/ONOO cycle and the production of the toxin peroxynitrite. More about peroxynitrite and these nasty bio effects later.

## Three Important Observations

**Firstly, at this point it might feel as though I'm trying to prove to you that EMFs are 100% dangerous. I'm not.** And I can't. I just want you to be *aware* of the overwhelming body of science which shows we *can't* suppose these technologies are safe. In any case, trying to prove that EMFs are 100% dangerous would be topsy-turvy. Remember these technologies were introduced without any pre-market safety testing; it should be for the industries which are selling these technologies to prove they are safe.

**Secondly, the thing to remember about nearly all of these studies is that they are looking at one EMF exposure in isolation.** Things don't happen like that in the real world. Pretty much everyone, every day is exposed to RF radiation, magnetic fields, electric fields AND dirty electricity. So, the fact that the studies are linking these exposures in isolation to all these different conditions and diseases is very problematic.

**Thirdly, the studies I've cited don't take into account that not only are we exposed to all these different kinds of man-made unnatural EMFs on a daily basis, but we also exposed to a bunch of other toxins at the same time.** Research has already pointed to the synergistic effect of EMFs. That's to say, when we are exposed to toxins from our food and water, air pollution, chemicals in skin products and furnishings in our homes, then in terms of our toxic exposure, instead of 2+2=4, when EMFs are added into the mix it becomes 2+2 = 10 or 100. This is the real problem.

Here's what you need to retain from this chapter:

- It's unlikely we will have incontrovertible proof of the cancer link anytime soon because of the long latency period and because of flawed research.
- Studies suggest that EMFs could be behind the slew of previously unknown chronic diseases and disorders, which have burgeoned in a 25-year period.
- The NO/ONOO cycle would appear to explain how EMFs are causing all these chronic diseases.
- There is an overwhelming body of science that shows we can't suppose EMFs are safe.
- EMF exposures are studied in isolation but in the real world we are exposed to many different frequencies simultaneously.
- Even more of a concern is the synergistic effect of EMFs + other toxic exposures; this is the most probable cause of the recent explosion in serious illnesses.

Chapter 6

# Choosing An EMF Meter

YOU MIGHT THINK, "WHOOOAH! DO I really need an EMF meter'? The short answer is yes! Perhaps not today, not this week but as you continue to read this guide you will (hopefully) begin to realize what an invaluable tool a good EMF meter is and, at some point, you will be ready to take the plunge.

All the following are types of EMF meter:

- RF meter—used to measure radio frequency radiation.
- Gauss meter or magnetic field meter—used to measure magnetic fields.
- Electric field meter—used to measure electric fields.
- Dirty electricity meter or Graham-Stetzer (GS) meter—used to measure dirty electricity.

**An EMF meter allows you to MEASURABLY reduce your exposures to EMFs—every home should have one.**

I guarantee that when you first start to use an EMF meter you will make some amazing discoveries.

EMFs have a habit of popping up in places you never thought imaginable. For several years I was experiencing headaches and hot head when I ate my meals in the kitchen. My first EMF meter was a cheapie and really didn't tell me anything useful. It wasn't until I bought the Acoustimeter AM-10 RF meter that I realized that it was the cordless phone on the other side of the wall in the living room that was the culprit. Needless to say, I quickly replaced it with a corded landline telephone.

## What's The Best EMF Meter?

I get asked this question over and over again. What people really mean is, "What's the best EMF meter for me?" Because it all depends on your circumstances and needs. For instance:

1. What is your biggest EMF concern? Next door's Wi-Fi? The overhead powerlines? First, get clear on your EMF concerns and then look at meters that can measure that type of EMF.
2. To measure the four types of EMFs (more on this later), you will eventually need at least two different meters. Which is another reason you need to be clear on what your biggest EMF concern is—first buy a meter which can measure that.
3. How technically minded are you? What's the use in a meter that is complex and gives you a lot of data if you're not able to interpret it?

Three more tips:

1. **Be methodical when using your EMF meter.** Have a notepad to hand where you note your readings in precise locations. That way you can keep track of them and refer back to them when you take subsequent readings in a few weeks or months.
2. **Get an EMF meter with a sound function.** This makes it easier to use and, with practice, you can distinguish between the noises that different devices emit—cell phones and Wi-Fi, for instance, make very different noises.
3. **You get what you pay for.** This is particularly true with EMF meters. There's plenty of cheap EMF meters out there, which are so insensitive and inaccurate they're a total waste of money. View your meter purchase as an investment. Do your research and invest wisely.

With 5G being rolled out things are changing fast in the world of EMF meters, so rather than include information here that will quickly become outdated you can see my latest reviews and recommendations for EMF meters here: www.electricsense.com/bookbonus

All the EMF meters I've reviewed are "consumer meters". They can supply you with invaluable information for reducing your EMF exposures in your home and workplace. But they don't offer the level of accuracy that professional instruments provide—which often require some technical knowledge and training to operate.

Lastly, buying an EMF meter does not make you an EMF expert. You may still want to engage the services of a qualified EMF professional to give your home a thorough EMF audit—you'll find you'll gain more from the visit having used your own meter/s.

Of course, the reason you're doing all this—reading this guide and trying to get your head around EMFs—is to make your home safe. Which leads us to the VERY important question, what the heck is safe?

## What's Safe?

In an ideal world, we shouldn't even have to ask this question because there would be safety standards in place that would protect us. But, as I explained in Chapter 3, there are no safety standards.

Fortunately, there are various independent bodies that give guidance on this question:

1. The Building Biology Institute—gives guidelines for sleeping areas with various levels of anomaly.[165]
2. BioInitiative Report—gives precautionary levels of EMF[166]
3. European Academy for Environmental Medicine.[167]

But none of these bodies are saying what's "safe". Because nobody knows what safe levels of exposure are for RF radiation, electric fields, magnetic fields, and dirty electricity.

> ***What I do in the bedroom areas, I've got at least four points or measurements, sometimes six, and I give you at least three types of exposure on these four points... I color code the numbers, so the client has got a color code chart. He has his report. He can compare the exposures we find to different suggested exposure guidelines. And he's the one that decides if it's high or not. I'm not the one to decide that.***
>
> —*STEPHANE BELAINSKY, ELECTROMAGNETIC HYGIENE TECHNICIAN.*

165 https://www.createhealthyhomes.com/richtwerte-2015-englisch.pdf
166 https://bioinitiative.org/
167 https://europaem.eu/en/library/blog-en/97-europaem-emf-guideline-2016

**What's safest, is to get your EMF exposure levels down to as low as possible.**

I know that's a bit vague, so I'm going to share with you are some benchmark levels for your bedroom.

| Benchmark Levels | | | |
|---|---|---|---|
| Radio Frequency Radiation | Electric Fields | Magnetic Fields | Dirty Electricity |
| 0.02 V/m | 1 V/m or 100 mV* | 0.5 mG | 50 GS units |

*mV is the body voltage reading.

Don't worry if this table doesn't mean much, I'm going to explore all this in detail in the upcoming chapters.

What's important is where you actually sleep in your bedroom (obviously, for dirty electricity you will measure the room). So make sure you measure RF radiation on the bed where you sleep.

Again, I'm not saying these are safe levels, but if, for instance, you can get RF radiation levels down to 0.02-0.06 Volts/meter (V/m) (1–10 microWatts/meter squared), then these are what I consider low levels. This might not be low enough for some people, but for most of you reading this guide these exposure levels will provide sufficient protection.

What you need to retain from this chapter:

- An EMF meter allows you to MEASURABLY reduce your exposures to EMFs—every home should have one.
- The best EMF meter for you depends on your circumstances and needs.
- Buying an EMF meter does not make you an EMF expert—you may still want to engage the services of a qualified EMF professional.
- What's safest, is to get your EMF exposure levels down to as low as possible—particularly in your bedroom.

For many of you reading this, your biggest single source of EMF exposure is your cell phone. In the next chapter, I'm going to share with you some of the many different ways you can reduce your exposure to this important toxin.

## Chapter 7

# Get Smart About Your Cell Phone

WE SLEEP WITH THEM. We eat with them. They tell us the weather, the time of day and connect us to friends and family. They find us dates (and sex!) and entertain us with music, films and games when we're feeling bored.

Most of us have one—there are around a billion more of them in circulation than there are people on the planet.[168] Of course I'm talking about cell phones! And not only are there an awful lot of them out there, but most of us can't stop using our phones. Research reveals we check our cell phones 2,617 times a day![169] Probably more if you're between 18 and 24 years old.[170]

According to one study, 96% of young adult Americans won't even go to the bathroom without their phone![171]

### How Does Your Cell Phone Work?

Ever wondered how it's possible to actually speak to your mum, dad or friend with your cell phone? When you turn your phone on to speak with a friend, radio frequency microwave radiation is sent to the nearest cell phone tower, even before you begin to talk. When you talk, a microphone inside your phone converts the vibrations of your voice into an information wave or signal that is then embedded onto a higher frequency signal. This is then divided up into short packets of information that your phone sends to the nearest cell tower, and it's passed quickly from cell tower to cell tower until it gets to your friend. Your friend's phone removes the high frequency signal, leaving the low frequency signal which the earpiece converts into the sound of your voice.[172]

---

168 https://www.bankmycell.com/blog/how-many-phones-are-in-the-world
169 https://www.businessinsider.com/dscout-research-people-touch-cell-phones-2617-times-a-day-2016-7
170 http://bit.ly/deloitte-mobile
171 https://www.pcmag.com/news/364244/who-uses-their-phone-on-the-toilet-most-of-us
172 Lyn McLean, 2015. *The Force: Living Safely in a World of Electromagnetic Pollution.*

The important thing to understand here is that to enable you to speak and text and so on, your cell phone uses high frequencies (in the gigahertz range) as a carrier signal AND low frequencies of data, which are introduced via modulation[173] of the carrier signal. These signals contain the data. Studies show that high frequency EMFs impact our health, but they also show that low frequencies are just as dangerous, if not more so. Meaning you have a double whammy of exposures.

**If you recall some of the studies I cited in the previous chapters, you'll remember that a good chunk of this radiation is absorbed by your head if you hold your cell phone against your head, or your body if you hold it against your body.**

One thing is for sure, cell phones are here to stay. Not only that, but it's quite possible that at some point in the not too distant future life is going to become incredibly difficult for the cell phone-less. Where I live in France, it's already happening. Certain administrative procedures and buying stuff online from certain websites can only be done if you have a cell phone number you can supply.

Given the dangers—what I talked about in Chapters 3, 4, and 5—and this increasing, albeit forced dependency on our cell phones, the question that needs answering is: how we can protect ourselves?

Not surprisingly, there are specific safety standards in place to protect you from cell phone radiation. Let me introduce you to SAR and SAM.

## SAR and SAM

No, SAR and SAM are not two conjoined twins. They're acronyms. Before a cell phone is allowed to be sold to the general public it has to undergo the SAR test. SAR stands for specific absorption rate. It's a measure of how much average radiation is being absorbed over one gram of human tissue.[174]

Different countries apply different SAR ratings. In the US, the SAR limit is set at 1.6 Watts per kilogram (1.6 W/kg). That means when a cell phone is tested under laboratory conditions the exposure must not exceed 1.6 W/kg.

173 Here, modulation means turning the carrier signal on and off in a certain rhythm, which contains the data.
174 http://bit.ly/electromagnetichealth-ExposureLimits

This is where SAM comes in. SAM stands for specific anthropomorphic mannequin, which sounds a bit fancy but it's not.

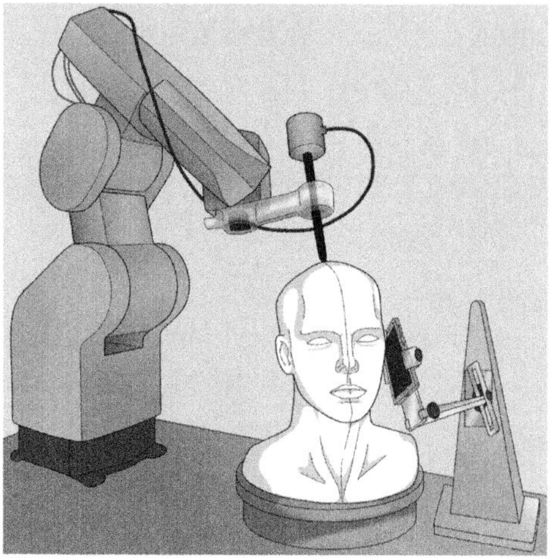

Basically, milk jug containers of fluids[175] of different densities are poured into SAM's head. In this head sits a probe that measures how much the temperature in the middle of SAM's brain increases. For six minutes he's exposed to the RF microwave radiation from the cell phone being tested.[176] If the probe measures less than or equal to an increase in temperature of 2°C or less,[177] which corresponds to 1.6 W/kg average absorption, the phone is given a thumbs up and can be sold. If the probe measures over 2°C it can't be sold until it is modified to pass the limits.

**This is why we call the SAR a thermal limit, because it's all about measuring the heating effect.[178]**

This means of safety testing is used pretty much all over the world, but different countries have slightly different SAR levels. In the European Union, for instance, the SAR limit is set at 2 W/kg but averaged over the 10g of tissue absorbing the most signal.[179]

You can check the SAR value on your cell phone by looking at the user manual that came with it or visit the manufacturer's website.

At this point, you might be thinking, good news! That means I just need to buy a phone with a low SAR. Then I'll know I'm safe. Not quite so fast...

## Heating Effect

Notice anything about the way they decide if cell phone exposures are safe or not? It's all about the heating effect, or what's known in the jargon as the "thermal effects".

This IS a big deal. Let me explain.

175 Devra Davis, 2010. *Disconnect: The Truth About Cell Phone Radiation.*
176 http://electromagnetichealth.org/electromagnetic-health-blog/fcc-limit/
177 Nicolas Pineault, 2017. *The Non-Tinfoil Guide to EMFs: How to Fix our Stupid Use of Technology.*
178 https://www.consumers4safephones.com/fccs-cell-phone-testing-dummy-is-larger-than-97-of-all-cell-phone-users/
179 https://en.wikipedia.org/wiki/Specific_absorption_rate

Cell phones *are* amazingly sophisticated devices. The strides that engineers have made in a few short decades are mind blowing. What once took up hundreds of square feet and was only available to the privileged few now fits neatly into the space in the back of your smartphone.

And yet despite this level of extreme sophistication, the technology used to ensure your cell phone is "safe" is downright antiquated. Manufacturers still use crude temperature probes introduced in the 1990s which measure... increases in temperature. The safety testing does not take into account biological effects.

Let me put it another way. Countless studies have shown that cell phone radiation exposures below the SAR values can cause:

- DNA damage[180]
- Oxidative damage in the heart
- Altered brainwave activity[181]
- Reduced neuron formation[182]
- Oxidative stress[183]
- Neurotoxic effects[184]
- Changes in microRNA expression.[185]

I could go on, but again, it's all these biological effects that are the problem because these bio effects are the foundation of disease.

**Safety standards do virtually nothing to protect us against the bio effects of cell phone radiation because they are only concerned with a heating effect.**

If you take you take two freshly hatched eggs from a hen, and then you boil one egg in a pan for five minutes and let it cool. When you hold those two eggs in your hands and compare them, on the outside they seem identical. But they're not. One of them, no matter what you do, is truly "cooked". The other, if put it back with the hen and given time, will probably evolve and develop into a healthy chick.

180 https://www.ncbi.nlm.nih.gov/pubmed/8627134
181 https://www.emf-portal.org/en/article/4766
182 https://www.ncbi.nlm.nih.gov/pubmed/19230827
183 https://www.emf-portal.org/en/article/17817
184 https://www.ncbi.nlm.nih.gov/pubmed/21524663
185 https://www.emf-portal.org/en/article/26684

Well, it's the same for us humans. From the outside we all look very similar but some of us who are heavy cell phone users and are overexposing ourselves to EMF technologies are slowly cooking ourselves, while others that are taking preventive action and connecting with nature have a good chance of continuing to develop and enjoy good health.

## Cell Phones Come With Warnings

The reason I'm making a very, very strong recommendation that you protect yourself from cell phone radiation is not just because I've experienced the debilitating effects of cell phone radiation firsthand, not just because there are thousands of studies linking these exposures to cancer and a long list of other serious diseases, but also because even the cell phone companies themselves warn you about the dangers.

- Apple
- Samsung
- Blackberry
- Google
- HTC
- LG
- Panasonic
- Sony
- Nokia

All these brands of phones come with warnings.[186] The Apple user manual tells you that for the iPhone radiation testing is done with a 5 mm separation from the head and that to reduce radiation exposure you should use a hands-free option such as speakerphone.[187] Samsung recommends keeping the phone 1.5 cm away.[188]

But when was the last time you read the user manual on your cell phone? And even if you did, chances are you'd miss the important bit because all these warnings are very discreet, and often hidden away in a lot of legal mumbo-jumbo.

**If you want to limit your radiation exposure to what is considered a safe level (or SAR), you should never use a cell phone against your ear to talk, hold it in your hand to text, or even put it in your pocket when it's turned on.**

I'm going to share with you my cell phone radiation protection tips. But first I want you to be 110% clear as to why you absolutely can't rely on SAM and SAR.

186 http://www.showthefineprint.org/see-the-fine-print
187 https://www.apple.com/legal/rfexposure/iphone12,5/en/
188 http://bit.ly/SamsungSARmodelSM-G920A

## 8 Reasons Why You Can't Rely On SAM And SAR

There are a lot of good reasons why you can't rely on SAR values. Here are some of them:

1. **SAM is based upon a 6'2" tall, 220 pounds male representing the top 10% of U.S. military recruits in 1989**—meaning that 97% of cell phone users are smaller than SAM. Also meaning that we CANNOT rely on SAR values to protect our children (I will talk about this more later on).[189]
2. **SAR values tell you a measurement of radiation exposure to the head assuming you hold the phone at the precise angle it was held during testing.** But if you hold your cell phone at a different angle the exposure will be different. More importantly, if you hold your phone directly against your head, like most people do, the SAR is much higher.
3. **SAR testing only reflects radiation exposure when you are actually using your cell phone**—it completely ignores day-long exposures when your cell phone is in your pocket and happily emitting radiation as it connects to cell towers, Wi-Fi devices, and so on throughout your day.[190]
4. **SAR tests give artificially low values because SAR testing uses average readings instead of peak readings.** Not surprisingly, SAR is highest in those parts of your brain and skull which are nearer to your phone's antennae. This peak SAR reading near the antenna is what we're interested in, and yet the temperature probe used for SAR tests takes measurements in a grid pattern inside SAM's head and gives an average value. This might seem like a small point but there is quite a lot of science (which I will talk about later) that shows why peak exposures are a better indication of dangers than average exposures.[191]
5. **Basing safety limits on a 2°C rise in temperature makes no sense at all.** This threshold was decided because it was observed that rats whose brain temperature rose by more than 2°C stopped eating—cell phone safety standards around the world are based on RF radiation affects a rodent's appetite!?[192]
6. **The use of the SAM dummy and the liquid inside it assumes radiation is absorbed in a uniform manner—this is not representative of the human**

189 https://ehtrust.org/sar-test-inadequate/
190 Martin Blank, 2015. *Overpowered: What Science Tells Us About The Dangers of Cell Phones and other WIFI Age Devices.*
191 https://ehtrust.org/sar-test-inadequate/
192 Nicolas Pineault, 2017. *The Non-Tinfoil Guide to EMFs: How to Fix our Stupid Use of Technology.*

**body**, which has dozens of different tissues. Radiation is absorbed differently by different tissues.

7. **Animal studies indicate SAR levels well below 1.6 W/kg can impact our health.** A level of 0.12W/kg can cause Parkinson's, ALS, early dementia and other neurological disease and exposures below 1.2 W/kg can cause brain tumors.[193]
8. **The FCC's own website admits that "a single SAR value does not provide sufficient information about the amount of RF exposure under typical usage conditions to reliably compare individual cell phone models."** Makes you wonder what the heck you *can* use it for.[194]

## Phonegate

You've heard of Dieselgate, where the big car manufacturers lied and cheated about the pollution emissions of their vehicles? It was such a big scandal that Volkswagen's boss was forced to resign and was very bad news for the planet.

Well, Phonegate is similar. But worse. People are being lied to and cheated AND their health is being put at risk, and particularly the health of children. Yet no one's resigning. In fact, hardly anyone's batting an eyelid.

In 2015, French physician Dr. Marc Arazi launched a campaign of public awareness, known as Phonegate, which led to the release of French government data showing that nine out of ten cell phones in Europe have radiation exposures which exceed the SAR safety limits. In other words, true radiation absorption levels are much higher than official radiation absorption levels, or SAR.[195]

Fast forward to 2019 and, not surprisingly, a US study has come to the same conclusion regarding the phones sold in the US.[196]

**A US study has found that nine out of ten cell phones violate US radiation safety limits.**

Worse still, in some cases the study found the safety limits have been exceeded by nearly four times the regulatory value.[197]

193 Katie Singer 2014. *An Electronic Silent Spring*, p.82.
194 https://www.fcc.gov/consumers/guides/specific-absorption-rate-sar-cell-phones-what-it-means-you
195 https://www.phonegatealert.org/en/about-international-phonegate-scandal-eng
196 https://ieeexplore.ieee.org/stamp/stamp.jsp?tp=&arnumber=8688629
197 https://www.phonegatealert.org/en/press-release-anfr-endangers-the-health-of-millions-of-mobile-phone-users

Does that mean that the safety limits would have been breached in the US and other parts of the world? Very probably, yes. A majority of the top-selling brands were cited, including Apple, Motorola, Samsung and Nokia.

What does all this mean?

> ***Stated simply, the SAR of your cell phone does not actually inform how much radiation you are exposed to by using that cell phone.***
>
> —*Martin Blank, Overpowered: What Science Tells Us About The Dangers of Cell Phones and other WIFI Age Devices.*

To put it another way, the whole idea that SAR somehow protects you is a sham.

And even if the SAR testing was given an overhaul to take on board the points I've laid out above, and if it did manage to somehow measure whole-body absorption instead of just absorption to the head, it would still only reflect cell phone radiation in isolation at a point in time. Whereas we are concerned with our CUMULATIVE exposure from multiple EMF sources—because it's this that impacts our health over the long term.

On the next page I'll share my cell phone radiation protection tips. But first let me share some cell phone stories. Pain in the hands and fingers are very common. Paul wrote to me saying that he'd been using his iPhone a lot to receive emails, containing long reports and research and so on. He'd gotten into the bad habit of holding his iPhone in his left hand, while reading and writing, sometimes for well over an hour. Sometimes he would notice that his left hand was getting hot whilst he was reading or writing.

> ***About a month ago, I started having light pain in my left hand. It got worse and now my hand is constantly sensitive and at times all the fingers are painful, restricting the full movement of the fingers. During the last week I wake up during the night due to very painful fingers in my left hand. I can barely make a fist, until I massage all five fingers.***

When I interviewed naturopathic physician and former EMF sufferer Dr. Garrett Smith, he shared a story with me about a woman who came to him suffering from insomnia. She said, "I don't sleep. I don't sleep at all."

Dr. Garrett's first question was, "Where do you keep your cell phone at night?" She replied with the worst thing that anybody could say. "I keep it on, under my pillow."

He gave her a B12 shot and told her, "You need to move that cell phone. It's best if it's off, but airplane mode is better than nothing. Move it at least six feet away from your head. The [charging cord and] plug needs to be six feet away from your head. More is better."

She did that and when she came back for her next consultation she said, "I slept eight hours straight and I haven't done that in years."

## Cell Phone Radiation Protection Tips—Free And Easy

**I don't own a cell phone, so my number one piece of advice here is—to stop using a cell phone.** What? Well, I just have to put that out there. Because for many of you reading this, your cell phone will be your EMF worst offender. Despite me telling you this, I know that some of you will want to/have to keep using your cell phone. Here is how you can make using your cell phone safer.

1. **Limit calls to those that are absolutely necessary.**

   Telling you to limit calls to those that are absolutely necessary and keep the length of your calls to an absolute minimum might sound boring as heck. But I have good reason to say this. Research has clearly identified a dose-response relationship[198] between the time you spend on your cell phone and your risk of disease—that means the longer you spend on your phone, the higher your risk of getting cancer or one of the other diseases I've been talking about.

2. **Avoid using your phone next to your ear.**

   It might sound silly, but you don't want to be using your cell phone next to your ear unless you absolutely have to. Radio frequency microwave radiation follows a rule of physics called the inverse square law. As a rule of thumb, signal strength falls off in proportion to the square of the distance to the source. So, if you double the distance to the source (the cell phone to your head, for example) your potential exposure is four times less, since two squared is four.

3. **Make Airplane Mode your best friend.**

   Your cell phone has three different kinds of wireless functionality. These are cellular (3G, 4G, and 5G.), Bluetooth and Wi-Fi. If you put your

198 https://articles.mercola.com/sites/articles/archive/2016/06/15/cell-phone-radiation-effects.aspx

phone in Airplane Mode, on most phones this will turn off all radiation emissions. BUT on some phones, it won't, so you'll need to deactivate Wi-Fi and Bluetooth manually.

The second point is that when you do software updates on your phone, sometimes this can cancel the Airplane mode. The best way to ensure Airplane mode is truly deactivating all wireless functionality is to test with an RF meter.[199]

4. **Avoid carrying your cell phone directly on your body.**

   Your cell phone pretty much zaps you 24/7, even when it's idle. Here's the scoop: your harmless looking cell phone is never really idle. Even on standby your cell phone may be communicating at *full power* with the nearest cell phone tower regularly (typically several times a second). If you're in a poor signal area, it may transmit more often to try and get a better signal. If you do have to keep your cell phone next to your body, keep it away from your major organs.

5. **Wise up about the bars.**

   There's no industry standard on the meaning of the signal bars on cell phones but you're best advised to only telephone when all the signal bars are showing. Some phones can ramp up their emissions 1,000,000 fold in areas where the signal is poor! This means that for each signal bar that is missing your exposure increases several thousands of times.

   Only use your cell phone in conditions of optimum reception. That means using it outside or near a window as much as possible. Avoid using it in a basement, underground station, elevator, and so on.

6. **Avoid using your phone in a moving vehicle.**

   This might be in a bus, train, or car. In a moving vehicle, the cell phone antenna is working overtime, constantly scanning for the nearest emitter and typically operating at maximum signal strength, hence zapping you even more.

199 Take readings with your RF meter with wireless connectivity activated then switch to airplane mode and monitor the readings for a few minutes to ensure that are no emissions.

7. **Avoid even using your cell phone in a parked car.**

   Would you consider sticking your head in a microwave oven when it's turned on? I don't think so. Using your cell phone in a car (or a bus or train) amounts to pretty much the same thing. In both cases, these are metallic enclosures where the effects of RF radiation are magnified.

   The RF radiation from your cell phone is reflected back by the car's metallic structure. It's called the Faraday cage effect. This radiation from your phone bounces around inside your car and is absorbed by your body at a higher level than would otherwise be the case.

8. **Never sleep with a cell phone switched on at night beside your bed.**

   Never even bring the cell phone into the bedroom. Why? Your cell phone has an uncanny ability to interrupt your natural sleep cycle and your hormonal processes—particularly production of melatonin (more on this later on).

   This can contribute to a host of ailments, like: irritation of allergies, heart palpitations, muscle pain, weakness and daytime irritability. These exposures can impede the function of your immune system and have long-term consequences—yes, cancer and the other diseases I talked about earlier.

9. **Prefer text to talk.**

   Text messaging also exposes your body to radiation, but most of the time at a lower level. When you speak with someone on the phone there's a tendency to have a conversation... about the weather, about what you had for dinner last night, and who knows what else. Texting tends to be more to the point and even if you do have a conversation your exposure will usually be less harmful—you don't text with the cell phone glued to your ear. Hold your cell phone away from your body when you press "send".

   Beware: texting is not without its dangers. A 2016 study[200] revealed that text messaging with smartphones can trigger a new type of brain rhythm.

10. **Go easy on the apps.**

    Minimize the number of apps running and disable any background services that are not absolutely necessary. Disabling "mobile services"/"data

200 https://www.ncbi.nlm.nih.gov/pubmed/27131913

network mode" makes your smartphone operate more like a conventional cell phone. So, when your smartphone is activated in wireless mode you can still be reached but you avoid unnecessary radiation from background data traffic.

A word about streaming. If you are watching a movie or listening to music on your cell phone, download it, then turn on airplane mode before watching the movie or listening to the music.

11. **Use a delaying tactic.**

    If you do put your cell phone next to you ear, wait until your recipient has picked up the communication. Some cell phones (particularly earlier models) are known to communicate at full power when connecting to a number. Hold your phone away from your body until you've finished dialing and put it to your ear when your correspondent answers. When receiving an incoming call, give yourself a second or two before putting the phone next to your head once you've accepted the call. Every bit helps.

12. **Use speakerphone.**

    Using your phone on speaker mode with the phone situated as far away from your body as possible is a smart move. The downside is that it can expose other body parts to more radiation, depending on how you hold your phone and depending on the design of your phone, the position of the antenna and so on. It also makes the battery work harder, thereby increasing magnetic field levels. The best is to not hold your phone at all when using speakerphone mode.

    A quick word about conventional headsets. A conventional headset has a wire cable. Wire has metal in it. Wired headsets can act as an antenna attracting ambient EMFs, transmitting radiation directly to your brain, thereby increasing your exposure. They should be avoided.

## Cell Phone Radiation Protection Tips—Intermediate

These tips are not really advanced, but they do mean buying something.

1. **Use an air tube headset.**

    As a rule of thumb, if you double the distance between you and the source of radiation (in this case, your cell phone) your potential exposure will be four times less, since two squared is four.[201]. Air tube headsets are a safe way of increasing this distance. The idea is simple: instead of using a wire, sound is transmitted by a part air tube cable and part wired cable. This air tube component converts the electrical signal into harmless airwaves. Some air tube headsets are better than others—there can be some loss of sound quality. Technology changes quickly, so I've put together a resource guide on my website for people who are interested in them. The guide will stay updated. See my video review for this air tube headset in the guide by going to this page: www.electricsense.com/bookbonus

2. **Use an EMF-blocking cell phone case.**
   Know this: all cell phone cases are not created equal. Some look pretty, and some are pretty effective radiation protection devices. For it to fit in this latter category, you want a shielded case which allows your phone to maintain connectivity whilst offering some degree of protection from radiation directed out of the front of your phone.

The Pong and Cruz cases are both brands I can recommend.

**Warning: Using a cell phone case like most people use can make your phone work harder and raise your radiation exposure.[202]**

I hate to sound like a broken record, but none of these tips will make using your cell phone "safe".

## Strategies To Reduce Your Cell Phone Radiation Exposure Exponentially

Even when your cell phone is switched off it may still be emitting radiation! Many cell phones now have GPS incorporated that periodically transmit to update their position, *even when switched off.*

201 The Inverse Square Law is a rule of physics which says signal strength (i.e. radiation) falls off in proportion to the square of the distance to the source. Note: this law has its limitations in real life because EMFs can bounce of buildings etc. and create localized hotspots.

202 https://www.ewg.org/research/does-your-cell-phone-case-raise-your-radiation-exposure

Here are three strategies I recommend:

1. Use airplane mode as much as possible. It's ALWAYS safer than having it on full wireless connectivity like most people do—the only way to know how truly effective airplane mode is on your phone is to test it with an EMF meter. To see me testing airplane mode with an EMF meter, see my two-minute video here: www.electricsense.com/bookbonus
2. Use a "Kill Tin". A Kill Tin is an amazingly effective and inexpensive way of shielding yourself from radiation emitted by your cell phone. When you're at home put your cell phone in any metal tin with a lid on it to kill the radiation emissions instantly—I've done multiple tests with different EMF meters it provides near 100% radiation protection.[203]
3. As a general rule, for incoming and outgoing calls, use a corded landline telephone or use corded VoIP applications like Skype via a hardwired computer. If you need to converse via text messages a lot, install a free app on your phone like "SMS to mail/phone – auto redirect" to send text messages to your email account. With an iPhone this feature is built in, go to Settings>Messages>Receive At and then choose Add An Email.

## Cell Phone Radiation Protection Tips—Advanced

If you find you are developing a sensitivity to EMFs after taking all these precautions, it might sound like a bitter pill to swallow, but my best advice is for you to stop using a cell phone. This would be a temporary measure while you focus on advanced strategies of EMF protection (I will talk about these in the upcoming chapters), which in time will enable you to recover and get back to some degree of cell phone use over time.

203 To be clear, both these solutions mean you can't make or receive calls or messages

If you really want to get smart about cell phone radiation, then you need to measure it with a good RF meter. When you first see your EMF meter flashing and buzzing as it measures the radiation from all the different signals your cell phone is emitting, that in itself is an eye-opener.

What you need to retain from this chapter:

- There are now more cell phones in the world than people
- Cell phone dependency is being forced upon us—increasingly, certain purchases or administrative tasks can only be completed if you have a cell phone
- The cell phone safety standards (SAR) are fundamentally flawed
- Since Phonegate, we know that most of the cell phones in the world don't even respect these (obsolete) safety standards
- Cell phones are so dangerous that even cell phone companies warn you about the dangers—but they hide the warnings in the fine print
- There are many free and easy ways to reduce your exposure to cell phone radiation
- Use a corded, landline telephone or VoIP as much as possible for calls
- More advanced means of protection include using an EMF blocking case and an air-tube headset.
- Reducing your cell phone radiation exposure is very important, but the real concern is your CUMULATIVE exposure from multiple EMF sources—this is what you need to do to safeguard your health over the long term and this is what I'm going to be talking about in the upcoming chapters.

# Chapter 8

# Taming Our Wireless World Gone Wild

IN MAY 2003, *WIRED MAGAZINE* published an article describing an emerging technology called "wireless fidelity" that would revolutionize our lives.[204] The internet, in the air? Who would have believed it?

Of course, they were right. How could they not be right? Wi-Fi is cheap, powerful, and, more importantly, it works. A paperback book-sized box costing no more than a decent dinner for two that magically distributes broadband Internet throughout your home, allowing you to surf in your bed, email in your backyard, and stream videos from your couch.[205]

## Wireless Words

Wireless means... without wires. No surprise there. More importantly, it means radiofrequency microwave radiation and it comes in many shapes and forms. A good way of understanding this is to look at some wireless devices:

- Wi-Fi routers
- Computers and tablets
- Cell towers
- Bluetooth headsets
- Cordless phones
- Smart meters
- Baby monitors
- Microwave ovens
- Game consoles.

What all these devices have in common is that they all emit radiation at similar frequencies, between about 1 and 3 GHz (this will change when 5G arrives). The exact frequencies vary according to where you live in the world, but Wi-Fi, computers, tablets, and their peripherals (keyboard, mouse, printer, etc.) typically use 2.4 GHz—most modern Wi-Fi routers now also have a 5 GHz antenna.

204 https://www.wired.com/2003/05/Wi-Firevolution/
205 https://www.wired.com/2003/05/Wi-Firevolution/

There's some confusion about 5 GHz Wi-Fi and 5G.

**If you have a Wi-Fi router that says "5 GHz", that just means it emits and receives wireless signals in the 5.8 GHz frequency range.**

Whereas 5G is the new standard for cellular technology, which uses lots of different and higher frequencies—I talk about this extensively in Chapter 12. It's quite different from 5.8 GHz Wi-Fi (and 5.8 GHz cordless telephones).

So far, I've talked a lot about cell phone radiation. But how bad is wireless and similar technologies?

## How Bad Is Wireless?

Here are a few of the stories my clients and website visitors have shared with me. Let's start with Tom and how Wi-Fi kept him from sleeping for the past three years...

> *For the last three years or so I've not slept more than three hours a night because I've been having terrible pains in my arms, legs, my testicles and in fact all over my body. I've been to my docs many times, had blood tests, scans of my testicles and many X-rays, all to no avail and in the end I got a letter from the NHS informing me there was nothing wrong with me... I read Lloyd's story and it just felt so much like what I'd been going through and I took his advice and turned off our Wi-Fi for the night and I had my first full pain-free night's sleep in three years.*

Robert has a similar story, his symptoms disappeared within 48 hours of turning off the Wi-Fi:

> *I turned [my Wi-Fi router] on to simplify my life (where was my brain?). For two months I had horrible headaches and very sick to my stomach. The doctors said they could find nothing wrong. Then, coincidentally, I went to an EMF conference. They said our bodies function at 7 (Hz) normally with the earth's gravity. Our cells recognize this frequency. They turned on the Wi-Fi router and the numbers escalated to 2000 (Hz). What a shock! I asked about my particular symptoms and they said yes, likely related. I went home*

***and turned off the Wi-Fi router and in 24 hours my symptoms subsided. In 48 hours, I was back to feeling good!***

Judy experienced a profound difference:

***Several weeks ago, I turned off Wi-Fi in my home, removed cordless phones, etc. The difference for me was profound. I am now without a sleeping disorder, amongst other health complaints. That is huge. I sleep like a baby!***

Karen experiences blurred vision whenever she is in a Wi-Fi area:

***Just wanted to say that when I am in a Wi-Fi area, such as a café, my vision becomes so blurry that I have to leave and have difficulty walking due to the change in my vision. The last time this happened, it took approximately 10 minutes after leaving the Wi-Fi area before my vision returned to normal.***

Let's look at what the EMF science tells us.

**Wi-Fi can cause cancer.** This is what recent studies by Dr. Martin Pall[206] are pointing to. Breast cancer and skin cancer are also a real possibility.[207] [208]

**Wi-Fi can impair brain function.** It can cause all sorts of effects on spatial memory, brain cell DNA and blood cell counts.[209] [210]

**Wi-Fi can reduce male fertility.** It can cause DNA damage in sperm cells and slow sperm mobility (how well it can swim).[211] The heat from a laptop can kill sperm cells.[212]

**Wi-Fi radiation can impact your heart.** Studies show a direct link between tachycardia (rapid heart rate) or arrhythmia (irregular heart rate) and exposure to Wi-Fi.[213]

206 https://www.sciencedirect.com/science/article/pii/S0013935118300355?via%3Dihub
207 http://www.ncbi.nlm.nih.gov/pubmed/25703814
208 http://www.ncbi.nlm.nih.gov/pubmed/22237725
209 http://www.jpier.org/PIERB/pierb29/02.11011205.pdf
210 http://www.ncbi.nlm.nih.gov/pubmed/25775055
211 https://www.sciencedirect.com/science/article/pii/S0015028211026781
212 https://www.defendershield.com/laptops-Wi-Fi-concern-male-fertility/
213 https://ecfsapi.fcc.gov/file/7520958029.pdf

Fewer studies have been done on the effects of Wi-Fi to your health compared to cell phones. But notice how the biological effects listed above are nearly identical to those of cell phone radiation. Not surprising, the frequencies are very similar—the big carriers in the US, like Verizon and AT&T, use 1900 MHz (or 1.9 GHz) and T-Mobile use 2.1 GHz.

Dr. Dietrich Klinghardt, who has been studying the health effects of EMFs for decades, says:

> ***The number one cause of death in women is neurological disease. It increased in the last 20 years by 663 percent. That's entirely and completely linked to the exposure to Wi-Fi.***[214]

## Why Is Wi-Fi So Wicked?

As humans, we've evolved in an environment where there are natural EMFs (see Chapter 2) like the static electric fields and geo-magnetic fields of the earth. Our bodies are designed to function quite happily in this environment.

In the last century, thanks to the work of Nikola Tesla, alternating current (AC) electricity was introduced into our lives. This was another big change, because before that we were only exposed to direct current (DC), and another big challenge in terms of our health—see Chapters 9 and 10 for more on this.

But when wireless was introduced decades later, and particularly cell phones, these man-made exposures exploded. There are two aspects to this:

1. The density of these exposures, all these different networks and frequencies (radio, TV, cellular, GPS, etc.) which were, and are still, continuously increasing. With Wi-Fi, for instance, get your cell phone or laptop out and look how many different Wi-Fi networks are showing.
2. The sheer technological complexity of these exposures.

Let me develop on this second point. I want to keep things simple, but the technology behind Wi-Fi is very complex.

For instance, I mentioned that most Wi-Fi uses a frequency of 2.4 GHz. This is true, but the 2.4 GHz is only part of the story. Similar to how cell phones work

214 Dr. Dietrich Klinghardt, EMF Health Summit interview

(which I explained in Chapter 6), the 2.4 GHz frequency acts as a carrier signal and is modulated. This modulation, which means how the carrier signal turns on and off in a certain rhythm, is how data is transmitted— the sounds, words and images.[215]

These modulations are more commonly known as pulsing—this is where we get to the nitty gritty.

**There is a good deal of science which shows that pulsed radio frequency radiation, as used by Wi-Fi and just about every other form of wireless you can think of, is a lot more dangerous than continuous wave radiation at the same frequency.**

As Prof. Magda Havas reminds us, literature from the Eastern European countries, including the former Soviet Union, have repeatedly reported that pulsed radio frequency radiation is more harmful than continuous wave radiation.[216]

Why is pulsed radiation more dangerous? We don't really know, but it's probably because:

- Our bodies are being subjected to jarring signals of varying intensities
- These brief intense bursts of energy or unlike anything that can be found in nature.

And the pulsing is also only part of the story. There are other parameters, like polarization[217] and field variability, which make these man-made EMFs particularly dangerous.

Dr. Andrew Goldsworthy argues it's the rate of change of the fields that does most of the biological damage, not their total energy.[218]

What has the telecoms industry been arguing (and still argues) about this? They say that it's all about thermal or heating effects, that there is no heating effect because there isn't sufficient energy, or power, to create one and that, therefore, these technologies are safe. It's true neither your smartphone nor your Wi-Fi has sufficient power (sufficient wattage) to heat your skin and organs in any significant way. But this is TOTALLY beside the point.

215 Information supplied by Jan-Rutger Schrader, PhD, founder of https://www.jrseco.com/
216 https://magdahavas.com/pick-of-the-week-12-why-pulsed-microwave-frequencies-are-more-harmful/
217 https://www.ncbi.nlm.nih.gov/pmc/articles/PMC4601073/
218 Andrew Goldsworthy, 2008. *Wi-Fi and Electromagnetic Fields.*

**Radio-frequency microwave radiation, as used by Wi-Fi, cell phones and other forms of wireless, is dangerous because of the complexity of the radiation, not because of its power.**

A quick word about penetration. Because the ability of wireless to penetrate is another important part of the puzzle.

By penetration, I mean the "ability to go through things"—because if this radiation couldn't go through things then we wouldn't have much of a problem, right? We could all just stay snug in our homes, cars and offices, because wireless from cell towers and other wireless sources wouldn't be able to reach us.

But this radiation does go through things. Most people's cell phones work at home, most of us can pick up our Wi-Fi in any room of our home and often that of our neighbors too. That tells you the wireless has good penetration.

This ability to go through things brings us back to the wavelength, frequency, power trio—in a nutshell, the shorter the wavelength, the higher the power, the greater the ability to penetrate. Which is why high frequency (short wavelength) gamma rays, as used in nuclear installations, are so dangerous and why X-rays, as used in a medical context, are also dangerous—because they can easily penetrate the human body.

What about Wi-Fi and different forms of wireless? This has good penetrative power, too. It can typically penetrate:

- Walls
- Floors
- Ceilings
- Wood
- Plastic
- Glass
- Most building materials
- The human body
- Plants and animals.

Wherever you can get a Wi-Fi signal, know that the radiation is penetrating the walls, floors and ceilings in your home and every cell in your body—if you live in a town or city, know also that your neighbors Wi-Fi will be doing the same.

But metal does deflect and reflect signals, as do certain other materials. I'll talk about how these can be used as a shield in Chapter 19.

Another important factor is the duration of exposure.

**Wi-Fi exposures are often 24/7 and for this reason alone Wi-Fi presents a serious threat to our health.**

You should now be clear why Wi-Fi is so wicked—it's clearly biologically active and it's this ability to create biological effects that is behind all these diseases I've been talking about.

## Wi-Fi Radiation Protection Tips—Nearly Free And Easy

After reading all this, are you sure you still want to keep your Wi-Fi router?[219] I hope you don't, but let's assume you are. Here are some tips to make your Wi-Fi safer.

1. **Move your router as far away as possible from the rooms where you spend any time.** This will probably be your office and (definitely) your bedroom. You might need to plug in your router in another room or move your bedroom or office so that they are further away. To do this, you might need to buy some Ethernet cable, also called LAN cable (I will explain below).
2. **Switch it off at night.** You can just unplug your router, but are you going to remember to unplug it every night? Instead, install a simple mechanical electrical timer (like the one shown here) on the outlet where you plug your router in. Set the timer to turn the power off during sleep time.

   Some more sophisticated routers let you turn the Wi-Fi signal off in the software settings—I'm always dubious of relying on this because software updates often cause the default setting to be reinstalled, which can mean you will be irradiated in your sleep without knowing about it.[220]

219 Some people also call this a modem. A modem and a router are quite different devices but, for simplicity I'm using the term router to refer to this kind of device.

220 There are also certain router models with a Wi-Fi on/off switch that reliably turn Wi-Fi off and keeps it off, so installing one of these routers is another option.

3. **Use an app to switch your Wi-Fi off.** There's a range of free apps (for instance, the Linksys app) that let you turn on and off your Wi-Fi whenever you need to by using your cell phone.[221] Obviously, it does mean you have to have a cell phone, but I know most of you reading this have, so that's not a problem. What I do like about this solution is that it gives you a lot of flexibility, and if you're not using your Wi-Fi regularly, then it means you can leave it switched off most of the time.

## Wi-Fi Radiation Protection Tips—Intermediate

1. **Use the software settings to reduce your exposures.** You might need to be a geek to be able to do this (or have a friendly geek on hand), but there are a couple of things you can do to turn down the Wi-Fi radiation coming out of your router and they are FREE.
   - **Reduce the transmit power**—a lot of routers have a setting to do this, but it's usually hidden away in the fine print. I've included detailed instructions here www.electricsense.com/bookbonus. This doesn't work for all modems/routers.
   - **Deactivate the second frequency**—if yours is a dual band router (that means it's transmitting at the normal 2.4 GHz frequency AND in the 5.8 GHz frequency range), make sure you turn off the frequency you aren't using.

Here are two other solutions, which are not free.

2. **Replace your existing router with a low EMF router.** One such solution is the JRS-Eco 100 Router which has auto Wi-Fi deactivation. That means the router automatically switches off its Wi-Fi signal when you stop using your computer or other Wi-Fi devices. When you power up your computer, the router senses a connection request and reactivates the Wi-Fi signal so you can surf the Internet. This solution ALSO enables you to reduce your Wi-Fi radiation exposure when Wi-Fi is activated in two ways, by:
   - Reducing the pulse frequency by ten times—traditional Wi-Fi pulses ten times a second, whereas the default setting for JRS-Eco Wi-Fi is one pulse per second.

221 Works with certain routers.

- Reducing the Wi-Fi transmit power by up to 95%—you can set your transmit power according to the range you require by going into the settings.

This reduction in exposure can be achieved without any reduction in performance. For a full review of this low EMF router, see: www.electricsense.com/bookbonus.

3. **Shield your Wi-Fi router.** There are lots of ways of doing this. The easiest is with a Signal Tamer, which is a pouch made with RF-shielding fabric. You put your Wi-Fi router in a special metal mesh cage to reduce your RF radiation exposures—the idea is that you still have enough signal coming out of the cage to have an Internet connection. These solutions will only work where the Wi-Fi radiation signal is already quite strong. This might be a good solution in an office, for example, if you can't replace your Wi-Fi router with a low EMF one.

## Wi-Fi Radiation Protection—My #1 Recommendation

I don't want to fool you into thinking that somehow having wall-to-wall Wi-Fi at home is okay. It's absolutely not. Remember, at one time I couldn't bear to be in the same room as a Wi-Fi router—the studies I shared above explain why.

**My number one recommendation in your home is to go hard-wired.** There's two ways of doing this:

1. **Replace your wireless router with a wired version and install an Ethernet cable.** I'm sure you'll know what I mean by Ethernet cable when you see the picture below.

Yes, going hard-wired is a bit more hassle. If your router and computer have an Ethernet jack or port, you can connect your computer by just plugging your Ethernet cable in when you want to use it.

For about two years, I used a very long Ethernet cable between two rooms before I got the electrician in to run the cables in the walls and install Ethernet outlets in each room. It was unsightly, but it was safe and did the job.

There are plenty of cheap wired routers you can use to give you an Internet connection without Wi-Fi, or even a wireless router with a proper button on the front or back so that you can switch the wireless off easily and leave it off.

2. **Use your existing coaxial cables to hardwire your Internet.** A lot of homes have coaxial wiring installed for cable or terrestrial TV.

The good news is that you can use this existing wiring to give you wired Internet access in any room that has a coaxial wall outlet. You use one adapter to convert the Ethernet, which is coming out of your router, into a coaxial and then you need a short coaxial cable between the adapter and the wall outlet. In another room, your living room or kitchen perhaps, where there is another coaxial outlet, you connect a coaxial cable between the coaxial wall jack and a second adapter. You use an Ethernet cable to connect between that adapter and your computer or other device you're wanting to connect to the Internet. The adapters you need to do this are called MoCA (Multimedia over Coaxial Alliance) adapters. There's more information on my resource page here www.electricsense.com/bookbonus on how to do this.

**Important: Remember to also disable the wireless function on your computer when you go hardwired.**

A LOT of people overlook this point. They think that when they use an Ethernet cable to connect their desktop, laptop or tablet to their router doing so will automatically switch off the Wi-Fi. Wrong. You have to actually go into your computer's settings and disable the Wi-Fi. While you're in there you can disable any other wireless signal it's pumping out. For instance, my Mac computer will radiate a Bluetooth signal if I don't switch it off.

**If, like many people, you get your Internet via your cable company, then the ideal set up is to replace the modem/router they supply with your own regular wired modem and a regular wired router.**

## Wi-Fi Radiation Protection—Advanced

If you're getting symptoms around Wi-Fi and similar devices, then that means you might want to take things a step further. It's not just about going hard wired, it's about going "low EMF hardwired". Because even a wired Internet system can cause health effects.

The irony is that the electronics industry has known about the effects of EMFs for a long time, and they've been quietly dealing with it. They call it electromagnetic interference or EMI. That's to say, what can have devastating effects on your health, can also have devastating effects on electronic equipment.

Most modems/routers use a switched-mode power supply (SMPS) which creates EMI. If you're using a modem/router that gives you a very fast connection, perhaps 1,000 Mbps download speed, there are two potential issues:

- EMFs on your Ethernet cable[222]
- EMFs on your electrical wiring.

In both cases, whether it's EMFs on your house wiring or on your Ethernet cable, there are potential dangers—I'll explain more about EMFs on wiring in the next chapter.

Here's what you can do:

- **Go for a lower bandwidth modem/router.** Are you going to be simultaneously downloading multiple big video files? My modem/router gives me 150 Mbps and it's plenty fast enough for me to stream my favorite movies on Netflix and YouTube. Look for how many Mbps your router has. It will say it on the packaging or if you look online it will probably say it in the title—1000 Mbps might sound sexy, but do you really need it?
- **Use a shielded Ethernet cable.** Most Ethernet cables are not shielded. The problem is AC electric fields can run up the Ethernet cable from the electricity provided to the router. This means that electric fields EMFs are being emitted from the cable and from the laptop in your hands. I

222 https://www.emfanalysis.com/low-emf-internet-connection/

recommend replacing your existing Ethernet cable with at least a Cat 7 SSTP (screened shielded twisted pair) Ethernet cable—the longer your Ethernet cable is, the more important it is to shield it.

- **Ground your Ethernet cable.** There are various ways of doing this, the easiest is with a network cable ground. It's a little kit which you can install yourself—it can be bought from LessEMF.

**Grounding your electrical equipment, particularly your computer or any other device you might be using for long periods of time, is THE most important thing to do—I'll explain more about this later.**

If your laptop or desktop is already grounded through its power supply, then grounding your Ethernet cable can create a "ground loop"—another source of EMFs. It's generally best to ground your computer installation in one place only to avoid ground loops. If you want to delve into this topic a bit more, I recommend you read this excellent article by Jeromy Johnson.[223]

## Broadband Over Powerline

This goes under various names: "Powerline Networking", "Broadband over Power Lines" (BPL) or "Powerline Ethernet". Special adapters, called Network Adapters, are used to send the Internet signal through your home or office electrical wiring. In one room you connect an Ethernet cable coming out of your router into a special adapter that you plug into the nearest electrical outlet. In another room, where you want to use the Internet, you plug in another special adapter into an electrical outlet and run an Ethernet cable from that adapter to your computer or laptop.

The good news is that you can surf the Internet in any room of your home where there's an electrical outlet—without exposing yourself to Wi-Fi radiation. The bad news is that these adapters introduce some degree of dirty electricity on to your house wiring.

Some people can actually feel this dirty electricity[224] on their house wiring. There is a long list of serious diseases, including cancer, associated with dirty electricity exposures—see Chapter 10. For this reason, I do NOT recommend Network Adapters.

223 https://www.emfanalysis.com/low-emf-internet-connection/
224 http://www.createhealthyhomes.com/safercomputers.php#1

Another variant of this idea of using the same wire to carry data and electrical power is Power Over Ethernet (PoE), which is the opposite of BPL. With PoE the Ethernet cables are used to carry electricity.[225] Typically, PoE cables are not shielded, so I do not recommend using PoE either.

## My Neighbor's Got Wi-Fi—Why Should I Bother?

Because I say so—haha. Just kidding. There are two good reasons why you should bother:

1. **Distance is your friend.** Every time you switch on your laptop at home you might see 25 other Wi-Fi networks. BUT, nine times out of ten, your router is the nearest and strongest signal. These exposures from all routers drop off quickly with each millimeter you put between you and the source—dealing with your own modem/router IS a priority.
2. **Nighttime EMF exposures are particularly harmful**. Even if you're being blasted by Wi-Fi and other EMFs all day long, you STILL want to deal with your Wi-Fi (and other) EMF exposures at home as a priority. In terms of your body's cells and your health, an hour of daytime is not equal to an hour of sleep time. Whatever your current state of health, creating optimal sleep conditions and reducing your Wi-Fi exposure at home should be high on your list of priorities—more about this in Chapter 10.

## My Neighbor's Got Wi-Fi—What Can I Do?

You can go and knock on their door and try and have a conversation about EMFs. They may not agree to hardwire their installation, but they may agree to using a Signal Tamer pouch or Wire Guard metal cage. It usually won't affect their own Wi-Fi coverage within their house.

> ***A lot of my clients will actually buy a Signal Tamer. It's a cloth product that you can put over routers that will actually decrease the radiation. I find that if they buy that for their neighbors – they're about $50 – and as long as it doesn't affect their neighbor's Wi-Fi, people are happy to do it.***
>
> *—Lee Sagula, Building Biologist, EMF Experts Solutions Club interview.*

225 It is a channel for low voltage "dirty electricity" current.

It's definitely worth a try. Failing that, then we are into more advanced solutions. Here are three possible ways of dealing with it:[226]

1. Paint the wall between you and your neighbor with Y-Shield shielding paint .[227] This will be the most effective shielding. You paint either your inside or outside wall, whichever is easier.
2. Copper, aluminum or steel roofing screen will stop 99% of the radiation and it costs about $5 per sq/ft.
3. Good old chicken wire is usually too wide a mesh to reduce transmissions to any extent. You have to use finer levels of mesh to achieve possibly 75%. This depends upon the frequency you are shielding from.

When you are doing any kind of shielding, the golden rule is to measure with your EMF meter, shield and then measure again. You always need to verify the effectiveness of your shielding.

## Public Wi-Fi From Your Cable Company's Modem/Router

Did you know that more and more cable Internet providers are offering public Wi-Fi via the Wi-Fi emitting from the modem/routers that they lease to you? According to one report, one in three home Wi-Fi routers may be doubling as a public hotspot—so you might already be sharing your router with other people without even realizing it![228]

**One in three homes have a Wi-Fi cable router that also provides a public Wi-Fi hotspot—creating a double dose of radiation.**

I don't have a complete list of companies that offer public Wi-Fi through private Wi-Fi routers, but here are some of them:[229]

- Cox
- XFINITY (part of Comcast)
- Spectrum (formerly Time Warner)

226 Eric Windheim, EMF Experts Solutions Club interview.
227 Y-Shield is a popular brand of special paint used to shield RF radiation.
228 https://www.juniperresearch.com/press/press-releases/1-in-3-home-Wi-Fi-routers-to-double-as-public-hots
229 https://www.lifewire.com/free-online-Wi-Fi-hotspot-locators-818276

- Optimum
- BT
- UPC
- Virgin Media.

Operators reassure people by telling them, "Oh, your data is quite safe, your private Wi-Fi is on a separate network to the public one." That is reassuring for your privacy concerns (because, yes, that is also an issue) but it is NOT reassuring for your health.

Few people are aware that their Wi-Fi router is also emitting public Wi-Fi.[230]

> ***While most operators now allow consumers to opt-out, if they so wish, most consumers simply have no idea that their routers are being used in this way...***
>
> —*Juniper Research*[231]

How to know if your router is equipped with public a Wi-Fi hotspot?

1. You can check the settings
2. You can ring your provider
3. Hold a smartphone near to the router and check for a list of available networks
4. Measure with an EMF meter.

You can easily check this with your EMF meter by deactivating your private Wi-Fi[232] and looking to see if your modem/router is still emitting a signal—Wi-Fi radiation has a very distinctive sound, which you can easily recognize with an EMF meter that has audio.[233]

The solution? Disable the public Wi-Fi. How exactly this can be done depends on who your provider is. For instructions on how to do this with different providers, see: www.electricsense.com/bookbonus.

230 According to Oram Miller, this is not a problem with the modem/routers provided by telephone companies in the United States, such as FIOS from Frontier and U-Verse from AT&T.

231 https://www.juniperresearch.com/press/press-releases/1-in-3-home-Wi-Fi-routers-to-double-as-public-hots

232 Check from time to time. Software updates can sometimes reactivate public Wi-Fi..

233 It sounds like a helicopter. Confirm that you have a Wi-Fi hotspot by unplugging your modem/router to see if the helicopter sound goes away

***Sometimes it may not be possible to disable the public Wi-Fi, in which case you will need to turn in your cable modem/router and purchase your own cable company-approved modem[234] and your own hard-wired router (or router with Wi-Fi on/off switch).[235]***

What you need to retain from this chapter:

- The science shows that Wi-Fi radiation harms our bodies in similar ways to cell phone radiation
- It's the complexity of this radiation that makes it particularly dangerous—not its power
- You can considerably reduce your exposure by moving your Wi-Fi modem/router away from rooms where you spend time and switching it off at night
- A free app can be used to turn off your Wi-Fi whenever you don't need it using your cell phone
- By replacing your existing router with a low EMF version, you can reduce your Wi-Fi radiation exposure by up to 100% when the router is on stand-by
- A Wi-Fi router shield can be used to reduce radiation levels while still allowing a sufficiently strong signal to connect to the Internet
- Ultimately, hardwiring is the safest—in many homes this can be achieved by using the existing coaxial network installed when your home was built
- More advanced strategies include shielding and grounding and are still fairly easy to apply and require no technical skills
- Network Adapters create dirty electricity on your house wiring and are to be avoided.

That's enough talk about wireless for the moment. Let's talk about its lesser known cousin, wired.

---

234 Such as the Surfboard modem from Motorola/Arris.

235 If you have a telephone company-provided modem you're okay. Currently, these do not have public Wi-Fi hotspots. You can usually disable the Wi-Fi on these modem/routers with two clicks of the mouse by going into their router control panel.

Chapter 9

# EMFs From Wiring

IF YOU'RE READING THIS INDOORS, just take your eyes off this page (or screen) for a moment and look around the room. Notice anything? Can you see the wires in your walls? Have you ever wondered how these wires function? Even if you can't see the wires, they pulsate with energy and some of that energy fills every room of your home.

A lot of people assume that the electricity in a wire stays in a wire. That's only partly correct. The energy in the wire will light up your house or drive your air conditioning, but some of that energy spills off of the wire and radiates outward into the environment that you live and work in, creating an energized area known—cue the drumroll—as an electromagnetic field.

**Wherever and whenever there is electricity, there is an EMF.**

These EMFs do not stay in the wire, even if the wire is in a wall. They can permeate out into the room and into you.

There are cases where these EMFs can be very high and yet you wouldn't know it because your electrical appliances and lights all work just the same.

Surely, building and electrical regulations protect us from these EMFs? Unfortunately, they do not. Even in "civilized countries" where building and electrical regulations require fuses, circuit breakers, grounding systems and the like, the focus is on protecting people from electrical shocks and fire hazards. Electrical codes do not address how electricity affects the human body—it's NOT about EMF protection.

Surely the World Health Organization or some other internationally recognized authority protects us from these dangers? Hardly.

**It's been known since the 1970s that magnetic fields thousands of times lower than international standards can lead to cancer in children.[236]**

There have been less studies done on wired EMFs compared to wireless, but there is sufficient evidence to show that wired EMFs also cause biological effects, such as:[237]

- Cellular damage
- DNA breaks
- Creation of free radicals
- Other synergistic effects.

You'll notice the biological effects from wired EMFs are similar to those created by wireless. Not surprisingly, the links to disease are also similar, namely:[238]

- Leukemia
- Brain cancer
- Breast cancer
- Diabetes[239]
- Obesity[240]
- Damage to the immune system.

## How Can Electrical Wiring Be Dangerous?

When electricity flows through electrical wires, this creates a strength of energy coming off these wires. It may be thousands and thousands of times less energy than what is needed to give you an electrical shock or cause a fire, but it can cause havoc with your health.

We generally have three areas of concern:

- Magnetic fields
- Electric fields
- Dirty electricity

236 https://www.ncbi.nlm.nih.gov/pubmed/453167
237 https://www.powerwatch.org.uk/library/downloads/pf-emfs-1-intro-2018-11.pdf
238 https://www.powerwatch.org.uk/library/downloads/pf-emfs-1-intro-2018-11.pdf
239 Paul Heroux PhD, EMF Experts Solutions Club interview.
240 https://microwavenews.com/news-center/emf-exposures-womb-can-lead-childhood-obesity

In this chapter, I want to talk about magnetic and electric fields from electrical wiring.

> ***While electric field exposures in homes create an agitating influence on the body that does not allow deep, restful sleep, magnetic field exposures, on the other hand, create what some consider to be a more harmful influence by depressing the immune system and vitality.***
>
> —*Oram Miller, Building Biologist.*[241]

First let's look at magnetic fields. Experts agree this is a BIG problem. Bigger than wireless EMFs? It's hard to tell, but high magnetic fields are a very common problem in homes.

Dr. Ross Andersen shared with me the story of one of his patients who was having major health challenges. This patient had an electrical panel was right below the floor under her couch where she sat for two or three hours a night watching TV. Dr. Ross helped her rearrange her furniture to get her away from the electrical panel and the wires that came out from it, and she got better.

> ***2/3 of homes have elevated magnetic fields and over 50% is due to wiring issues.***
>
> —*Walter McGinnis, master electrician, EMF Experts Solutions Club interview.*

In a federal housing authority study in Canada, which analyzed hundreds of residences coast-to-coast, over 70% of all the problems of excessive magnetic fields were wiring errors.[242]

Building Biologist Alex Stadtner explains:

> ***We show up to someone's house who has none of these obvious exterior signs and the moment you turn on the bathroom exhaust or you turn on the kitchen lighting or the pump goes on for the garage or the pool, and all of a sudden the magnetic fields in that entire property can be much higher than what you will find immediately underneath a high voltage transmission line [particularly along the path of certain circuits due to wiring errors].***

241 https://www.createhealthyhomes.com/articles_magnetic_fields.php
242 Andrew Michrowski, EMF Experts Solutions Club interview.

## Magnetic Field Sources

Your electrical wiring is not the only thing which creates magnetic fields in your home. Magnetic fields are also caused by:

- Refrigerators
- Electric stoves
- Fans
- Transformers in computers etc.
- Anything else with a motor or transformer.

The problem is, magnetic fields are NOT stopped by building materials or any commonly found metals. They go through just about everything. So, what can you do to protect yourself?

## Magnetic Field Protection Tips—Free And Easy

Distance is your friend when it comes to magnetic fields. There are two types of sources of magnetic fields:[243]

1. **Linear sources**, for example, as emitted from a circuit with a wiring error or from a metal grounding path, such as a metal water pipe or TV cable sheathing.
2. **Point sources**, for example, as emitted from motors in devices like refrigerators, stoves, fans or transformers (as found on computers and the like).

**Magnetic fields from linear sources drop off in direct proportion to the distance from the source.** So, twice the distance from an electric wire with a wiring error would mean two times less exposure.

**Whereas, magnetic fields from point sources drop off even quicker, because the strength of the field drops off exponentially with distance.** For example, if you are two feet from a transformer, you would expect a certain field strength. But if you're 20 feet away, the field strength will be more than ten times less.

In normal day to day operation, magnetic fields from point sources can be very powerful, but fields from these sources drop off in intensity quite quickly. The fields from a mis-wired electrical circuit, however, can be just as strong, but they reach much farther.

243 https://www.createhealthyhomes.com/articles_magnetic_fields.php

**This distinction between point and linear sources is a bit academic, but they each have their own characteristics and mitigation strategies. In either case, you need an EMF meter to know your exposures.**

Often, point source magnetic fields can be dealt with just by moving your furniture, moving your bed, or by moving your couch.[244] Ideally, you would want an EMF meter to help you with this, but just from a common sense point of view, in any room where you spend any time where you've got electronics with transformers or motors in them plugged in and switched on (e.g. fans, computer equipment, older TVs), if you can get 3 or 6 feet away from them, you will have greatly reduced your exposure to magnetic fields.

## Wiring 101

Let's talk wiring for a moment. If you live in the US, this should look familiar:

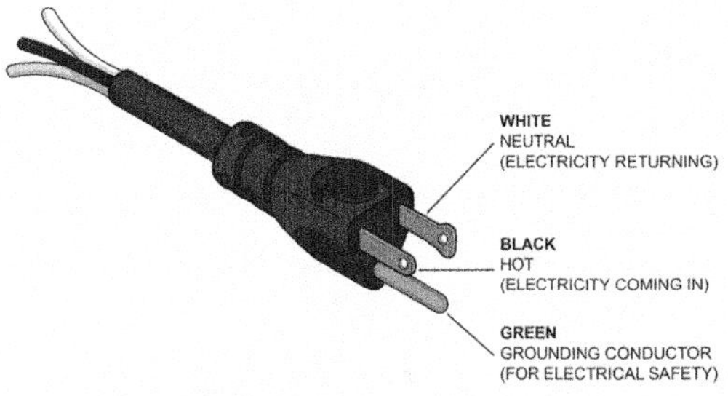


USA TYPE PLUG

It's a standard electrical plug that has two blades and one prong. Each blade and prong corresponds to an electrical wire.

**Black wire**: hot wire or phase (carries electric current coming from the breaker panel)

**White wire**: neutral wire, also known as the "grounded" conductor (carries electric current going back to the breaker panel)

**Green wire**: "grounding" conductor (for electrical safety, to trip the breaker in case of a hot to ground fault).

All homes have an electrical system with a main electrical box with different circuits. Lighting and other electrical devices plugged into outlets are on these different circuits. If it's a bigger property, you might have smaller, additional electrical boxes (all called sub-panels) located throughout the house.

All this wiring has to be done in a certain way in accordance with electrical codes. Different countries have different electrical codes. In the US, it's called the National

244 Anne Stewart - EMF Experts Solutions Club interview.

Electrical Code (NEC). Electricians performing electrical work have to comply with this standard.

> ***All it needs is for there to be one single wiring error anywhere on your wiring and you can have high magnetic fields all over your home.***
>
> *—Spark Burmaster, EMF Experts Solutions Club interview.*

There are all sorts of wiring errors that can give rise to serious EMF issues.

**Very often it's because your electrical system is not balanced, unbalanced loads are where the magnetic fields don't cancel each other out—this can create really big magnetic field problems.[245]**

Here are some typical wiring errors that can cause high magnetic fields as well as cause shocks or a fire hazard:

- A disconnected wire (causes the light bulb to not light up)
- Corroded wire at the contact (also causes the light bulb to not light up)
- Wires not connected properly (causes magnetic fields)
- Hot and neutral wires are not kept together in the same circuit (causes magnetic fields)
- Combining of neutrals from different circuits (causes magnetic fields). They cannot be connected to each other in a junction box[246]
- Neutral wire, which is normally connected to the grounding system in the breaker panel at the start of the circuit, is also connected to the grounding system somewhere else, such as your metal water pipe or incoming TV cable sheathing (causes magnetic fields).

In many of these cases, your electrical system would appear normal (except with a disconnected or corroded wire). When you plug things into an outlet, they will work. When you switch on a light, it will work. And yet any of these last four scenarios can create high magnetic fields that can have serious consequences to your health.

245 That's to say your electrical system has unbalanced loads of current on hot wires compared to current on neutral wires within circuits that have wiring errors. So the magnetic fields created by current running on the hot and neutral wires don't cancel each other out.

246 Unless designed specifically for that purpose, such as so-called "12-3" or "14-3" circuits.

You may even have a neighborhood problem with magnetic fields. If your neighbors do not have a good neutral connection to the electric utility's neutral wire[247] in their main electrical panel or anywhere along the path of their utility's electrical service return neutral wire, then some or all of their return neutral current can go onto shared metal grounding paths going into other homes in the neighborhood. This will include your metal grounding paths, such as metal water service pipes and TV cable sheathing, and enter everyone's electrical panel, including yours. This causes a—sometimes huge—magnetic field.

In such cases, the neighbor with the loose or broken electric utility service neutral is effectively using everyone else's, and your, service neutral as the sole path for their return current to get back to the transformer. This return current travels through everyone else's neutral connections creating a potentially humongous magnetic field.

**Warning: You should not try and fix any of these wiring errors yourself. Your ONLY concern at this stage is to determine if there are EMF issues with your wiring.**

Dealing with these errors might involve any or all of the following steps:

- Reconfiguring connections between certain circuits, or rarely rewiring circuits (eliminates magnetic fields)
- Putting all wiring in metal conduits (reduces electric fields)
- Replacing plastic jacketed wiring with shielded wiring (reduces electric fields)
- Repositioning your chairs, couches, desks, beds and wherever you spend time away from the electric meter and breaker panel (eliminates magnetic fields)
- Removing dimmer light switches and replacing them with conventional switches (reduces dirty electricity, more on this in Chapter 10)
- Inserting a dielectric coupling, AKA a plastic section, in the incoming metal water service supply pipe if current is present on it (eliminates magnetic fields)[248]
- Inserting a cable TV isolation filter into an incoming TV cable, if current is present on it (eliminates magnetic fields).

247 The electric service cables to a residence in North America consist of two insulated hot wires wound around a bare, braided neutral/ground/guy wire. That bare wire has three functions: it carries return current from the electric loads on circuits in the house back to the neighborhood transformer, as well as functioning as a ground for the house electrical system to the ground wire(s) at the utility pole or ground-mounted transformer, and finally, as the guy wire that holds all three wires up.

248 Typically, this requires a plumber and an electrician.

If you're thinking "this sounds complicated", you're right. It is. And working with electricity is dangerous if you don't know what you're doing. Which is why you need to get in a competent electrician to do this work, preferably under the guidance of an EMF consultant.

Some EMF consultants will consult with your plumber and electrician over the telephone and via the Internet to help guide them to take the proper steps to make the required repairs. Do NOT attempt these repairs yourself, unless you are a licensed electrician.

I'm going to explain how to get an electrician to fix your EMF issues. But first, a quick word about troubleshooting.

## Magnetic Field Protection Tips—Advanced Tips

**The next step in finding out if you have any magnetic fields from wiring is to take readings with an EMF meter, commonly called a Gauss meter.** This will NOT tell you precisely which circuits have the wiring errors but, if you use it properly, it should tell you if something is wrong and that you need to bring in an electrician to find and fix any wiring errors. This is all you are interested in anyway.

How to use your EMF meter to troubleshoot:[249]

1. **If you're standing near a light switch, you hold the Gauss meter about a foot away from the wall and turn on the light**—if the magnetic field reading on the Gauss meter jumps up, then you've got a possible wiring error.
2. **Do the same for other circuits carrying current to the other electrical devices in the rooms in your home**—you should be able to turn on anything in any room without the magnetic fields jumping up.
3. **Finally, put your Gauss meter next to your incoming metal water service pipe**—if you've got current on your water pipe, the Gauss meter reading will go up.[250]

So, if you turn the switch on for anything and the magnetic fields jump up, that says you likely have a wiring error.

249 Spark Burmaster, EMF Experts solutions club interview.
250 This means you've got some kind of wiring problem, meaning a neutral-to-ground connection somewhere in your electrical circuits or in a sub-panel.

Your EMF meter will give you a reading in Gauss or Tesla. I've created a short video showing you how to do this with an EMF meter and explaining the "safe" readings you need to achieve. See: www.electricsense.com/bookbonus

Magnetic fields are by far the hardest type of EMF to shield from. I explain how to do this in Chapter 19.

## Getting An Electrician In

**When you get your Gauss meter out and your testing indicates you have high magnetic fields, that's when you know you need to get in an electrician.** Your goal is to be able to talk intelligently to an electrician about this.

A lot of people assume that electricians know about EMFs. Wrong. Electricians are trained to do electrical work. EMFs are another kettle of fish. Finding an electrician who is willing to help you with your EMF issues can be a tall order, but you'll have success if:

- You find an electrician with an open mind who is sympathetic to your needs
- You assure him or her that you are not going to ask them to do anything that is not in code
- For any work that they do, you are able to check with your EMF meter that it's had the desired effect of reducing the magnetic field level.

**The other important point is that you want a *licensed* electrician.** Or you could find yourself solving one problem and creating another (bigger) problem. In many parts of the world, including some states in the US, anybody can do electrical work—they don't need a license. In the US, you can verify if a contractor has a license by going to Licensedelectrician.com.

When you're calling around looking for an electrician, there are certain do's and don'ts.

**Things you shouldn't say:**

- I've got magnetic fields. I'm going to die. Come out here and fix it.
- I've got scientific studies. My wiring is giving me cancer.
- I've got a bad case of EMFs.
- There's something wrong with my electromagnetic fields.

**Things you should say:**

- I think I've got wiring errors.
- I'm wanting a wiring upgrade.
- I want to bring my electrical system up to code.

Remember, electricians want to fix electrical things. They don't want to be dealing with magical, mystical magnetic fields or other EMFs. So, you have to speak their language.

Once the electrician has turned up and you've got some rapport going, then you can get your EMF meter out and show him what happens when you flip the light switch on or when you hold your Gauss meter near your water pipes. (For current on metal water pipes, you will also need the services of a plumber.)

What's important here is that you have some basic understanding of the situation so that any electrical work that is done actually fixes your magnetic and electric field EMF issues.

Confused? We have got a bit technical here. To better understand this subject, two resources I recommend are a 22-minute video by Karl Riley to learn more about tracing errors on building wiring and a video by Building Biologist Oram Miller on common wiring errors. Both these videos are referenced here: www.electricsense.com/bookbonus.

These are technician-level videos that you might want to share with your electrician.[251]

## Wiring Errors Can Make Your Hair Fall Out!

Having intact neutral wires between every house and the utility pole is super important. If the electric utility service neutral wire in your or any other house in the neighborhood becomes loose or broken, it can literally make your hair fall out and cause many other health problems. A broken neutral does not happen often, but when it does, it can cause big magnetic fields.

251 According to Building Biologist Oram Miller, many people in the EMF community think that the only magnetic field from circuits is the localized magnetic field on top of the wire, which can be quite high. This occurs when current is flowing through the hot and neutral wires within the circuit and the two epicenters of the magnetic fields they produce are separated by a quarter of an inch inside the circuit or conduit. As long as the current loads are balanced, this field drops off within a few inches. This is normal. The solution to magnetic fields, according to many, is to twist the wires to take care of that separation. Twisting plastic Romex with a drill can actually break the wires inside. Building Biologists are fine with Romex. They say the real causes of magnetic fields from circuits are wiring errors. They don't recommend twisting, they recommend fixing and avoiding wiring errors.

When I interviewed Building Biologist Diana Schultz on my podcast, she shared the amazing story of how she was using her EMF meters regularly to monitor her own home. She noticed when she was taking a shower that her EMF meters would start clicking. "It was a humongous magnetic field coming out of the water pipes in my front yard, coming up over top of the house and halfway into the backyard. The whole house. And all the houses down the street. It was amazing."

She realized the magnetic field was coming from her neighbor's house.[252] For three months, Diana tried contacting them without any success. During that time, her hair started falling out and a weird freckle on her collarbone started to grow. She also noticed that her pet cockatoo had developed a nasty looking tumor growing out the side of her beak.

The neighbors finally got their wiring issue fixed. Since then, the magnetic field reading on Diana's EMF meter has never risen again in her house, all her symptoms went away, and her cockatoo's tumor dried up and fell off.

Building Biologist Spark Burmaster shared with me the story of a lady on Long Island, New York, who had tiny warts all over her body. She spent over $20,000 on rewiring, creating a whole new electrical installation, but she hadn't dealt with what was causing her symptoms. In the end she ended up paying a plumber to fit a dielectric coupler into her water service pipe to prevent the electric current from flowing under her house and all her little warts went away.

**A dielectric coupler, also called a dielectric union, is a connector which, when fitted into the incoming metal water service supply pipe, provides a plastic ring between the two metal pipes, thereby preventing electric current from flowing.**[253] The lady told Spark, out of all that stuff, out of all that money, rewiring, new panels, new everything, the thing that had the most effect on her health was to put the plastic insert into the incoming metal water pipe to get rid of all the current on the water pipe.[254]

Oram Miller points out that a 1 Amp current load on a water pipe, which is not uncommon (or a similar amount of net current on a circuit with a wiring error), will emit a magnetic field that takes six feet before it reduces below our target goal of roughly 1.0 mG (in daytime) and farther than six feet, to reach our nighttime goal of being below 0.5 mG.[255]

---

252 Oram Miller comments that "the most likely explanation is a broken neutral wire in the electric utility's service cable between a neighbor's house and the utility's transformer. That pushes most or all of the return current for that one house onto the metal grounding paths (like water service supply pipe and the sheathing of the incoming cable TV cable) running through all neighboring houses, including her's."

253 Building Biologists are trained to guide a plumber and electrician in the proper installation of this remedy.

254 Spark Burmaster, Building Biologist, EMF Experts solutions club interview.

255 The Institute of Building Biology + Sustainability makes a distinction between daytime and nighttime readings.

**"Pipe current", as Spark Burmaster calls it, runs constantly, day and night, possibly under a first-floor bedroom, whereas the magnetic fields from wiring errors go away when you turn off lights and other electrical devices.**

Building Biologist Shaun Kranish recommends inserting two dielectric couplers into your copper pipe. Each dielectric coupler has a steel side and a copper side on it, so you insert a short steel pipe in between. That way, you can safely connect copper to copper and steel to steel.[256]

Another solution is to install two feet of plastic piping into your water pipe. This will create the same effect.[257]

*90% of houses I've checked have electrical current on the water pipes.*
*—FRANK DICRISTINA, BUILDING BIOLOGIST, EMF EXPERTS SOLUTIONS CLUB INTERVIEW.*

To see a video on how to insert dielectric couplers onto your water pipes, see my resource page: www.electricsense.com/bookbonus

## Grounding Errors

On a different topic, if your home is improperly grounded, this can mean you may have stray current or stray voltage EMFs. (So-called "stray voltage" is really "stray current", according to Spark Burmaster.) There's been a lot of studies done on this with cattle. In the 1970s, they noticed cows that were dying, weren't producing milk and had trouble reproducing.[258]

The studies showed that stray current causes milk production to go down. If you've got stray current wandering around your backyard, home or workplace, it's not difficult to imagine how this could affect your health.

I'm not going to explain to you how to ground, that's too technical. But what I can do is explain things so that you have some idea of how grounding should work so when you get an electrician out to check your grounding system, you avoid not getting the repair you need because your electrician doesn't fully understand what you need them to do.

256 Shaun Kranish, EMF Experts Solutions Club interview.
257 Joe Darnell, EMF Experts Solutions Club interview.
258 https://articles.mercola.com/sites/articles/archive/2017/05/28/dirty-electricity.aspx

## Grounding—What You Need To Understand

**Your grounding system is made up of two types of grounding: a system ground and an equipment ground.**[259] They could be on one and the same wire. Your system ground is typically a ground rod, which is a stake driven into the earth upon which your home is built. This ground rod is connected by a wire to the neutral/ground bar in your main service panel, which will also have current-carrying neutral wires from circuits connected to it.

Every house is supposed to have a system ground. Its purpose is to ensure that if lightning hits your house, that lightning has a path to get into the earth. That's it.[260]

**Quite separate is the equipment ground, which protects you if there's something wrong with the wiring in your house.** The equipment ground is the third wire in your circuit and in a grounded cord. The green or bare wire in the circuit is the equipment ground. If a hot wire touches the equipment ground, the purpose of the equipment ground is to provide a lowresistance path all the way back to the transformer that immediately trips the circuit breaker to protect you from shock.

**The bottom line is your grounding system, whether it is a system ground or an equipment ground, is not supposed to be carrying any current on it (except in a lightning strike or to trip a breaker).** That's one of the reasons why wiring errors exist, because there's no requirement in the electrical code for when the electrician wires something up to get out his clamp-on ammeter and verify that 100% of the current that goes out on the hot wire returns on the appropriate neutral wire of that same circuit, and that there is no current on the ground wire. Current always travels out to an electrical device on the hot wire of a circuit, and no other path. Current on the hot wire is normally not shared with any other wire.

**The return current on the neutral wire is often shared with other neutral wires or grounds. When that happens, you have a wiring error.**

Electricians in some countries (like France and Australia) have had ground fault-protected circuits in breaker panels for decades, wiring errors are therefore not present.[261]

259 https://www.thespruce.com/what-is-grounding-1152859

260 Oram Miller comments, "Technically, if your house does not have a ground rod, your house is always still grounded through the neutral/ground wire of the overhead or underground electric utility service cable, which is connected to ground rods out at the utility pole or at the ground-mounted transformer if you have underground electrical service."

261 Oram Miller comments that in the US, ARC-Fault breakers have been recently required by code in almost all circuits in new and permitted remodeled homes. This should result in far less magnetic fields in new and remodeled homes in the US in the coming years.

In summary, the electrician's job is to make it so that everything works, that there's no shock hazard, and that their wiring installation job passes electric code.

**The electrical code in the US doesn't require that absolutely every single circuit be tested to verify the absence of "net current".**

It's not that unusual for older properties to have no ground at the house.[262] It's also not unusual for homes of any age to have grounding wiring errors.[263]

## Identifying Grounding Errors—Intermediate

One way to take the guesswork out of identifying ground errors is to use a circuit tester.

It costs $10–$15. You plug it into your wall outlet, and it has LEDs that indicate some wiring issues.

There are different versions of this device, but the one I recommend (shown on the left here)[264] is a slightly more advanced version than some you can buy. It can identify several different scenarios where you can have incorrect wiring.

Here's how to interpret the LEDs when you plug it into an outlet:

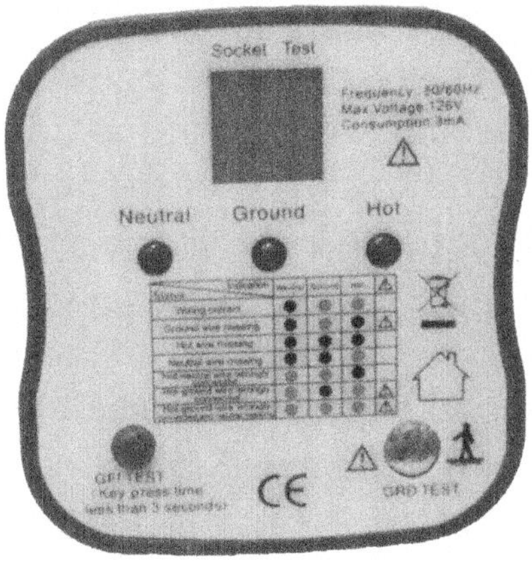


| Status / Indication | Neutral | Ground | Hot | ⚠ |
|---|---|---|---|---|
| Wiring correct | ● | ○ | ○ | |
| Ground wire missing | ● | ○ | ● | ⚠ |
| Hot wire missing | ● | ● | ● | |
| Neutral wire missing | ● | ● | ○ | |
| Hot-neutral wire wrongly connected | ○ | ○ | ● | |
| Hot-ground wire wrongly connected | ○ | ● | ○ | ⚠ |
| Hot-ground wire wrongly connected and neutral missing | ○ | ○ | ○ | ⚠ |

262 But again, the house is still grounded out at the utility pole.
263 Spark Burmaster, EMF Experts Solutions Club interview.
264 Image supplied courtesy of LessEMF.com

As Building Biologist Oram Miller explains:

> ***The only thing a plug-in circuit tester can tell you that would have EMF ramifications is an open ground, when only the middle light lights up but the outer light is dark or dimly lit. In the first case, when it is dark, the ground is non-existent, non-functional. When the outer light is dim, it means the ground wire is loose, which is as good as no ground at all.***

The circuit tester can also test your outlets with GFI capability (applies to North American homes). Your GFI or GFCI (Ground Fault Circuit Interrupter) outlet monitors the flow of current on the circuit it's fitted to and will immediately cut the power if it detects a ground fault. That problem does not cause magnetic field EMFs, but it will protect you from a shock.

Press the button on the bottom left of your circuit tester to test that the GFCI is wired correctly and press the button on the bottom right to test for voltage on your ground wire.

The picture on the left here shows a GFI outlet as can be found in many homes in North America.

Just to be clear, the circuit tester is an easy and inexpensive way to get certain information on your electrical system. But it cannot identify complex wiring errors such as neutral-to-neutral nor neutral-to-ground wiring errors, which cause most magnetic fields.

So, use this as a starting point before moving on to the more advanced steps, including having an EMF consultant guide an electrician in testing for wiring errors that cause magnetic fields, which, again, circuit testers do not test for.

## Resolving Grounding And Wiring Errors—Advanced

When you call an electrician in, you want to ask him to check your grounding and wiring system, which should include:

- Checking that there is a system ground and it is effective (an electrician can easily measure its resistance)

- Checking the equipment ground to make sure it is properly connected
- The electrician particularly needs to check the return neutral wires of every circuit to ensure that 100% of the current that goes out from the breaker panel on hot wires comes back from the device on the corresponding neutral wire within that circuit, and only on that path
- There should be no current on ground wires within individual circuits
- Likewise, there should also not be current on the ground wire that runs between sub panels and the main panel.

**Resolving grounding issues is complex.** Sometimes even otherwise competent electricians and EMF consultants can be baffled by grounding errors. Using your circuit tester and Gauss meter does not turn you into a grounding ninja, but it will help you understand if the contractor you've hired has done a good job. In particular, your Gauss meter will ensure that any neutral-to-neutral or neutral-to-ground errors (which again will not show up on any circuit tester) are fixed when he is done, because the magnetic field you measured before will be gone when devices are turned on.

## Electric Field Issues

I mentioned in Chapter 2 that wherever current flows in an unbalanced way between the hot and neutral wires, there is a magnetic field and wherever there is voltage, there is an electric field. The truth is it's a bit more complicated than that, but if you keep that idea in mind, you won't go far wrong.

Remember, electric fields will exist even when there is no current flow. Like magnetic fields, electric fields are in the walls, floors and ceilings of all of our homes and buildings because that is where plastic-jacketed wiring circuits are located. Like magnetic fields from circuits with unbalanced loads with wiring errors, electric fields can jump out of the walls many feet and zap you, especially when you sleep. Your body is a natural conductor. So, wherever the electrical fields are in your home, the electric fields are constantly wanting to jump into the human bodies (yours, your spouse, your kids, etc.) that are right next to it.

**Electric fields can act as a micro stressor. This is not something that will knock you over like a freight train.**

**It's a cumulative small stress. It has a toxic influence that's invisible but it's slowly breaking you down.**

The problem is, the more you are exposed to these electric fields, the more cumulative exposure you have and the more severely they affect you.

Electric fields are potentially as much of a concern as magnetic fields for two reasons:

1. **Electric fields on electrical wiring consistently radiate out six to eight feet through drywall and most building materials from every plastic-jacketed circuit, as well as from every plastic lamp cord when plugged in.**[265] Magnetic fields, on the other hand, will only extend out a certain distance depending on how much current is flowing in a circuit with a wiring error.
2. **Electric fields are present whether you have the device switched on or not.** A bedside lamp, for instance, will emit electric fields regardless of whether the lamp is switched on.

Again, take a moment to look up from what you're reading and look around you. Are you more than six to eight feet from the nearest visible electrical wiring that is plugged in? Are you more than six to eight feet from the nearest light switch or wall where there is likely to be a hidden electrical wire? If not, then that means you are engulfed in the electric field of that wire.[266]

If you have a bedside lamp plugged in but switched off, its electric fields are engulfing you, zapping you and everyone and everything within a six to eight foot radius.

**When electric fields envelope the body, they place an electrical charge on the body that can be measured as a body voltage** (more about this in Chapter 16). This can lead to insomnia, nightmares, fatigue, low immunity, and so on. Your body was not designed to live in an electrified environment, much less sleep in it.

> ***People are more sensitive, in terms of adverse effects—headaches and things—to electric fields than they are to magnetic fields.***
>
> *—Electrical Engineer Alasdair Philips, EMF Experts Solutions Club interview.*

265 Oram Miller, Building Biologist - EMF Experts Solutions Club interview.
266 According to Walter McGinnis, electric fields can radiate out up to 12 feet!

## Studies On Electric Fields

The most compelling research I can share on electric fields is that of Dr. Samuel Milham. He studied a whole bunch of historical US vital statistics documents over a 50-year period during the first half of the twentieth century. Because electricity was introduced much earlier in some parts of the US than in others, he was able to compare the death records of two big populations, one of which was electrified and one of which wasn't. What he found blew him away—death rates were significantly higher in urban areas that were electrified compared to rural areas that were not electrified.[267]

Was it the 60Hz electric fields or magnetic fields that caused this? We don't know.[268] There is something of a gaping hole in the EMF research with regards to electric fields and particularly electric fields in the home (residential electric fields). It's the aspect of EMFs that has been the least studied.

One of the reasons is because when we look at the EMFs on your household wiring, there is always an electric field and a small magnetic field.[269] Of course, if the current is not flowing, there is no localized magnetic field. But when the 1979 study was published[270] showing a clear association with cancer from low level magnetic fields on wiring, that's where all the research was directed, while electric field research got side-lined.

Yet there is an almost widespread agreement amongst those in the know, including hundreds of independent scientists, EMF consultants and Building Biologists I've interviewed, that electric fields are possibly the biggest EMF elephant in the room.

Fortunately, the saving grace of electric fields is that they are easy to measure and easy to control.

## Electric Field Protection Tips—Free And Easy

Here are two easy ways to deal with electric fields:

1. Move
2. Unplug.

267 https://magdahavas.com/electrification-caused-diseases-of-civilization/
268 This was before the days of dirty electricity, which Dr. Milham has pioneered the awareness of—dirty electricity has its own electric and magnetic fields from frequencies above 60Hz, see Chapter 10.
269 This can become a big magnetic field when a wiring error is present.
270 https://www.ncbi.nlm.nih.gov/pubmed/453167

Sometimes you can just rearrange your furniture. Look at your favorite couch and rooms where you spend the most amount of time, particularly where you sleep. Think about the six to eight feet, look at what wiring and electrical appliances are within that distance, and remember that electric fields go straight through walls. Try and get yourself outside the field of action or as far out of it as possible—it's better to be three feet from electrical wiring than six inches.

Often you can unplug. Manual and remote outlet shut-off switches can be purchased to easily do this. There are lots of things you can easily unplug when you're not using them, like:

- Lamps
- Fans
- Computers.

Some computers, laptops for instance, can still be used on the battery when unplugged. Does unplugging your laptop always mean a reduction in electric field exposures? No, unfortunately not, particularly if you are trying to reduce your RF exposure by plugging in an Ethernet cable. It's not as simple as that—I explain how to tackle this in Chapter 13.

Does this mean you need to run around your house unplugging everything and anything? No, only for the cords within six to eight feet of your body. But in your mind's eye, collapse all walls and think about the six to eight foot rule and unplug what you can. The room where it's most important to get serious about reducing your electric fields is in your bedroom. Unplug the cords for all the electronics and lamps you have right next to their bed—in Chapter 11, I explain in detail how you can reduce EMFs in the bedroom.

## Electric Field Protection Tips—Intermediate

**The second takeaway with electric fields is that they lower with grounding.** So, make sure all electrical items you use on a regular basis that are plugged in are on a grounded cord; one with three prongs. That third prong is what grounds. (In some countries, it's not a prong on the plug, but the principle is the same).

The way this works is that the ground wire bleeds off some of the electric field coming off the live, hot wire (with 120 Volts in North America), which is the source of the electric field in the cord. The neutral wire, being the "ground*ed*" conductor, already bleeds off some of the electric field. Adding a ground wire, the so-called "ground*ing*" conductor, adds a second grounded wire, thereby bleeding off more electric field from the hot wire. Rewiring your lamp cord with shielded cord completes the reduction and eliminates the electric field altogether.

If you are using electrical equipment and it's not grounded, then this can mean that you become the path of least resistance and the electric field is more drawn to you—electricity follows ALL paths, with its preference being the path of least resistance.

## Electric Field Protection Tips—Advanced

You're already unplugging where possible and where you are using appliances, you're making sure they have a grounded cord. Beyond this, advanced solutions for reducing exposure to electric fields in places you occupy during the day and evening time revolve around a combination of grounding and shielding. The bedroom needs special attention and has its own mitigation techniques, including shutting off circuits at night or shielding walls and floors, which I will explain in Chapter 11.

Most homes are fitted with plastic jacketed circuits in walls and floors. The whole electrical system is done out with plastic covered wires because it's cheap. Unfortunately, plastic coated wires do not "contain" electric fields. Two solutions are possible. Replace with:

- Shielded wiring for cords you plug in, and
- Metal clad wiring for circuits in walls and floors—that's to say, wiring in a grounded metal sheath or conduit.[271] This is an option for those places in the house where you sit for extended periods of time, such as at a desk, easy chair or couch, or a play area for children.

In both cases, the idea is the same. You are putting a conductive, grounded surface between you and the source of the radiation—that's to say the wiring. In both cases you would ground the shielding material to make sure any electric fields are dissipated.

The good news is that this is very effective and, if done carefully, you should be able to get your electric field exposures right down to around 1 V/m or thereabouts. The less good news is, in both cases this requires a LOT of work and needs to be carried out by a licensed electrician. And for most people, this is not feasible, except

271 Metal-cladding, either flexible metal conduit as in MC cable or "flex", or solid metal pipe conduit as in electrical metal tubing, does not hold in magnetic fields, especially from wiring errors. Circuits wired with MC cable that have wiring errors can produce magnetic fields that are just as strong and extend just as far into the room as plastic Romex circuits with wiring errors.

perhaps if you're renovating an old property and have to re-do the wiring in any case, or perhaps you're having a new property built and you can install it from scratch.

Some people will have their electrician drop in a new, dedicated metal-clad circuit into a home office or other room they occupy a lot. The occupant shuts off the plastic circuit in the walls of that room. You must then make sure that cords you plug into the new outlet are themselves shielded, such as shielded power cords for computers and monitors and shielded power cords that you can rewire lamps and other appliances with.

You can also rewire lamps with a shielded power cord, such as Mu-Cord from LessEMF (best done by an electrician).

**What's important is to measure your electric fields so you can mitigate effectively—and not blindly.**

There are two ways of doing this:

1. By measuring the ambient electric fields throughout your home and particularly in rooms where you spend a lot of time, using a sensitive, accurate electric field meter. To see a short video on how to do this, see: www.electricsense.com/bookbonus
2. By measuring electric fields on your body using a body voltage meter—I explain how to do this in Chapter 16.

In both cases you would take readings, mitigate (by following some of the strategies laid out in this chapter), and then take readings again to make sure your mitigation has been effective.

What you need to take away from this chapter:

- Electricity in a wire does not stay in the wire. It permeates out into the room and into you
- There are cases where the EMF from this electricity can be very high and yet you wouldn't know that because your electrical appliances all work just the same
- Studies show these EMFs from wiring can have devastating consequences on your health
- Some experts estimate 2 out of 3 of homes have elevated magnetic fields and that over 50% is due to wiring issues

- Move three or four feet away from any electric wires with electrical appliances switched on to greatly reduce your exposure to electric fields
- An easy way to take the guesswork out of magnetic fields on wiring is to use a Gauss meter to help you identify if you have a problem
- You should NOT attempt to resolve wiring errors yourself. You need to get a licensed electrician and be able to speak "their language"
- Having an electrical system that is properly grounded is important for your health —a licensed electrician can easily check this for you
- Electric field issues in the home can be potentially as dangerous as magnetic fields—but they are usually easy to resolve by unplugging and/or moving
- Make sure all electrical items you use on a regular basis that are plugged in are on a grounded cord and that your electrical system is properly grounded—using shielded cord is even better
- To take this to the next level, take readings with an EMF meter and have shielded wiring or metal clad installed in the areas where you spend time in the day and evening
- Reducing electric fields in bedrooms when you sleep at night is crucial, and is covered in Chapter 11.

We like to think of the place where we rest every night as our nice, safe, sweet home. This is what it should be. Unfortunately, for many people, it's not. For many of us, our homes have become an electrical cage. You and your family are living in an increasingly dense electrosmog, which is impacting your health in subtle but powerful ways. Contributing to this are the several thousand feet of wire running through all the rooms, walls and ceilings of your house acting like an antenna emitting all these man-made EMFs.

Keep reading. By the end of this guide, you will have a very clear idea of how to significantly reduce this electrosmog and turn your home into a safe haven.

## Chapter 10

# Dirty Electricity

SO FAR, WE'VE TALKED ABOUT magnetic fields, electric fields and radio frequency radiation. Well, there is a fourth main category of electropollution that is zapping you and your family in your home and workplace, and it's growing at an alarming rate. It goes under different names: intermediary frequencies, electrical noise, dirty power or, more commonly, dirty electricity.

If you live in the US, the electrical wiring system in your home and place of work will be a 60 Hertz alternating current (AC) electric system (50 Hertz if you live in Europe). Once upon a time, when I was a boy, 60Hz was all there was running through those wires—that means 60 cycles a second.

Times have changed. Some devices, like laptops and tablets, run better and more efficiently with a low voltage direct current (DC) power supply, while others run better with higher voltage. But one of the big reasons that 60Hz AC is no longer the sole frequency on your electrical wiring is because when the energy crisis hit the world in the 1970s, it suddenly became important to economize resources. So, engineers came up with all kinds of novel ways to make devices work by using less power. One of the most ingenious of these involves the use of switch mode power supplies (SMPSs). The use of SMPSs in our electrical devices has become rampant.

**SMPSs do a wonderful job of making our favorite electrical devices more energy efficient and help to save the planet but, unfortunately, they introduce a potent form of electrical pollution on our wiring... dirty electricity.[272]**

272 Some experts also include "stray voltage" within the definition of dirty electricity, see Chapter 9 for more on this.

They do this by chopping the waveform of the current, sometimes 20,000 times a second.[273]

Here are some devices that can cause dirty electricity:

- Light dimmer switches
- Computers, printers and scanners
- Induction hobs
- Energy-efficient light bulbs
- Solar power installations
- Televisions
- Music entertainment systems
- Video game consoles
- Cordless telephones
- Microwave ovens
- Smart meters and smart appliances
- Routers and modems
- Battery chargers for cell phones, etc.
- Blenders and mixers
- Hair dryers
- Multi-speed fans

**If you have fancy gadgets and electronics in your home, then I can guarantee you are exposed to dirty electricity.**

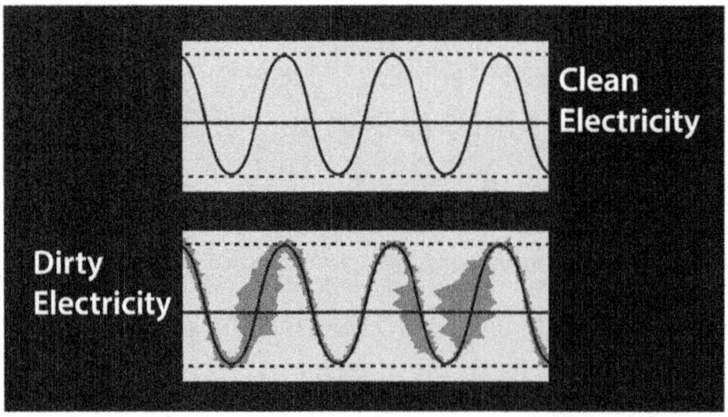


If you were to look at a 60Hz electricity power supply on an oscilloscope (a device that electricians and electrical engineers use to see the quality of the electrical

273 Lloyd Morgan, EMF Experts Solutions Club interview.

waveform), it produces a nice smooth sine wave. Devices fitted with SMPSs interrupt and disturb the sine wave, causing spikes and surges, otherwise known as "harmonics" and "transients", as shown in the above diagram.

Most of the devices listed above cause dirty electricity in your home. Once it's created, dirty electricity flows throughout your home because no device can use it.

Many of these devices create a combination of EMFs. Take induction hobs for instance. When in use, they emit high levels of dirty electricity AND high magnetic fields. The magnetic fields impact whoever is doing the cooking, whereas the dirty electricity pollutes your entire home.[274]

## Is Dirty Electricity Dangerous?

There is a growing body of research which suggests that dirty electricity is very dangerous to our health.

> ***There is a high likelihood that most of the twentieth century "diseases of civilization", including cardiovascular disease, malignant neoplasms (cancer), diabetes, and suicide, are not caused by lifestyle alone, but by certain physical aspects of electricity itself.***
>
> *—Dr. Samuel Milham, Dirty Electricity: Electrification and the Diseases of Civilization.*

This is a bold statement for anyone to make. But when you know it comes from the mouth of one of America's most esteemed epidemiologists of the last 50 years, it does get you thinking.

Power expert Dave Stetzer, who did pioneering research on dirty electricity with Dr. Martin Graham, also says it's dangerous.[275] The earliest research on this is believed to have been done by the Russians at the end of World War II. They called it radio wave sickness, even though the harmonic frequencies of dirty electricity are not in the radio wave bandwidth. The Russians identified that the following symptoms could be associated with dirty electricity exposures:

- headaches
- nausea
- flu-like symptoms

274 According to Alasdair Philips, when in use induction hobs can impose at least 1000 GS units of dirty electricity on your kitchen circuits and several hundred GS units in other parts of your home. I will explain what this means below.

275 Much of the information shared in this chapter is gleaned from my talks with Dave Stetzer.

- cancers
- memory loss
- depression.

Prof. Magda Havas, a researcher at Trent University in Canada, links dirty electricity with ADD, ADHD and chronic fatigue.

## Cancer Clusters

In 2003, the teachers at La Quinta Middle School in California were complaining that cancer rates amongst their colleagues were alarmingly high. There was found to be a threefold risk of cancer in teachers at La Quinta compared to California residents as a whole. Why? When dirty electricity measurements were taken, it was found that in one quarter of the classrooms, the dirty electricity readings were so high they overloaded the meter.

At the time of the study,[276] which was published in 2008, there were 11 reported cancer cases. Unfortunately, things have evolved since then, for the worse. Twenty-four teachers and staff have now had cancer and 49 students have developed cancer in their 20s. Six teachers and staff have now died, and six students have now died.[277]

## Why Is Dirty Electricity So Dangerous?

Obviously, dirty electricity is dangerous, because it can cause cancer and all these other terrible diseases. But how? And why? The how and the why is thought to be linked to the range of frequencies associated with dirty electricity. All the electronic devices mentioned above create pollution in the kilohertz range, which unfortunately doesn't stay on your wiring. That electrical pollution permeates out into the room and into your body if you are also in the room.

Research shows that when you are exposed to alternating current (AC) harmonic frequencies in the kilohertz range, (thousands of hertz as opposed to the 60Hz that should be on your electrical wiring), then these frequencies have the ability to "go internal". These harmonic frequencies oscillate at thousands of Hertz, as opposed to frequencies at 60Hz, which should be the only frequency on your electrical wiring.

276 http://bit.ly/High-frequency-voltage-cancer-incidence-in-teachers-in-a-California-school
277 Bill Cadwallader, EMF Health Summit interview.

**When you have 2 kilohertz (kHz) of dirty electricity on your electrical wiring, you are particularly vulnerable.**

At these frequencies the EMFs have the ability to "go internal", that's to say your skin resistance doesn't really come into play anymore. EMFs from dirty electricity penetrate directly into your cells, tissues and organs.[278]

## Dirty Electricity Protection Tips—Nearly Free And Easy

The number one way to deal with your dirty electricity exposures is to minimize or eliminate the devices that are causing these exposures. That might not sound very practical but look through my list of devices above. Which of those devices do you have in your home? Do you really need to use a cordless phone, a hair dryer, energy-efficient light bulbs, dimmer switches? There are some things, like your cordless phone and your energy-efficient light bulbs, that are going to be easier to replace than others, like your dimmer switches. Go for the easy wins now. Cell phone chargers are another one. Unplug them when they are not in use.[279]

To make this slightly more scientific, you can use a regular AM radio as a dirty electricity detector. A good choice is the Radio Shack 12-467, which sells for under $20. You don't have to buy this model, but you want a radio without noise suppression technology—you might already have one lying around.[280] Here's a picture of the old Sony radio that I use.

Here's how you can detect dirt electricity with your AM radio:

1. Turn your radio dial to the white noise between stations, where there is no radio signal, particularly at the low end of the dial
2. Move around the room turning your radio antenna in all directions
3. When you hear the radio start to hiss and crackle, this means you are picking up static and that there is a source of dirty electricity nearby.

278 Dave Stetzer, EMF Experts Solutions Club interview.
279 Avoid charging on the mains power at night—use battery operated power banks to charge your phone instead.
280 https://www.emfanalysis.com/how-to-measure-dirty-electricity/

The frequency of the dirty electricity being created depends on the device. For instance, energy efficient lighting tends to be higher frequency, so you want to move the dial of your radio up to the top of its range, about 1600 kHz. To see a video of me detecting dirty electricity from a low-energy light with my AM radio, go to this page: www.electricsense.com/bookbonus

How to use your AM radio to detect dirty electricity from different sources:

1. Place your AM radio near any of the devices listed above. Switch on, switch off and listen to what happens. Do this a few times.
2. Move around your home holding your portable AM radio near your electrical outlets. If your radio starts to hiss as you are moving about, this is a good indication that you have DE on the circuits in that room.

Using an AM radio does have its limitations. It detects dirty electricity, but it doesn't measure it. For that, you will need a dirty electricity meter.

## Dirty Electricity Protection Tips—Intermediate

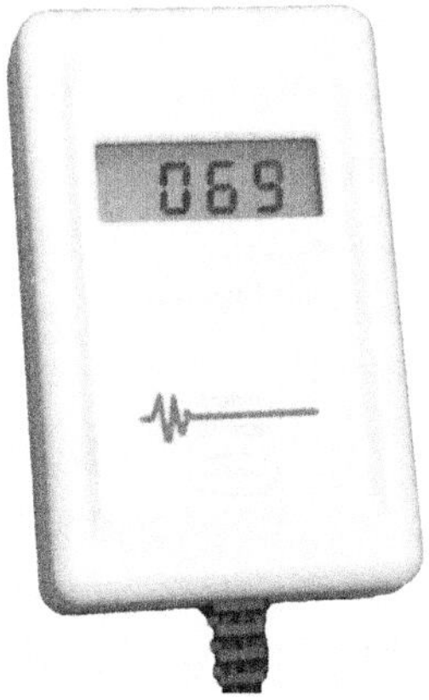


The easiest way of measuring dirty electricity in your home is to use a Stetzerizer® Microsurge Meter.[281] I like this meter because it's so easy to use.

You just plug your microsurge meter into any outlet in your home and it gives you a GS (Graham Stetzer) reading between 0—2000. For the scientifically minded, this corresponds to frequencies between 4 kHz and 100 kHz. The manufacturers recommend taking corrective action (doing something to reduce your DE levels) if your GS reading is above 50 Units. The first thing you want to know is if the dirty electricity is coming in from outside of the home (for example, from your neighbors) or if it is being created by the appliances you have in your home, or both.

You can do this by switching everything off in your home, even unplugging them if you can, and then going to the electrical outlet that is nearest the breaker panel in your home and plugging in your GS meter. If your meter is reading over 50 GS units with everything switched off, you know that the problem is external to your house.

281 Image courtesy of LessEMF.com

In which case, try to insert one or two filters into the closest outlet to the panel that's on two different circuits, with one circuit on each of the two legs of electricity coming into the house.[282]

A simpler solution to reducing dirty electricity that comes in from neighbor's homes is to have an electrician mount a metal box next to your main breaker panel and then install two regular two-gang (double) outlets in the box, one connected to Leg A and the other to Leg B in the main panel. Then, plug your favorite plug-in dirty electricity filter (Stetzer, Greenwave, or some other company) into each of the four outlets and you will successfully reduce the incoming dirty electricity from neighbors' houses. This will cost you more than the other approach mentioned above, but it is somewhat more effective at blocking incoming dirty electricity.

If you're two people testing dirty electricity in your home together, you can then go room by room and one by one switch lights on and turn every electrical appliance on. You're trying to identify which devices cause high readings. You can then make a decision: Do I need to keep this device or not? If you can't eliminate it (this will be the case for essential appliances like refrigerators, washing machines, etc.), then you can install Stetzerizer® or Greenwave filters to get your readings down to a "safer" level.

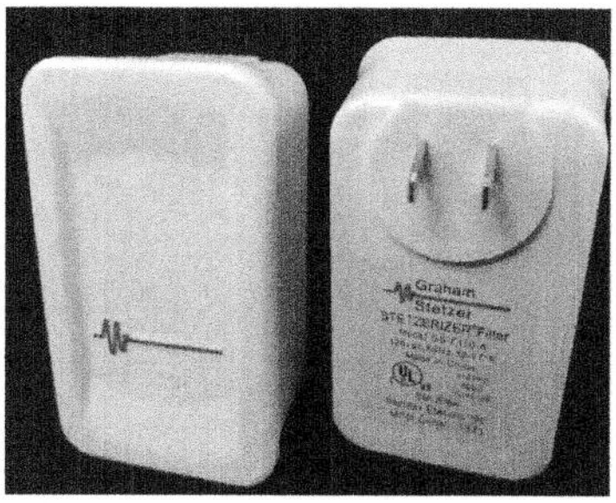


Installing the filters[283] is really easy. You don't have to insert them into the outlet where the device is causing dirty electricity. You can just put them in an outlet in the same room, which will likely be on the same circuit. The number of filters you'll need varies. In my home, I need two filters to get below 50 GS units. In some homes, 15 or 20 filters will be needed.

Where you have several circuits, which is the case in all homes, it's a good idea to install at least one filter on each circuit particularly in rooms that you occupy the most.

282 Oram Miller explains, "the electric utility sends electricity into your home on two separate insulated hot conductors wound around a bare neutral/ground guy wire that holds up the whole electric service cable. Those two insulated hot wires are on opposite 'legs', as electricians call them, bringing 120 Volts of power on each leg into every home in North America (to provide 240 Volts of power to certain appliances, such as your electric oven, hot water heater, dryer and air conditioner compressor motor) all the rest of the 120 Volt circuits then come from either Leg A or Leg B with half of the circuits on each leg. You can tell what leg each circuit is on by counting the breakers in your breaker panel. The two breakers at the top of the panel (if your panel has two parallel vertical rows of breakers side-by-side) across from each other are on one leg, which you can arbitrarily call Leg A. The next two breakers down on each side would be on Leg B, and the third row would be on Leg A again, and so on. Make sure to distinguish between regular and mini-breakers. These thinner mini-breakers take up the space of one regular breaker and are thus on the same leg."

283 Image courtesy of LessEMF.com

## Greenwave

An alternative to using the Stetzerizer® Microsurge Meter and their filters is to use Greenwave filters. Greenwave also have their own meter, which you plug into electrical outlets to measure dirty electricity. I've never used the Greenwave filters, but I have heard good reports about them and know they can also be effective.

## Practical Tips

There are a few things you need to know about dealing with dirty electricity:

1. **Buy and use the meter BEFORE investing in filters.** In my experience, all homes have dirty electricity, but you might be able to eliminate it by not using/replacing the devices that cause it.
2. **Stetzerizer®, Greenwave and other capacitive plug-in filters can increase the currents on your house wiring.**[284] If your house contains any wiring errors or has current running on the grounding system, installing filters can generate high magnetic fields. See Chapter 9 for tips on dealing with wiring errors.
3. **Some electrically hyper-sensitive (EHS) people don't get on well with either the Greenwave or the Stetzerizer® filters.** These devices do change the quality of the electrical energy in your home, sometimes leading to people not feeling well. But this feeling can be a temporary detox reaction. Try one or both of these filters out for a couple of weeks before making your decision that you are not tolerating them well. You may find that after a few weeks, you no longer have the adverse reaction and you feel the benefits of reducing dirty electricity.

I have to admit to being slightly biased towards the Stetzerizer® filters (some people call them Graham-Stetzer filters, GS filters or Stetzer filters). They work well for me and I know they work well for other people.

284 According to Oram Miller, this is because the filters draw one-half to almost one Amp of current on their own, which is an electric load like having many incandescent lamps on at one time. The higher the total electric load on a circuit with a wiring error, the higher the magnetic field is and the further it extends into the room. Also, the way in which plug-in dirty electricity filters dissipate the dirty electricity itself puts more magnetic fields onto circuits, again when wiring errors are present. It is true that the current load generated by capacitive filters is a reactive current load, but Building Biologists still measure that magnetic field in the room with their Gauss meters and EHS clients feel the presence of that magnetic field. We want to avoid that.

Here are some of the stories people have shared with me via my website, taken from comments on ElectricSense.com:

*I was diagnosed with MS in 2001. For the next six-to-seven years I was pretty sick, having a bad relapsing—remitting Multiple Sclerosis condition and having moved to an area on the north side of Sydney, next to a railway line, three TV stations and plenty of mobile tower booster stations, it became worse. Everything I did, in terms of rebuilding my immune system, stopping free radical damage with nutrition and other things worked, and then only temporarily.*

*In 2007, I installed around 15 Graham-Stetzer Filters... The MS improved considerably, able to walk better, improved balance and less fatigue. Now I have the MRI scans to prove that this condition has changed, from definite lesions (plaques) readily seen, to very reduced plaques in both the size and prominence. It is my conviction that MS and many autoimmune disorders are affected by environmental EMR. The neurologist was shocked but showed many other neurologists the difference in the scans from 2001 to 2008. It should have been worse! Stetzerizer® Filters and a low EMF environment certainly aided this healing process as nothing else was changed.*

Anne-Marie says:

*I used a GS meter to check for dirty electricity in my home. Shockingly, the levels were so high (1900 and higher) in many areas and the meter shut down in some cases due to high levels. I purchased many filters and replaced halogen bulbs with incandescent bulbs and keep many gadgets unplugged. I now have levels in the range of 20 to 35 in most areas. Where I could not plug a filter into the wall, I plugged into surge protector strips and found this was very effective and recommended by Greenwave for those few places that had gadgets that can't be easily unplugged, such as the burglar alarm. Of course, my husband and I both noticed a remarkable improvement in our sense of well-being the day after the filters were installed.*

Sophie says:

*I've had very positive results with the Stetzer filters. I suffer severe EHS and was staying in a place that I had shielded well from EMR (as shown*

> ***on my Acoustimeter), but was feeling extremely unwell, with typical EHS-type symptoms. I read about dirty electricity, borrowed a meter from the local supplier, and saw the GS levels were huge. I installed some filters, and immediately my disabling headache dissolved, and the stress in my body also. It was quite extraordinary. I've used them ever since and they make places that would be unlivable for me, bearable.***

But some people, particularly those who are EHS, need more advanced solutions.

## Dirty Electricity Protection Tips—Advanced

What I like about the solutions I've mentioned so far is that they're relatively inexpensive, depending on how many filters you need to buy, and they're all "plug and play"—you can get readings for dirty electricity and then you plug in filters without needing to call in an electrician.

But there are times when you need to go one step further, particularly if you have symptoms around EMFs. Nearly everyone needs filtering and sensitives often need further help via dirty electricity shielding and filtering.[285]

The shielding will usually take the form of special paints or wall papers—see Chapter 19.

**For people that want to take their filtering to the next level, Geobiologist Brian Hoyer recommends the SD Power Perfect Box,** which does a great job of filtering at the panel and preventing any dirty electricity coming in on your electrical supply from getting on your wiring. He's installed a number of these filters and has been very pleased with the results. This solution offers several advantages over the plug-in filters mentioned previously:

1. Sometimes 20 to 40 plug-in units might be required to get the dirty electricity down to acceptable levels. All this can raise ambient magnetic fields, as mentioned above, when wiring errors are present, whereas the SD Power Perfect Box doesn't create magnetic fields.
2. It also acts as a surge protector, thereby correcting any voltage spikes and protecting your electrical equipment.

285 Brian Hoyer, Geobiologist, EMF Experts Solutions Club interview.

Two other points that Brian makes:

1. Plug-in units (like Stetzerizer® filters) might still be needed where you have devices in the home creating DE, but only a few. Again, you can check this with your Stetzerizer® or Greenwave meter.
2. Since all residences have two supply lines coming in from the electrical company, you would need two SD Power Perfect Boxes. One filter is needed for each service entry point.

The downside is the cost, over $1000 per box, and this does need to be installed by an electrician.

## Solar Power

**Solar power installations deserve a special mention. They are one of the most challenging sources of dirty electricity to deal with.** This is because they can create SO MUCH dirty electricity.

Isn't it ironic that so many people choose solar power because they want to do the right thing for the planet, yet few of them realize the dangers?

**The problem is not with the solar panels or the electricity that the solar panels generate. It's the inverters that cause the problem.** The inverter is the device which converts the DC electricity generated by the panels into AC electricity, which the appliances in your home can use directly or which is sent back to the electric utility if you "net meter" with them.

When I spoke to Building Biologist Eric Windheim about this, he explained that some solar power inverters are so dirty that an inverter installed on just one home can create dirty electricity in neighboring homes up and down the block. In some cases, the dirty electricity readings are so high that often the cheapest solution is to just get rid of the dirty inverter and replace it with a model that is much cleaner. The brand that Eric and other Building Biologists recommend is the SUNNY BOY SMA.

Many Building Biologists advise their EHS clients to avoid solar panels altogether. This means, don't install them on the home you live in and don't buy or rent a home that has them already in place. Too many people are saying, "I can't be in my house anymore since the solar panels (and inverter) were installed." It's not worth the risk.

> ***You can defend yourself, but it is far better to just get a product that doesn't have a problem in the first place.***
>
> —*ERIC WINDHEIM, BUILDING BIOLOGIST, EMF EXPERTS SOLUTIONS CLUB INTERVIEW.*

The worst thing you can do with dirty electricity is to ignore it and pretend it's not there, as Building Biologist Oram Miller explains:

> ***These harmonics of dirty electricity... affect your health, whether you feel it or not, on a cellular level. They're from many different sources that did not exist 50 years ago or so.***

Here's what you need to retain from this chapter:

- Dirty electricity is a form of electropollution that can lurk on your house wiring
- Studies show this pollution does not stay on your wiring. It permeates out into your home and into your body
- It can cause a variety of symptoms and life-threatening diseases, including ADHD, chronic fatigue and cancer
- If you have energy-efficient lights and modern electronics in your home, then you most likely are exposed to dirty electricity
- The number one way to deal with dirty electricity is to minimize or eliminate the devices that are causing these exposures in the first place
- You can detect dirty electricity in your home with a basic AM radio, which sells for under $15
- You can easily measure the dirty electricity on your electrical wiring by plugging a specially designed meter into one of your electrical outlets
- First take readings in your home with a dirty electricity meter, then if you need to, you can install filters to get your readings down to a "safe" level
- Before installing Stetzerizer® or Greenwave filters, check your house for wiring errors to avoid aggravating magnetic field issues
- A more advanced solution is to install whole-house protection units, which would need to be installed by an electrician
- Some brands of solar power inverters can cause extremely high levels of DE—sometimes the best solution is to replace the inverter.

All this might sound complicated, but I've found dirty electricity to be one of the easiest aspects of EMFs to deal with. As with all these devices, buy and try. See what works for you and make sure you buy from a reputable retailer that gives you at least a 30-day money back guarantee so you can get reimbursed if you need to.

The last point I want to make is that dirty electricity is really just an electric field in a higher frequency so if you reduce your electric field exposures you ALSO reduce your dirty electricity exposures.[286]

In the next chapter I'm going to explain exactly how you can do this because this is one of the keys to living a healthy life.

286 Michael Neuert, EMF Experts Solutions Club interview.

## Chapter 11

# The Foundation Of A Healthy Life

***Number one, you've got to make your bedroom into a safe haven. That is your healing haven. That is where you spend a third of your life. So you want to make that into the safest room in your house.***[287]

ROUGHLY **20% OF AMERICANS HAVE** a **sleep disorder:**

- Sleep deprivation costs the US $411 billion annually[288]
- 30% of people experience insomnia at some point in their lives
- A decrease in sleep by 1.5 hours reduces performance by 32%.

Sleep is a big deal. When I first started reacting to my cell phone I tried sleeping more. But no matter how much I slept, I woke feeling tired. I didn't know what to do to change that and had no idea that the EMFs in my bedroom could in any way be impacting my sleep—yet these stories show they do.[289]

***I got very sick last summer with the usual host of symptoms. Luckily, I recognized what was happening and was able to take action. I broke my lease with an inner-city home in Calgary, Canada, that was inundated with Wi-Fi and cell frequencies. I moved to the country, did qigong daily in bare feet by the river, and recovered well. I choose to remain living in the country and protect my precious sleep. (I also love it out here). I have been forced to (blessed by) changing how I run my business and how I use my devices. I am far more productive now, working only 20 focused hours per week***

287 Ann Louise Gittleman, *Zapped*
288 The first two points, reference to: https://www.thegoodbody.com/sleep-statistics/
289 Source: comments made on ElectricSense.com

*instead of 40+ mediocre hours. Not an easy path, but I am living a higher quality life for it.*

—*Patrick in Seattle*

*Some things I've been doing are switching off the breaker to my bedroom, which happens to be the furthest from the smart meter, and I unplug my modem in the next room at night. I've filled my room with lots of plants and I bought a nontoxic mattress with organic sheets. I do seem to sleep better now.*

—*Nicole in San Francisco*

*I have been having ringing in my ears lately that I have never had before. I heard about RF possibly causing it. So, I started unplugging my home Wi-Fi at night when I go to bed and all of a sudden the ringing went away. Whew... finally a good night's sleep.*

—*Eve in Wyoming*

*The way I found out EMFs were causing my insomnia was there was one place in my life that I slept like a baby. It was at my in-law's house in Pennsylvania... I said, "Let me buy an Acoustimeter and bring it down there, see what happens, what kind of reading I get." I turned the meter on, and it has colors, green, yellow and red. It's the first time that since I had owned the meter that it was green. In New York, I never got a green level.*

—*James Finn, Building Biologist*

These people were able to connect the dots on EMFs. But a lot of people don't. EMF's zap them in their beds every single night when they are the most vulnerable, and they remain ignorant to their effects until perhaps something drastic happens. Like with electrical engineer Lloyd Morgan.

Friday, April 28, 1995 was just like any other day for Lloyd Morgan. He was lunching in an Indian restaurant with a work colleague. Then, half-way through the meal, his body started convulsing violently, uncontrollably and he lost consciousness. He suffered a 45-minute "Grand Mal" brain seizure—they rushed him to hospital in an ambulance where the doctors told him he had had a massive brain tumor. Lloyd spent the next eight days in intensive care fighting for his life. Fortunately, the MRI scan showed that the tumor was operable, after a grueling 12-hour operation the tumor was removed. During the post-surgery follow up there was one question and one question only on Lloyd's mind: "How did I get this thing?" When he was able to ask the neurosurgeon, the surgeon replied, "Perhaps electromagnetic fields."

Lloyd was stunned because he thought he knew all about EMFs. As an electrical engineer he'd undergone substantial scientific training, he'd worked in electronics for decades and even in high school was involved with ham radio. On returning home, he did some testing with an EMF meter in his home and discovered the clock radio in his bedroom that was about four inches from his head was emitting a 12 milligauss magnetic field. It was this realization that instigated his subsequent EMF research and his work with the Environmental Health Trust.

## The Golden Chain

"Sleep is that golden chain that ties health and our bodies together," Thomas Dekker supposedly once said that back in the seventeenth century. Whoever said it, it turns out he was right. Today, there's over 50 years of research on sleep and what we know for sure is that sleep is not the passive state it was once thought to be.

Sleep heals illness. Sleep reduces stress. Like diet and exercise, sleep is a pillar of wellness.

**Sleep is a highly active process that needs to be nurtured.**

Your immune system does its major repair work while you sleep. It's when your body's cells regenerate, rejuvenate and detoxify. On a cellular level this means that if at night your cells and organs are not able to perform these processes and your cell membranes are subjected to constant stress, you probably won't heal as well as you should. Healthy cells can be damaged while unhealthy cells, infections, mutations and neural disorders, can proliferate. You can see where I'm going with this...

**If your bedroom isn't totally conducive to optimum recuperation, you need to make changes—the sooner the better.**

Reducing nighttime exposures to EMFs is a HUGELY important part of this.

*When I work with people, one of the first things we do is try to get the electric fields really, really low where they sleep. What's amazing about that is how often people will have better sleep, deeper sleep, longer sleep, wake up more refreshed.*

—*MICHAEL NEUERT, EMF EXPERTS SOLUTIONS CLUB INTERVIEW.*[290]

Let's see what EMF science has to say about the golden chain.

## EMF Sleep Science

Nighttime is when your pineal gland produces melatonin, a hormone that helps to regulate sleep and contributes to many vital bodily processes.

**Melatonin has its own special membrane receptors that are found in almost every cell and tissue in the body from epithelia to neurons to smooth muscle.**[291]

Melatonin is considered by many experts to be the master hormone. Studies show it has a role in bolstering your immune system,[292] fighting cancer[293] and anti-ageing.[294]

It even has a role as a powerful antioxidant[295] and can protect against oxidative damage caused by EMFs.

**Multiple studies, stretching back over two decades show that EMF exposure at night reduces melatonin production.**[296]

It's thought that EMFs have this effect because the pineal gland interprets night-time EMFs as light. Thus explaining why EMFs cause a deregulation of the body's sleep-wake cycle, known to be vital for your health.

290 Michael Neuert is founder of https://emfcenter.com/
291 https://www.zrtlab.com/blog/archive/melatonin-importance-is-so-much-bigger-than-sleep/
292 https://www.ncbi.nlm.nih.gov/pmc/articles/PMC3645767/
293 https://www.ncbi.nlm.nih.gov/pubmed/12790777
294 https://www.ncbi.nlm.nih.gov/pmc/articles/PMC3583885/
295 https://www.sciencedirect.com/science/article/abs/pii/0024320594006660?via%3Dihub
296 http://www.neilcherry.nz/documents/90_b1_EMR_Reduces_Melatonin_in_Animals_and_People.pdf

Researchers at the University of Melbourne[297] found that exposure to weak 50 and 60Hz EMFs, as found on the electrical wiring of many homes, may lead to long-term health effects. Another study conducted on employees in a high voltage electrical substation found that workers exposed to EMFs enjoyed less sleep and a lower quality of sleep compared to the control group.[298]

An animal study,[299] which exposed rats to different kinds of radio frequency microwave radiation, found the sleep cycle was disturbed and that the REM (rapid eye movement) sleep of rats to be more susceptible to modulated radio frequency radiation as used by cell phones compared to non-modulated radiofrequency radiation fields.

**Your ability to enjoy REM sleep plays a vital role in your health and well-being.**

In a study that deprived rats of REM sleep it was found that doing so significantly shortened their life span from two or three years to five weeks. The implications of this are significant; it's possible that this is the single most important way EMFs impact our health.[300]

**What's clear is that EMFs can affect BOTH the quantity and quality of your sleep and possibly reduce your life span.**

This could explain why, when I became symptomatic, despite sleeping for 10 or 12 hours, I would wake up feeling tired and drowsy. It could also explain why millions of people are affected by insomnia.

**The US Centers for Disease Control and Prevention (CDC) has declared lack of sleep a public health epidemic.[301]**

Insufficient sleep is linked to a wide variety of health problems, including heart disease and strokes.

297 https://www.ncbi.nlm.nih.gov/pubmed/23051584
298 https://www.ncbi.nlm.nih.gov/pmc/articles/PMC3561068/
299 https://www.sciencedirect.com/science/article/pii/S2090123212000034
300 https://valleysleepcenter.com/3-things-you-should-know-about-rem-sleep/
301 https://edition.cnn.com/2015/02/18/health/great-sleep-recession/index.html

Lack of sleep also diminishes your ability for learning and critical thinking[302] and increases your risk of depression[303] and loneliness.[304]

Exposure to blue light also has a role to play in all this.

## Blue Light

You've probably heard or read somewhere about the dangers of blue light. But did you know it's also an EMF? Well it is, it's on the EMF spectrum just below the frequency of ultraviolet light.

Ironically, sunlight is the main source of blue light. Sunlight is more than just one type of light; all the colors of the sun are in there from red to blue and even invisible rays like UVB and infrared.[305]

There are many man-made indoor sources of blue light, including:

- Fluorescent lights
- LED lighting
- Flat-screen TVs.

Smartphones, computer displays, electronic notebooks and similar digital devices also emit blue light.

**Although the amount of blue light emitted by our devices is only a fraction of that emitted by the sun—the problem is it's totally unnatural.**

This blue light exposure is unnatural by virtue of:

1. The inordinate amount of time we spend using these devices
2. How we use these devices—that's to say proximity of the screen to your face
3. When we use these devices—at night.

302 https://thesleepdoctor.com/2018/04/17/heres-why-you-cant-think-straight-when-youre-sleep-deprived/
303 https://share.upmc.com/2018/01/connection-sleep-and-depression/
304 https://www.nature.com/articles/s41467-018-05377-0
305 https://primalhacker.com/blog/nutrient-sunlight

Relaxing in the evening in front of a movie on a flat screen TVs, surfing the Internet on a smartphone or tablet, all these have become the norm for many of us.

Some people are even doing this in bed! Yet, clearly these practices are not conducive to optimum health.[306]

They can cause insomnia by down-regulating your melatonin production and stimulating cortisol production—just the opposite of what you want to achieve at bedtime.[307]

They may cause cancer, diabetes, heart disease and obesity.[308]

Other issues include:

- Possible long-term effects on eye health, including accelerating macular degeneration a leading cause of blindness[309]
- Chronic bright light exposure can release dopamine neurons—implicated in the development of Parkinson's[310]
- Encourages you to miss out on valuable sleep.

In short, exposure to blue light at night aids and abets the damage caused by EMFs. Still want to watch movies in bed?

## Bucking The Trend

The challenge is how to continue enjoying the wonders of living in the twenty-first century without putting your health in danger. The best way of doing this is to reinforce your body's natural wake/sleep cycle by:

1. Exposing yourself to natural full spectrum sunlight or daylight in the morning to sync your pineal gland so it can produce appropriate quantities of melatonin at night
2. Avoid blue light at night ideally for about two hours before bedtime.

306 https://articles.mercola.com/sites/articles/archive/2018/08/29/blue-light-blindness-study.aspx
307 Jason Bawden-Smith, 2016. *In The Dark.*
308 https://www.health.harvard.edu/staying-healthy/blue-light-has-a-dark-side
309 https://www.nature.com/articles/s41598-018-28254-8
310 https://www.ncbi.nlm.nih.gov/pubmed/23462874

**It's a two-step process, you need to get the natural blue light in the morning AND avoid man-made blue light at night.**

Besides the question of blue light, there are other issues you need to be aware of with regard to modern lighting:[311]

1. Compact fluorescent lights (CFLs)—studies show they generate high electric fields, dirty electricity[312] and UV radiation. Many CFLs also contain high levels of mercury[313]—one of the most potent neurotoxins known to exist.
2. LEDs—many LEDs have SMPS chips fitted, which create dirty electricity.

Safer forms of lighting are halogen incandescent light bulbs or old-style incandescent lights—what we all had until about ten years ago!

I recommend you test any light bulbs you use in areas you spend any time with a dirty electricity meter. Do this by taking readings before switching the bulb on and after.

Three ways to reduce exposure to blue light:

311 https://www.createhealthyhomes.com/lighting.php
312 https://www.electricsense.com/wp-content/uploads/2013/02/08_Havas_CFL_SCENIHR.pdf
313 https://www.maine.gov/dep/homeowner/cflreport.html

1. In the two hours before bedtime, avoid fluorescent lights, CFLs and LEDs, which give off a very white unnatural light—prefer old style incandescent light bulbs
2. Wear blue light blocking glasses at night when watching movies and such— instead of avoiding blue light from screens two hours before bedtime, perhaps you can cut it down to one hour
3. Install a (free) blue light filter app, like f.lux, on all your devices to minimize your melatonin getting zapped.

Does wearing blue light blocking glasses[314] and using blue light filter apps mean you can have your cake and eat it? No, I don't believe this is as effective at jump-starting your natural wake/sleep cycle as total avoidance of blue light two hours before sleep. BUT if you are in apparent good health, your body can probably tolerate this.

Neurosurgeon Dr. Jack Kruse stresses the importance of exposing yourself to natural light, which contains blue light, first thing in the morning to activate your pineal gland:

> ***Blue light has amazing effects. It actually turns on your pituitary gland in the morning... I see the sun rise every morning.***[315]

Often referred to as the "master gland" of the body, the pineal gland produces many hormones that travel throughout the body, directing bodily functions or stimulating other glands to produce other hormones.

So, blue light is not all bad. What matters is how and when you expose yourself to blue light. By simultaneously following the above tips to optimize your exposure to light and reducing your exposure to other man-made EMFs, particularly at night, you can do yourself a LOT of favors.

Here are some more tips to take this process a step further.

## Low EMF Bedroom Tips—Free And Easy

1. **Eliminate cell phones from your bedroom.** Why not just switch your cell phone off, I hear you say? Are you ALWAYS going to remember to switch

314 For my recommendation on the best blue light blocking glasses, see: www.electricsense.com/bookbonus
315 Dr. Jack Kruse, EMF Health Summit interview.

if off? Bringing your cell phone into your bedroom exposes you to the risk that your phone may be zapping you at close proximity all through the night while you are trying to sleep. Instead, get into the habit of switching your cell phone to airplane mode at night (with Bluetooth and Wi-Fi off) AND putting it well away from your bedroom. This goes for any other personal wireless devices like watches and fitness trackers.

2. **Move your bed away from the wall.** Most homes have electrical wires in the walls behind the bed. Even if you've got nothing plugged in and no lights switched on, those electrical wires generate electric fields that can and will zap you every night, throughout the night. Move your bed six-to-eight feet from the walls. If that's not practical, then six inches or a foot is a good start.

## Low EMF Bedroom Tips—Intermediate

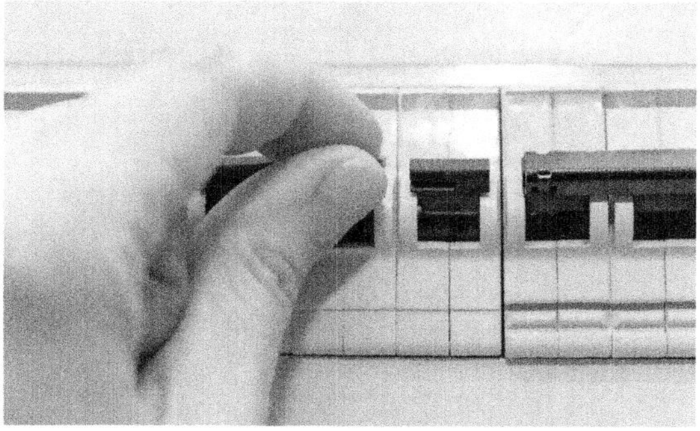

1. **Switch the power off at the breaker switch.** Go to your main electrical breaker panel, identify which circuit your bedroom outlets are on (by flipping the breaker, then going to your bedroom to see if there is any power in those outlets) AND identify surrounding circuits and also flip those breakers off at night.

   The reason we need to kill the surrounding circuits is because the six-to-eight feet electric field can radiate out from the circuits for surrounding rooms. So, if you sleep above your office, you'd need to flip the breakers on the office lighting circuit as well to avoid being zapped by wiring going to the ceiling light in your office.

   **Warning:** sometimes switching off the power on just your bedroom circuit can cause an INCREASE in electric fields in your bedroom (due to non-cancellation of electric fields).[316]

316 If you don't have an EMF meter to measure this, it's safer to flip the circuits on surrounding rooms also.

2. **Eliminate ALL electrical devices from the bedroom.** This might sound like I'm being a party-pooper, but creating a sleep sanctuary is sooo important for your overall health and well-being. If the power is off at the breaker, what's the point in removing electrical devices from your bedroom? Well, what's the point in having them? Even if you are being super EMF conscious there will still be some low-level EMFs in your bedroom—radio frequency radiation is practically inescapable—removing electrical devices (which have metal components) will avoid any unwanted antenna effect with these devices.

## Low EMF Bedroom Tips—Advanced

Can you see the problem with everything we've done so far? It's all guess work. Flipping breaker switches might be very effective but until you actually take some readings you don't know what your EMF exposures are in your bedroom.

Remember, your bedroom IS the most important room in your house as regards EMF exposures so it's definitely worth doing this properly. You need to take readings for:

- Electric fields
- Magnetic fields
- Radio frequency microwave radiation
- Dirty electricity.

Then you need to interpret those readings—that's to say, decide on what readings are too high and where you need to take action to mitigate your exposures.

All this might sound complicated, but it's not. You can get all these readings with just two EMF meters in under an hour. To get my cheat sheet with step-by-step guidance on measuring EMFs in the bedroom, go to www.electricsense.com/bookbonus

Left unchecked, EMFs will zap you every single night in your bed when you are the most vulnerable. The long-term consequences can be devastating.

Here's what you need to take away from this chapter:

- Sleep is not a passive state, it's a highly active process which needs to be nurtured
- Reducing nighttime exposures to EMFs is a HUGELY important part of this nurturing process

- Multiple studies, stretching back over two decades, show that EMF exposure at night reduces melatonin production
- What is clear is that EMFs can affect BOTH the quantity and quality of your sleep, and possibly reduce your life span
- Exposure to blue light at night aids and abets the damage caused by EMFs
- To buck the trend, you need to get the natural blue light in the morning AND avoid man-made blue light at night
- Avoid blue light exposure from screens and modern artificial light in the two hours before bedtime, wear blue light blocking glasses to mitigate adverse effects
- Switch your phone to airplane mode at night AND put it well away from your bedroom—the same goes for any other personal wireless devices
- In many cases, switching the power off on your bedroom circuit at the breaker panel is an easy and inexpensive way to drastically reduce your nighttime exposure to electric fields
- Ultimately you need to take the guesswork out of dealing with your EMF exposures in the bedroom by taking readings with an EMF meter.

## Chapter 12

# 5G—How To Protect Yourself

It seems George Orwell wasn't far wrong. The next chapter in the wireless colonization of the globe is 5G and the Internet of Things (IoT), which will connect everything! Exciting times, eh?

In this world where it seems everyone wants "more", 5G promises to deliver. More data, quicker data, faster downloads, all in more real time. By all accounts, it will enable your cell phone to download a Hollywood movie at the blink of an eye.

**5G will support at least 100 billion devices and will be 10 to 100 times faster than current 4G technology—4G was already about 10 times faster than 3G.**

5G, the latest generation of cellular technology, is mainly about connecting people, whereas the IoT is about connecting things, objects. Lots of objects, actually. Billions of them. It's quite a double act.[317]

We are talking toothbrushes that can make a 3D map of your mouth and report your dental record to dentists, toasters that can ping you on your smartphone when your toast is ready, cars that drive themselves, washing machines that order their own detergent and softener, refrigerators that will send out for milk, butter or eggs when you're getting low. On the supply side, your every whim will be pampered by companies running automated platforms with deliveries assured by self-piloting drones.[318]

Everything you buy will be smart, also called a smart connected thing (SCoT). That's to say a "product, asset and other things embedded with processors, sensors, software and connectivity that allow data to be exchanged between the product and its environment, manufacturer, operator/user, and other products and systems".[319]

317 http://fortune.com/2017/01/04/att-5g-directv/
318 Cindy Russell, *A 5G Wireless Future: Will it give us a Smart Nation or Contribute to an Unhealthy One?*
319 https://en.wikipedia.org/wiki/Smart_object

Further down the line it could mean the creation of "smart cities". In Asia and Africa, brand new smart cities are already on the drawing board.[320] Elsewhere, existing cities will undergo a gradual transformation to make them "smarter".

The end goal of the visionaries (lunatics?) behind these technological advances is the eventual connection of everyone and everything on earth.

> ***If something can be connected, it will be connected in a 5G world. Hundreds of billions of microchips will be connected in products from pill bottles to plant waterers, requiring massive deployment of small cell antennas in cities and towns.***
>
> —*Tom Wheeler, former chairman of the FCC.*

## Wireless Cell Antennas Galore

5G offers this mind-blowing data capability and connectivity by using largely untapped bandwidth of very short wavelengths (less than 10 millimeters) called millimeter waves (mmW) in the frequency range 20 GHz to 300 GHz. 5G, however, will also make use of upgraded 4G LTE signals at lower and mid-range frequencies, from 600 MHz to 6 GHz.[321]

**Specifically, 5G proposes to bring 3G, 4G LTE,[322] Wi-Fi and new 5G antennas closer to people through millions of small cell antenna arrays.[323]**

These higher frequencies of mmWs will not have the same ability to penetrate buildings as existing frequencies. They won't travel so well through buildings and will tend to be absorbed by rain and tree leaves, which will interfere with the signal.

To counter this problem, 5G will use advanced technologies, such as massive MIMO (Multiple Input Multiple Output) carrier aggregation, full duplex and beamforming that will send powerful and brief signals targeted to your cell phone and fixed Internet consumer equipment units (CEUs) when you use them. In the US alone, this will mean millions more antennas and globally, tens of millions more.

320 https://www.weforum.org/agenda/2018/08/smart-cities-forest-city-belmont/
321 https://spectrum.ieee.org/video/telecom/wireless/5g-bytes-millimeter-waves-explained
322 The terms 4G and 4G LTE (Long Term Evolution) are sometimes used to mean the same thing. 4G LTE is a more advanced form of the technology.
323 https://buildingbiologyinstitute.org/free-fact-sheets/5g-understanding-the-technology-protection-strategies/

**This could mean wireless antennas on lamp posts, utility poles, homes and businesses throughout entire neighborhoods, towns and cities.**

As if that is not enough, wireless signals at millimeter wave frequencies will be raining down on us from the skies. Plans are already underway to launch 20,000 satellites and drones to send focused beams of microwave radiation over the earth.[324] This might all sound like science fiction but it's already happening. In May 2019, SpaceX launched its first batch of satellites. OneWeb and Amazon are following hot on their heels.[325]

All these antennas and satellites will add ANOTHER layer of man-made EMFs beyond that which already exists. 5G combined with existing EMF frequencies will create a soup of electrosmog with a level of density that our planet has never previously experienced.

## Should You Be Concerned?

What this comprehensive global digital connectivity means is we're going to have radio-frequency microwave radiation blanketing and permeating our homes, cities, counties and airspace like never before.

324 http://bit.ly/20000-Satellites-5G-greenmedinfo
325 http://bit.ly/activistpost-60-Satellites-Into-Space-5G

I'm all for progress, but there are reasons for concern:

1. **Skin diseases.** Industry is downplaying the health effects of this technology by saying that the mmWs will only penetrate skin deep. This may be the case, yet effects on the skin are the biggest concern. Dr. Ben-Ishai of Hebrew University in Israel explains that our sweat ducts act like "an array of helical antennas when exposed to these wavelengths", meaning that we become more conductive. Research on millimeter waves conducted by Dr. Yael Stein of Hebrew University found that these frequencies can cause physical pain, the possibility of many skin diseases, and even cancer.

   Millimeter waves have been used by the U.S. Army in crowd dispersal weapons. It's also known that U.S., Russian and Chinese defense agencies have been developing weapons that use the mmW frequency range to cause burning sensations on the skin as a form of crowd control.[326]

   Last, but not least, your skin plays an important part in your immune system. The concern is that mmWs in zapping your skin will zap your immune system.

2. **Cataracts and eye damage.** A 1994 study[327] found that low-level millimeter microwave radiation produced lens opacity in rats, which is linked to the production of cataracts. An experiment conducted by the Medical Research Institute of Kanazawa Medical University found that 60 GHz "millimeter-wave antennas can cause thermal injuries of varying types of levels".

3. **Heart rate changes.** A 1992 Russian study[328] found that frequencies in the range of 53–78 GHz (that which 5G proposes to use) impacted heart rate variability in rats, an indicator of stress. Another Russian study on frogs whose skin was exposed to mmWs found heart rate changes (arrhythmias).[329]

4. **Profound immune system effects.** A 2002 Russian study[330] examined the effects of 42 GHz microwave radiation exposure on the blood of healthy mice. It was concluded that "the whole-body exposure of healthy mice to

326 https://ehtrust.org/key-issues/cell-phoneswireless/5g-networks-iot-scientific-overview-human-health-risks/
327 https://www.ncbi.nlm.nih.gov/pubmed/7897988
328 Cindy Russell, *A 5G Wireless Future: Will it give us a Smart Nation or Contribute to an Unhealthy One?*
329 Cindy Russell, *A 5G Wireless Future: Will it give us a Smart Nation or Contribute to an Unhealthy One?*
330 https://www.ncbi.nlm.nih.gov/pubmed/11855293

low-intensity EHF (extra high frequency) EMR has a profound effect on the indices of nonspecific immunity".

5. **Depressed cell growth rates.** A 2016 Armenian study observed the effects of mmWs at low intensity (mirroring future 5G environment) on E-coli and other bacteria. They found that the waves had depressed cell growth as well as "changing properties and activity" of the cells. The concern is that it would do the same to human cells.

Other cited effects of 5G are possible antibiotic resistance,[331] not to mention effects on plant health and disruption of our ecosystem generally—notably impacting bird, bee and insect populations,[332] which appear particularly vulnerable.

Just to be clear, all of the health effects on humans and effects on plants and animals listed above are in ADDITION to the adverse effects of EMFs that I've already talked about so far in this guide.

**5G, because of the frequency that's going to be used and because of the extraordinarily high pulsation level that will be used, is a much bigger threat to our health than the things we already have, which are very substantial threats to our health.[333]**

Dr. Pall's name pops up a lot, I know. But he's not the only scientist out there voicing concerns about this technology. In 2017, 180 doctors and scientists from 35 countries signed a petition calling upon the European Union to enact a moratorium on the rollout of 5G until potential hazards for human health and the environment have been fully investigated by independent scientists.[334]

Another issue few people are paying attention to is the bandwidth.

## Flying Blind

Let's not forget, the reason 5G and the IoT are on the agenda is because consumers want more, more, more. It's an evolution of technology to meet consumer demand.

331 https://articles.mercola.com/sites/articles/archive/2016/09/20/stop-antibiotic-resistant-bacteria.aspx
332 https://www.nature.com/articles/s41598-018-22271-3
333 Martin L. Pall, PhD, Professor Emeritus of Biochemistry and Basic Medical Sciences, Washington State University.
334 http://www.5gappeal.eu/the-5g-appeal/

So, while this hyper connectivity is a new thing, most of the technology behind it has been under development for decades. The earliest applications of millimeter wave technology were in radio astronomy back in the 1960's and the military has had millimeter wave applications since the 1970s.

**Previously, these technologies were used in discrete point-to-point connections. What's significant today is the scale of application of these technologies.**

The truth is no one really knows what the health impacts of 5G and the IoT are going to be because the data and studies we have to date are not "genuine 5G" studies. They were done on EMFs in the same frequency range as 5G, but they didn't use pulsed radiation.[336] The science shows very clearly that pulsed, modulated radiation is a lot more dangerous than non-pulsed radiation.[337]

The other big unknown is the bandwidths. The bandwidths being used for 5G are increasing. Without getting overly technical, bandwidth is like the wideness of the road. To transmit the data faster, the road needs to be wider. More bandwidth combined with increased signal strength and compression technology means higher data transmission speeds. Unfortunately, that also probably means more biological impact.[338]

**We are flying blind with all this. The reports I've seen so far from people that have been exposed to 5G are not encouraging.**

Residents of Geneva, Switzerland, reported feeling bad "literally overnight" following the installation of 5G antennas in the city. Common symptoms reported were insomnia, tinnitus, and headaches.[339] The deployment of 5G was subsequently put on hold.

For Maria, it started when 5G was installed in a lamppost next to her home:

---

336 https://www.radiationresearch.org/research/dr-martin-palls-latest-compilation-of-emf-medical-research-literature/

337 https://magdahavas.com/pick-of-the-week-12-why-pulsed-microwave-frequencies-are-more-harmful/

338 Pawel Wypychowski, EMF Experts Solutions Club interview.

339 https://www.illustre.ch/magazine/5g-sentons-cobayes?

> ***5G fitted in a lamppost outside my home. Ears ringing, can't sleep, moody, balance disorientation. I'm laughed at. I know 5G started these symptoms.***[340]

Dr. Lyn Patrick shared with me that since 5G has started to be rolled out in Dallas, Texas, her colleague Dr. Stephanie McCarter has seen a significant increase in the number of young people who have the common symptoms of EMF sensitivity. People recalled that their hands started heating up when they held their cell phone and computer in their hands. Then that evolves to other symptoms, such as agitation, anxiety, insomnia, fatigue, skin rashes, numbness, tingling, and heart palpitations.

Dr. Stephanie McCarter explains:

> ***We have seen an escalation of intermittent symptoms, like burning of skin or tingling while holding a cell phone, that is episodic, escalate to full blown sensitivities of headaches, insomnia, tremors, difficulty concentrating, short-term memory loss, indigestion, fatigue, burning all over, anxiety, depression and heart palpitations with placement of 5G antennas. Patients have become very EMF sensitive and cannot tolerate being indoors in public places due to wireless routers, towers, etc.***

## What Is 5G Really About?

5G is the latest generation of cellular technology. So, yes, you are going to be able to do even more amazing things with your cell phone. But there is more to it than that.

Forbes claims that 5G and the IoT are at the center of a battle for high-tech supremacy, principally between America and China, and that whoever wins this struggle will become the dominant superpower in the twenty-first century.[341]

Some argue that the real reason for this heightened connectivity is about energy efficiency. "5G is itself more cost effective and energy efficient than past generations of wireless technology, thus making its own contribution to energy savings".[342]

These energy and cost savings would be facilitated by all these connected electrical devices in our homes and businesses as part of an enlarged smart grid. They would be used to monitor and track energy-usage patterns and help us make choices that hopefully result in energy savings. In a world with rapidly dwindling resources,

340 Story submitted to ElectricSense.com
341 https://www.forbes.com/sites/arthurherman/2018/10/17/the-war-for-the-worlds-5g-future/
342 https://www.engerati.com/article/5g-%E2%80%93-what-will-it-bring-energy-sector

anything that can ensure that these resources are better used would seem to make a lot of sense.

This is a persuasive argument, if it were true.

### Swiss IT magazine reports that 5G systems have triple the energy consumption of 4G.[343]

French researchers also suggest that significant pollution will be caused through processing data. A recent study found that riding for an hour and a half in a self-driving car generates as much data as 3,000 people using the Internet for one day. Processing this data will produce the equivalent of 26 g/kilometers of carbon emissions.[344]

These new data streams also raise questions about privacy issues. There are reports that 5G and the IoT will be used to spy on you, that your most intimate personal data will not only be used by intelligence agencies but would also be shared with private companies so they can profile you, as revealed by former NSA technical director William Binney, the man who designed the NSA's automated surveillance systems.[345]

Behind all the smoke and mirrors, what's obvious to me is that 5G is ultimately about creating more demand to sell more devices, so big corporations can make more money.

## Is This Really As Bleak As It Sounds?

Perhaps not, because although 5G is being rolled out, we are still a long way off from having the infrastructure necessary for full 5G deployment.

All this will cost money—LOTS of money. The economics of this are such that governments will sell off parts of the frequency spectrum at exorbitant prices (because they need the money) to telecom companies who will invest in infrastructure to create the "5G product" in the hope that they can profit by selling their product to the public and businesses. The socioeconomic impact of 5G is estimated to be $2.2 trillion over the next 15 years.[346]

343 https://www.itmagazine.ch/Artikel/70199/5G_hat_ein_Energieproblem.html
344 http://bit.ly/2qUynQi
345 https://www.youtube.com/watch?v=uYg_0Imrnr4&mc_cid=e642a09eee&mc_eid=788abdf1b1
346 http://bit.ly/gsma-Poorly-Designed-Spectrum-Auctions-Risk

Yes, there is a LOT of money to be made. But 5G is a huge gamble. Firstly, for our governments, it's a huge gamble with our health. We must ask what the long-term consequences will be. Secondly, for the companies that are investing in 5G, the gamble for them is that sufficient numbers of people "buy into" this new technology to make it profitable AND that there is no public backlash.

## What Can You Do To Protect Yourself?

On a collective level, I encourage you to be part of this backlash. No, you don't have to become a revolutionary overnight. But around the world, people are saying no.

Brussels, Belgium, was the first city to decide against a 5G rollout.

> ***The people of Brussels are not guinea pigs whose health I can sell at a profit.***
> —*Céline Fremault, Environment Minister commenting on the proposed 5G rollout.*

Geneva, Switzerland, has called for a moratorium on 5G,[347] and several other cantons have said NO.[348] In the Netherlands, parliament insist that research must be carried out before any approval of the 5G network.[349] The mayor of Florence, Italy, has refused to grant permission for 5G towers[350] and the Prime Minister of Poland has personally signed an International Appeal to stop 5G.[351]

Local rallies are taking place all over the US. The Environmental Health Trust[352] has compiled an analysis of dozens of states and cities taking action against 5G. Here are some of them:

| | |
|---|---|
| **Hallandale Beach, Florida** | Resolution passed calling the state federal government to initiate a study of the health effects 5G and to develop installation guidelines |
| **Fairfax, California** | Urgency Ordinance to Establish New Regulations for Wireless Telecommunications Facilities |
| **Portland, Oregon** | The City of Portland has voted a resolution to require the FCC to investigate the health effects of 5G and to make the information available to the public |

347 https://www.letemps.ch/suisse/geneve-adopte-une-motion-un-moratoire-5g
348 https://www.thelocal.ch/20190729/swiss-5g-rollout-slowed-as-opponents-fight-antenna-plans
349 https://www.ad.nl/tech/kamer-wil-eerst-stralingsonderzoek-dan-pas-5g-netwerk~ab567cd6/
350 http://bit.ly/OasiSana-5G
351 https://www.counterpunch.org/2019/06/11/prime-minister-of-poland-signs-global-appeal-to-stop-5g/
352 https://ehtrust.org/usa-city-ordinances-to-limit-and-control-wireless-facilities-small-cells-in-rights-of-ways/

| | |
|---|---|
| **Mill Valley, California** | The City Council voted to prohibit new towers in residential areas and to require a minimum distance of 1,500 feet between small cells |
| **Monterey, California** | The city denied Verizon's application for a small cell tower to be placed in a residential area |
| **Mason, Ohio** | Passed an ordinance prohibiting small cells within 100 feet of a residential dwelling |
| **San Rafael, California** | Passed an ordinance establishes a 500-foot setback from residential districts and 500-foot separation between small cell wireless facilities |

This backlash can take many forms, including marching in the street, joining a local activist group, and signing a petition. Do what feels right for you on a collective level.

For a list of organizations that are working to bring awareness about 5G and stop 5G at a local and national level, see: www.electricsense.com/bookbonus.

**Remember, this is not just about saying NO to 5G. It also means saying NO to antennas being added in front of your home for 5G and existing 3G and 4G LTE technologies.**

## Take Action On A Personal Level

In terms of your home and work environment, you can and must take your EMF protection to another level.

It might seem that 5G is a juggernaut that's going to slowly crush us all, but hopefully you are beginning to realize to what extent the power is in your hands to determine just how much (or how little) 5G, the IoT and everything "smart" are going to impact your health.

**There is a lot of fear around 5G—take action instead of being fearful!**

The good news is that much of what I've laid out above is not going to happen tomorrow. 5G is being rolled out, but the frequencies and technology being used currently, including in the low-to-mid-range, are akin to what is already being used now with 3G and 4G LTE.

There are two phases in the 5G roll-out:[353]

| Phase | Frequency | Implementation |
|---|---|---|
| 1 | Below 6 GHz | Now |
| 2 | 6 GHz to 80 GHz | Underway in test cities worldwide |

The exact frequencies being used in each phase depends upon where you live in the world. Different countries are using different frequencies.[354] BUT no matter where you live, currently phase one is the primary activity being introduced. Phase one uses the same frequencies that are being currently used for 3G and 4G LTE. These are in the low-band range of 600 MHz to 2 GHz, and the mid-band range of 2 GHz to 6 GHz.

## 5G Action Plan

Your best 5G action plan is to:

1. Do everything you can NOW to protect yourself from phase one AND the other EMFs I've talked about so far in this guide
2. Be part of the collective movement at the local, national and international level to raise awareness and stop 5G, including stopping more cell antennas being added for existing 4G LTE technology.

**Focus on phase one.**

EMF exposures are cumulative. The problem is not just the magnetic fields from wiring errors on your electrical wiring, or the electric fields in your bedroom, or the radio frequency radiation from your router, cell phone, tablet, laptop or cordless phone, or your car. It's ALL these exposures.

353 https://www.rfpage.com/what-are-5g-frequency-bands/
354 According to Oram Miller, for the foreseeable future cell carriers in North America will use frequencies from 600 MHz to 6 GHz, and from 24 GHz to roughly 39 GHz (with plans to use 60 GHz and higher frequencies in coming years).

Dealing with all these exposures will put you in a VERY strong position if and when phase two is introduced in your neighborhood.

There's something else I want to say. 5G does represent a new spectrum of dangers being introduced into our lives, but in some ways it's a good thing. It might sound like a topsy-turvy thing to say, but people who never would have realized their cell phone or their Wi-Fi could be dangerous are now talking about 5G. There is a growing awareness.

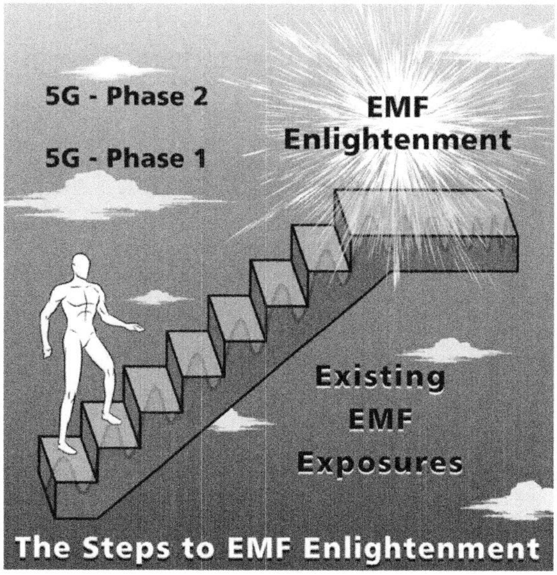


This WILL lead us into a new age of EMF enlightenment. As you start making changes to your life that reduce your EMF exposure, this will have a filter-down effect on the people around you. As a result, friends, family, and work colleagues will be brought into the conversation.

**The best way to protect yourself from 5G phase One is to apply as many of the EMF protection strategies and tips I've laid out in this guide.**

As and if 5G phase two is rolled out where you live (and hopefully as the message of this book is spread, we can keep it from ever being fully rolled out), you'll discover new ways to protect yourself and your family.

## The Saving Grace Of 5G

According to the Building Biology Institute,[355] another particularity of 5G is that numerous engineers say that 5G transmitters using beam-formed technology in the mmW band above 20 GHz will only emit a signal when a cell phone initiates a connection. That makes it essentially on-demand.[356] [357]

355 https://buildingbiologyinstitute.org/free-fact-sheets/5g-understanding-the-technology-protection-strategies/
356 This is at least true if you are away from dense urban areas, where beam-formed 5G signals will primarily be deployed and where the environment will be saturated with beam-formed 5G signals.
357 5G small cell antennas have been found to emit a very weak "reference SSB" signal to look for consumer units (cell phones) in their service are (information related to me by Oram Miller).

Secondly, the beam from a 5G antenna that is sending data is quite focused, somewhere between 2 and 15 degrees wide, not 120 degrees as with always-on, stronger 4G LTE signals. So, the 5G antennas would NOT be constantly transmitting as is currently the case with existing 3G and 4G LTE. This would seem to be a saving grace in so far as 5G goes, at least in your home, *if* you don't bring technology into your home that will draw that narrow, beam-formed signal right in through the walls and windows, such as a 5G-enabled cell phone.[358]

**You will be able to shield your home from 5G signals in the mmW band above 20 GHz with materials that also work in the low-to-mid-band ranges, such as RF-shielding paint and building foil.[359]**

But the other materials successfully used in the low-to-mid-band range, like mesh and fabric, are not expected to work as well in the mmW high-band range above 20 GHz.

The third important point is that 5G mmW, because of the high costs involved in its deployment in mmWave band, will primarily impact urban areas and to a lesser extent suburban areas. It is unlikely to impact rural areas away from towns.[360]

Measuring 5G in the mmW band above 20 GHz may not be possible for a while with affordable meters. However, existing RF meters will still able to measure 4G LTE transmitters on new small cell antennas, along with 4G transmitters when they are upgraded to 5G in the low-to-mid bands, because they measure in these bands already.

**Activists believe the vast expansion of always-on 4G LTE and Wi-Fi antennas close to homes in residential neighborhoods to be as much of a health risk as 5G beam-formed signals.[361]**

Given that these always-on 3G and 4G LTE technologies use frequencies in the range which we can easily measure and shield, this is all the more reason to focus

358 That includes new 4G/5G hybrid cell phones, which are on the market now, 5G-enabled fixed wireless Consumer Equipment Units (CEUs) for new Internet service from cell companies, and new 5G-enabled routers and smart speakers.

359 According to information related to me by Building Biologist Oram Miller.

360 People that are EHS will be able to seek refuge in rural areas because rural areas will likely only have enhanced 4G in the low-to-mid-band and not the full-fledged 5G in the mmWave band.

361 https://buildingbiologyinstitute.org/free-fact-sheets/5g-understanding-the-technology-protection-strategies/

on dealing with these new and existing 4G LTE exposures and frequencies in the low-to-mid-band as best we can.

## Fiber Optic—A Safer Alternative To 5G

Despite the current push for 5G and wireless generally, fiber optic[362] is in so many ways the better choice. First and foremost, it's safer because fiber-optic cables use light instead of current (EMFs) to transmit data.

Many broadband services marketed as "fiber" are only part fiber. They use fiber to the cabinet in your street, and then switch to copper cabling to your property. Full fiber is the safest and fastest.

**Full fiber optic is generally low EMF.**

But fiber optic systems, through their power supplies and operation, can generate EMFs that piggyback on the copper cable and phone lines into our homes. This can be resolved in various ways, for instance by disconnecting these existing cable and telephone lines from the cable provider.[363]

Fiber optics offer:

- Better stability
- Larger data quantities and speed
- Easier service to upgrade.

But the big advantages of wireless are its cost and ease of deployment.

> ***Microwave does not have high costs in running fiber cables down the pavement or a busy road. Deployment is quick and microwave can access environments where there are hills, mountains and buildings, assuming good line of sight and availability of licensed spectrum from the relevant government body. Users can be online within a week or so, even before planning for road closures has begun for its fiber foe.***[364]

362 Also called Fiber To The Premises (FTTP).
363 As reported by Jeromy Johnson, see https://www.emfanalysis.com/fiber-optics-increasing-electrical-sensitivity/
364 https://www.vostronet.com/blog/fibre-vs-microwave-the-future-of-fast-internet/

But given that, ultimately, we all want more, more, more and faster, faster, faster, fiber optics can give us this in generally a much safer way than wirelessly over the air.

Even conventional cable and telephone (DSL) wireline Internet services are generally faster than the fastest wireless, and fiber optics are way faster.[365]

5G operators are talking of being able to provide above 1 Gbps—one billion bits per second—if and when they are able to push 5G through. Fiber optic cables have been proven to offer speeds of over 1Tbps (1 trillion bits per second), a thousand times faster.[366]

Nearly 100 cities[367] around the world are already saying yes to fiber optic broadband, including Chattanooga and Longmont in the US[368] and more than two dozen cities in the UK.[369] The Science, Law & Public Policy Institute reports that the municipal fiber optic systems introduced in Chattanooga as "exemplar of a successful municipal broadband fiber 'Network' and a real boost to the local economy".

5G is not a done deal. The continued deployment of 3G and 4G technologies is not inevitable. If 5G does come to pass, it will be through our individual action—in particular, spending money on telecom products—and collective inaction. Meaning, we will have let it happen. Start participating in initiatives on a collective and community level to say no to 5G and take action to enhance your personal EMF protection.

Here's a summary of what you need to retain from this chapter:

- 5G is the latest generation of cellular technology. It promises to deliver more data, quicker data, and way faster downloads than previously available
- 5G goes hand in hand with the Internet of Things (IoT), which will connect billions of objects, taking us into a world of unprecedented global digital connectivity
- 5G proposes to bring 3G, 4G LTE, Wi-Fi and new 5G antennas closer to people through millions of small cell antennas dotted around neighborhoods, known as antenna densification
- 5G will first be rolled out in dense urban neighborhoods and in certain suburban neighborhoods
- 5G technology has not been safety tested (and there are no plans to do so!)—and yet, studies point to a number of adverse health effects

365 *Re-Inventing Wires: The Future of Landlines and Networks* by the National Institute for Science, Law & Public Policy Washington, DC.
366 https://www.dailydot.com/debug/fastest-internet-speed-ever-recorded/
367 https://en.wikipedia.org/wiki/Fiber_to_the_premises_by_country
368 *Re-Inventing Wires: The Future of Landlines and Networks* by the National Institute for Science, Law & Public Policy Washington, DC.
369 https://www.cityfibre.com/gigabit-cities/

- Some experts fear it is a much bigger threat to our health than existing EMF exposures
- There are reports that 5G and the IoT will be used to spy on you, that your personal data will be used by intelligence agencies and shared with private companies so they can profile you
- Ultimately, 5G is about creating more demand to sell more devices, so big corporations can make more money
- Dozens of cities and states around the world are putting the brakes on 5G—get involved at a local and/or national level to let your voice be heard
- In terms of your home and work environment, you can and must take your EMF protection to another level
- It's possible that the expansion of always-on 3G, 4G and Wi-Fi small cell antennas close to homes may be as much of a health risk as 5G beam-formed signals
- Fiber optics are generally a much safer technology than wireless and should be endorsed.

# Chapter 13

# Simple Safety Tips For Computers, Laptops, And Bluetooth Devices

Desktops, laptops, tablets, who doesn't use some type of computer these days in some form or other? Guess what? They all give off EMFs, too. But there are solutions!

## Computer Protection Tips—Free And Easy

**Keep your computer a safe distance from your body.** What's a safe distance, I hear you say? Of course—you probably know what I'm going to say—there is no absolutely safe distance!

**Even the FCC acknowledges that mobile devices like laptops and tablets should be used at least 20 cm (almost 8 inches) from the body.[370]**

**Desktop**—if you're using a desktop, move the Central Processing Unit (CPU), or computer tower and peripherals as far away from your legs and feet as the wires will let you. You can even buy USB and VGA extension cables. A wired desktop with an Ethernet connection and all wired peripherals are as safe as you can get from an EMF viewpoint (without measuring with an EMF meter). Even though it is wired, you must still turn off Wi-Fi and Bluetooth.

**Laptop**—don't use it on your lap! I know a laptop sounds as if it's made to be used on your lap, but don't. Not unless you want to expose yourself to high electric, magnetic and radio frequency fields. Using your laptop on your kitchen table or desk

370 https://transition.fcc.gov/Bureaus/Engineering_Technology/Documents/bulletins/oet65/oet65.pdf

is MUCH safer. And again, hardwire your Internet, disable your Wi-Fi and Bluetooth, and use only wired peripherals.[371]

**Tablet**—these devices are designed to be held and used in close proximity to your body. My recommendation is the same as for your laptop: use it sitting down at a desk so it's away from your body—there's a workaround for hardwiring iPads, too (not free, see below).

## Computer Protection Tips—Intermediate

1. **Go hardwired.** It's less convenient and less sexy, I know, but do you really want to zap your private parts with radio frequency microwave radiation? Laptops and tablets are particularly good at this, but wireless desktops have a lot to answer for too—they all emit RF radiation in close proximity to your body. The solution is to go hardwired using an Ethernet connection.

**When your computer is on a wireless Internet connection, you get zapped with RF radiation from your modem router AND from your computer.**

**Desktop**—this is the best set up. **But don't assume that just because you're on a hard-wired connection that your Wi-Fi is deactivated. BIG mistake.** In most cases (all that I'm aware of), you have to go into the settings on your computer and disable the wireless functionality— otherwise you'll still get zapped with RF radiation from your computer.

For instructions on how to disable wireless on Windows and Mac computers, go to www.electricsense.com/bookbonus.

371 Laptops with solid state drive (SSD) microprocessors emit far less magnetic fields than older spinning hard drive motors because SSDs have no moving parts.

**Laptop**—the trend IS towards wireless. Some laptops, like the new MacBooks, don't even have an Ethernet port anymore. But there are adapters you can use so you can use it hard wired—remember to deactivate the wireless.[372]

**Tablet**—these are not designed to be used on an Ethernet connection but, in most cases, there is a workaround. For the iPad it involves:

- A Lightning-to-Ethernet adapter
- A shielded Ethernet cable
- An Ethernet Grounding Adapter Kit.

For a video on how to do this, go to www.electricsense.com/bookbonus. If you have an Android tablet, just Google "Name of your tablet hardwire" or something similar for instructions.

2. **Ground your device.** If your computer isn't grounded, that very probably means you're exposing yourself to electric fields totally unnecessarily! How do you know if your computer is grounded or not? Look at the plug. You want a nice three-prong plug (shown below, left). That way, you know you are grounded.

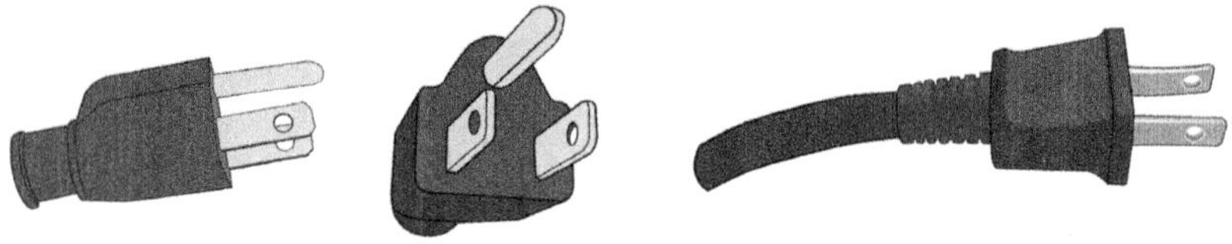

Grounded Plug Ungrounded Plug

**Desktop**—you'd think all desktops were grounded. Unfortunately, not so. The simple workaround is to use a USB ground cord or use an alligator clip on a wire (like in the image here to the right). One end clips onto a screw or something metal on your computer, the other you connect to ground by plugging into the ground hole in an electrical outlet.

372 Apple's adapter is called a Thunderbolt to Gigabit Ethernet Adapter.

**Laptop and Tablet**—it's the same principle. A USB ground cord will usually be the easiest way of doing it. This plugs into a properly grounded outlet at one end and into a USB port on your computer at the other, thereby grounding the metal chassis of your laptop. If there is no USB port, it might mean using multiple adapters. Where there's a will, there's a way!

Remember: if you're grounding via your electrical outlet, make sure the electrical ground is working and reliable—for a refresher on how to do that, read Chapter 9.

3. **Shielding.** Placing your laptop on a laptop shield when you use it, instead of placing it directly on your lap, does make using your laptop or tablet safer to use. But don't make the mistake of thinking that a laptop shield gives you total protection from EMFs. It doesn't.

**Laptop and tablet shields primarily protect you from magnetic fields, they do not protect you from full body RF exposures. When using them, I recommend that you shut off the Wi-Fi (and Bluetooth) and use a hardwired Ethernet connection.**

The three brands of shields that I'm familiar with are Harapad, Defendershield and SafeSleeve. All have a good reputation, and all make laptop shields and tablet shields. To see my video of how a laptop shield can protect you from magnetic fields, go to www.electricsense.com/bookbonus

## Computer Protection Tips—Advanced

This is more advanced, but this is my preferred way of dealing with any form of EMF; taking measurements with an EMF meter. All computers emit:

- Radio frequency radiation
- Electric fields
- Magnetic fields
- Dirty electricity.

**Radio frequency radiation**—the easiest way to check for RF from your computer is to have your RF meter switched on as you power up your computer. Let it boot up completely and then switch your computer off, all the time watching your RF meter.

**If there is no significant fluctuation in RF readings corresponding with the power up and power down of your computer, you're good.**

If there's a lot of background RF radiation where you use your computer, this test might be difficult to do. If that's the case, try doing the test in a basement or area where the ambient RF is lower. If your readings spike when you switch your computer on, go into the settings to deactivate Wi-Fi and Bluetooth (and anything else that possibly causes this).

To do this on a Mac, find the Wi-Fi icon on the upper right of the menu bar (it looks like a piece of pie). Click on it and click on, "Turn Wi-Fi Off". The curved lines in the icon will disappear. The Wi-Fi is now off, so you will now need to insert an Ethernet cable to get on the Internet. On a PC with Windows 10, go to the icon in the lower right corner and enable Airplane mode. Make sure Wi-Fi and Bluetooth are not still enabled. With earlier Windows operating systems, you will have to go into the control panel, click on to Network and Sharing Center, then click on "Change Adapter Settings" in the left-hand margin, and then find the Wi-Fi icon. It will say, "Not Connected". That is not the same as being completely off. Your computer can still send out an RF signal. Right click on the icon and on the drop-down menu, left click on the word "Disable". The words "Not Connected" will change to "Disabled" in the Wi-Fi icon. Now the Wi-Fi is completely off.

**Electric and Magnetic Fields**—you need to test where you sit and over the keyboard area. These are the kinds of readings I would typically expect to see:

| Position | Magnetic Fields | Electric Fields |
|---|---|---|
| In your seat | 0.1 mG | 0.5 V/m |
| Immediately above your keyboard | 0.5 mG | 2 V/m |
| *N.B. these are not 100% accurate readings, but they give you an indication.* | | |

If your readings are significantly above these levels, then you need to explore different mitigation options, perhaps grounding if it's a high electric field or perhaps using a different external keyboard if there is a high magnetic field.

**Dirty electricity**—check the dirty electricity reading in your office to begin with. With the Stetzerizer® Microsurge meter you would ideally want readings below 50 GS Units. It may well be that your computer equipment causes dirty electricity, in which case, assuming there is no item of computer equipment you can replace or do without, you want to filter to get the readings below 50 Units.

## Computer Peripherals

EVERYTHING you connect to your computer is a source of additional EMF exposures. Individually these exposures may be small, but they all add up. Here are some of them:

**Wireless peripherals**—a lot of people use a wireless mouse, wireless keyboard, wireless printer, and so on, because it's so easy. Don't. This means additional layers of radio frequency radiation exposure. All these devices need to be hardwired. Hand pain and tendon pain in the arm are common complaints of people using a wireless mouse and keyboard.

Be careful when you swap out your wireless mouse and keyboard with wired models. On a PC, pull out the dongle that you plugged into a USB port. On a Mac, go to System Preferences and open Bluetooth. If it says, "Bluetooth: On", you must click on the words, "Turn Bluetooth Off". Then it will say, "Bluetooth: Off". BE SURE to do this only after you have plugged in a wired mouse, or you will lose control of your computer.

**Power strips**—these are notorious for emitting high levels of magnetic fields, especially from the transformers that are all plugged into them. Most homes have got these strips and particularly around computers because there are so many things to be plugged in: CPU, modem, printer, monitor, desk lamp, and so on. The problem is that often power strips are put under the desk, right where you put your feet. Move the power strip at least three feet away from your body.

**Wired peripherals that emit wireless**—I've seen this countless times with printers. Sometimes it's an oversight. You plug in the Ethernet or printer cable but forget to deactivate the wireless.

Last year my son was studying in Bordeaux, France. Because he was away from home, he bought a printer. The following year he went to study abroad, so we brought the printer home. My wife started to use it with her laptop. By chance one day I switched my Acoustimeter on and noticed there was a massive Wi-Fi signal in the house. It was coming from the printer, even with wireless deactivated. It still emitted RF radiation! We still have the printer, but we leave it unplugged all the time. My wife plugs it in when she has something to print out and is careful to unplug it afterwards.[373]

## Is Bluetooth Bad?

Notice how more and more things you buy have the cute little Bluetooth logo on them?

At one time, it was only to be found on things like cell phones, headphones, hands-free kits on cars, things like that. But now Bluetooth is popping up everywhere.

I bought my wife an exercise machine last year that has Bluetooth functionality. The year before that we bought a leaf blower for the garden. That has it, too.

What does the Bluetooth logo mean or, more precisely, what does Bluetooth mean? Bluetooth is "a proprietary open wireless technology standard for exchanging data over short distances".[374]

The Bluetooth logo means your device can transmit radio frequency microwave radiation in the 2.4 GHz band—that's the same frequency most Wi-Fi routers use.

There are three power classes for Bluetooth and it's these power classes that are your best indicator as to what level of Bluetooth radiation you're exposing yourself to:

**Class 1 transmitters**—these are the most powerful. They have a range of 100 meters and a peak transmission power of 100 mW (milliwatts)

**Class 2 transmitters**—these have a range of ten meters and operate at 2.5 mW peak transmission power

**Class 3 transmitters**—these are the weakest and operate in a range of less than ten meters and have a peak transmission power of 1 mW.

In this respect, Class 1 Bluetooth devices are the worst offenders. Class 3 are much lower power and therefore less harmful. So, is Bluetooth safe? Is using Class 3 Bluetooth safe?

## What Does The Science Say?

Science doesn't say anything much about Bluetooth, per se. But don't be fooled. Bluetooth is just a fancy word for radio frequency microwave radiation. It uses the

373 Some other manufacturers have *two* Wi-Fi transmitters in their printers. The first is regular Wi-Fi, the second is called "Wi-Fi Direct", which allows you to print directly from your smartphone or tablet. If you are unable to fully deactivate Wi-Fi in the settings the best solution is to unplug.

374 https://en.wikipedia.org/wiki/Bluetooth

same frequency as Wi-Fi and the same frequency that microwave ovens use... to cook your food! This is also a very similar frequency to that which cell phones use. There is a LOT of very compelling evidence to show that these exposures are very dangerous (see Chapter 3).

These exposures are weak but, like cell phones and Wi-Fi, they are pulsed.

> ***Pulses carried by microwaves are particularly dangerous. This is because their very short wavelength allows the transmission of pulses with extremely rapid rise and fall times, and it is the rate of change of the fields (rather than their total energy) that does most of the biological damage.***
>
> —*Dr. Andrew Goldsworthy*[375]

So, everything else being equal, lower power is safer than higher power. But the complexity of this radiation, which I talked about at length in Chapter 8, is the real culprit. This is one of the main reasons even Class 3 Bluetooth devices are dangerous.

## What Is The Worst Form Of Bluetooth Exposure?

If distance is your friend, then proximity is your foe. The worst Bluetooth exposures are those that are in close proximity to your body, especially your brain—namely Bluetooth headsets and earpieces. Bluetooth hearing aids would also go in this category. The worst is using a Class 1 Bluetooth headset or earpiece with your cell phone.

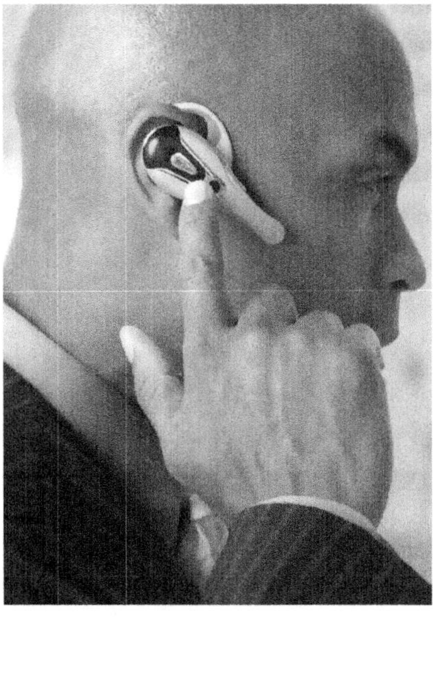

The main reason why using a Bluetooth headset and cell phone together is to be avoided is because **your radiation exposure when using a Bluetooth headset is the sum of cell phone radiation and Bluetooth radiation.** So even if it were true that Bluetooth

375 http://bit.ly/2lx8Z0v

radiation is less dangerous than cell phone radiation, when you use a Bluetooth earpiece you are always exposing yourself to radiation from both devices.

**It's the double whammy of cell phone radiation plus Bluetooth radiation in very close proximity to your brain that makes Bluetooth headsets a particular concern.**

## Tips For Avoiding Bluetooth Radiation

**A much safer alternative to a Bluetooth headset is to use an air tube headset.**[376] With a classic headset, sound is conveyed from your cell phone to the speakers in your ears by a wire. An air tube headset uses a part air tube cable and part wired cable. This air tube component converts the electrical signal into harmless airwaves. The problem with wired headsets is that the wire can act like an antenna and transmit ambient radiation all the way up to your brain. With any headset, you don't have the freedom of movement that you get with a wireless Bluetooth connection and the sound quality may not be optimum, but it is MUCH safer.

**Avoid Bluetooth devices where possible.** This might seem like a hard line to take, but these devices do ramp up your radiation exposures unnecessarily. I'm not saying zero Bluetooth, that's for you to decide. Frankly, if you are already experiencing symptoms around EMFs, I strongly advise it. Some Bluetooth exposures are considerably less dangerous than others, so there may be situations where you feel Bluetooth use may be tolerated:

| | Bluetooth levels of concern | | |
|---|---|---|---|
| | Acute | Moderate | Low |
| Bluetooth headset/earpiece | x | | |
| Wireless mouse, keyboard, sound system and other types of prolonged exposure | | x | |
| Brief exposures like transferring photos from your camera to your computer | | | x |

376 For an air tube headset to be effective, be mindful of where your cell phone is. Keep it as far away from your body as possible.

Perhaps you are in a situation where you have to use a Bluetooth headset for some reason. If this absolutely cannot be avoided, then ideally you should prefer a Class 3 device to a Class 1 device. There are two problems here:

1. Class 3 devices, because they offer a limited range, are practically obsolete
2. Unfortunately, manufacturers are not obliged to say what classification their device is rated at.

Fortunately, by looking at the product description, you should be able to deduce the classification of any Bluetooth device. The product description will generally boast about the range and how far away you can use it. If they say it's got a range of 100 meters, that means it's Class 1. In that case, avoid it like the plague.

**If you absolutely have to use a Bluetooth device, look for one that is as low power as possible—ideally it should have a range of ten meters or less.**

Lastly, in your home and work environment and in your car, be vigilant about anything containing Bluetooth. Like Wi-Fi, you can usually deactivate Bluetooth without too much difficulty. Be aware that software updates or replacing batteries can cause the Bluetooth emitter/receptor to be switched back on again. The best way to know if you're being exposed—in some cases the only way to know if you are being exposed—is to measure with an EMF meter.

## Microwave Oven Radiation

Of all the devices you have in your home, the one which has the ability to zap you the most is your microwave oven.[377]

There are two issues with microwave ovens. The first one is... EMFs, of course. Microwave ovens give off VERY high magnetic fields AND they leak radio frequency microwave radiation (2.45 GHz), in spades. They leak RF radiation through the door seals. Even brand-new microwave ovens leak significant levels of RF radiation. I've tested more than ten microwave ovens and they all leaked. This page has a link to where you can see my video on this: www.electricsense.com/bookbonus

377 Considered so dangerous that they were banned for a time by Soviet Russia, because it was considered the dangers outweighed the benefits, see https://www.powerwatch.org.uk/rf/microwaves.asp

***Radiation from a microwave oven can be measured at 30 to 40 feet.***
— *DIANA SCHULTZ, BUILDING BIOLOGIST - EMF EXPERTS SOLUTIONS CLUB INTERVIEW.*

That's right, so if you literally measure 40 feet from your microwave oven on the floor with your feet and then imagine the radiation going up and down in all directions, you will get some kind of idea of the area that gets zapped with RF radiation when your microwave oven is in use.

Added to this are the very strong magnetic fields generated. How bad this is depends on the power rating of your microwave. A smaller microwave might have a 700-Watt power rating whereas a heavy duty one might be 1500 Watts or more. With the microwave switched on and cooking, I've measured 100 mG of magnetic field at two feet on a 1500-Watt microwave oven.

**I've measured 100 mG of magnetic field at two feet from a microwave oven (when cooking). Levels of 3 mG are associated with cancer.[378]**

The other thing I need to mention while we are on this subject is what microwave cooking does to your food. Microwave cooking can cause a 40% decline in mineral content in fresh produce,[379] reduce vitamin content,[380] and strip vegetables of up to 97% of their beneficial antioxidants.[381]

**Microwave cooking seriously zaps your body and zaps your food.**

For the two reasons I outlined above, I believe that using a microwave oven long-term can seriously damage your health.

378 https://www.bems.org/node/1069
379 D. R. Davis, 2009. "Declining fruit and vegetable nutrient composition: What is the evidence?", American Society of Horticultural Science.
380 U Kidmose and Kaack K. Acta, 1999. Agriculturae Scandinavica B, 49(2).110–117.
381 http://www.greenmedinfo.com/blog/studies-show-microwaves-drastically-reduce-nutrients-food

## Microwave Oven Protection Tips—Free And Not So Easy

The very best advice I can give you is:

1. If you're thinking of buying a microwave oven, DON'T.
2. If you already own a microwave oven, don't use it EVER again.

It depends what you're cooking, but all that a regular microwave oven does is re-heat your food. There are various ways you can reheat food:

1. Using a cooker top gas ring or electric ring
2. If it's frozen food, you want to defrost first, then use a bain-marie—which is just a fancy term for putting whatever you take out of the freezer in a hot water bath.

## Microwave Oven Protection Tips—Intermediate

The MUCH healthier and safer alternatives to using a microwave oven are:

1. Use a steamer. This is about the healthiest and most nutritious way you can cook your food
2. Use a countertop convection oven.

If you want to be really stubborn about this and fly in the face of my recommendations—because, yes, I do understand how inconvenient it is to not use a microwave oven—at the very least, I recommend using your microwave oven the absolute minimum you can and keeping pregnant women, children and the elderly well away when you do use it.

Here's what you need to retain from this chapter:

- Keep desktops, laptops and tablets as far away from your body as possible when you use them
- Always use wired connections for your computer devices—remember to deactivate the wireless functionality on your modem AND on your computer
- Ground your computer—laptops and tablets can be grounded using a three-pronged power cord, a USB ground cord or clips

- Advanced tip—use an EMF meter to ensure that your computer is not emitting radio frequency radiation, magnetic fields, electric fields and dirty electricity
- There are different classes of Bluetooth—the lowest power and safest is Class 3, which has a range of less than ten meters
- Even Class 3 Bluetooth devices are dangerous—Bluetooth headsets and earpieces are the worst kind of Bluetooth device
- A much safer alternative to a Bluetooth headset is to use an air tube headset
- There are two issues with microwave ovens—they give off VERY high magnetic fields AND they leak radio frequency radiation
- The third EMF-related issue is that microwave cooking seriously zaps your body and zaps your food.

Chapter 14

# Cell Tower Protection

CELL PHONE TOWER, MOBILE PHONE mast, cellular base station, they go under various names and various guises. Strictly speaking, the "tower" is the structure upon which antennas are attached. The antennas are the real culprit here. But cell tower is the popular term, so I'll stick with that. They can look like this:

But they can also look like this:

That's right, they can be hidden. Other common disguises are silos, cactus plants and church steeples. Newer 5G antennas will look like square and rectangular boxes.

Not only that, in many countries, telecom companies have the right to erect a cell tower pretty much wherever they see fit, like next to sensitive locations like schools and hospitals, and there's not a lot you can do about it. In the US, for example, the Telecommunications Act of 1996 and the more recent 2018 Order FCC-18-133[382] did a great job of taking power away from individuals and communities and giving it to the cell phone companies.

**In the US a cell phone tower cannot be opposed on health or environmental grounds.[383]**

## What's The Problem?

Cell phones operate by sending and receiving radio frequency microwave radiation from their antennas to a nearby cell tower. Cell towers consist of antennas and other electronic equipment that transmit this radio frequency (RF) radiation to enable cell phones to function. Cell towers and cell phones are inextricably linked—without one you wouldn't have the other.[384]

The telecommunications industry say's we have nothing to worry about. That cell tower radiation exposures are at very low levels. It's true, these exposures *are* at very low levels, particularly when you get out to the limits of their range.[385] No one is disputing that. But cell tower radiation is relentless, it's 24/7 and studies tell us that even when the signals are low in power, it's the complexity of the radiation that is dangerous.

**Cell towers function 24/7 with an intermittent but persistent pulsed radiation emission. It's the cumulative exposure over time that poses a problem.**

382 https://www.fcc.gov/document/fcc-facilitates-wireless-infrastructure-deployment-5g/ and https://inside-towers.com/cell-towers-news-fcc-small-cell-order-18-133-become-effective-january-14-2019/
383 Telecommunications Act of 1996 https://www.fcc.gov/general/telecommunications-act-1996
384 5G cell phones work slightly different to this, as outlined in the previous chapter.
385 Which is generally one to one and a half miles

Common health problems associated with cell tower radiation are:[386]

- Headaches
- Sleep disturbance
- Memory-related disorders
- Fatigue
- Buzzing in the head
- Joint pain
- Miscarriages
- Cancer.

Arthur Firstenburg reports[387] that when cell towers were first activated on a mass scale in New York City on November 14th, 1996, within 24 hours he experienced headaches and similar symptoms, despite having no warning about the cell towers. He subsequently discovered that hundreds of other people reported similar symptoms at exactly the same time.

There are numerous cases of cancer clusters being linked to cell tower radiation exposures. Likewise, cell tower-related cancer clusters in schools[388] are a particular concern. There's also science to back this up.

A German study carried out to examine whether people living close to cell towers were more susceptible to developing malignant tumors found a significantly higher incidence of newly developing cancer cases among people who had lived the past ten years within 400 meters of a cell tower compared to those living further away.[389] [390]

Another study carried out in Brazil's third largest city found that over 80 percent of people who succumbed to certain types of cancer lived within a third of a mile of one of the hundreds of cell phone antennas that cover the city. The study established a link between over 7000 cancer deaths and cell phone tower radiation exposures.[391]

Similarly, an Israeli study, published in *The Lancet*, found a significantly higher incidence of cancer in people living in close proximity to a cell phone base station.[392]

386 Reply to ASSOCHAM comments on Prof. Girish Kumar's presentation at the ASSOCHAM EMF Workshop 7th Feb 2012, New Delhi.

387 Arthur Firstenburg, EMF Experts Solutions Club interview.

388 https://articles.mercola.com/sites/articles/archive/2019/04/16/cell-tower-emf-radiation.aspx

389 Horst Eger, et al. 2004. The Influence of Being Physically Near to a Cell Phone Transmission Mast on the Incidence of Cancer. Umwelt·Medizin·Gesellschaft [Internet]. [cited 2018 Feb 1]; 17: 326–32.

390 http://www.wifiinschools.com/uploads/3/0/4/2/3042232/eger_2004.pdf

391 Adilza C.et al, –Mortality by neoplasia and cellular telephone base stations in the Belo Horizonte municipality, Minas Gerais state–, Federal University of Minas Gerais 2011.

392 http://www.thelancet.com/journals/lanonc/article/PIIS1470-2045(11)70147-4/fulltext

Another study, carried out to analyze the relationship between cancer and proximity (within 10 km radius) to cell tower antennas, found a significant decrease in risk of brain cancer with increasing distance from the transmitter.[393]

**Studies indicate that the closer you live to a cell tower, the higher your risk of developing a brain tumor.**

Cell tower radiation is also linked to childhood leukemia[394] and DNA damage,[395] but most worrying are the effects on our children when cell towers are placed near schools.

An Australian study found that children schooling within 300 meters of cell towers had a total RF radiation exposure about 3.5 times higher than children with cell towers further away.[396]

3G is being gradually phased out and replaced. In the US, most operators are planning on a 3G sunset —total phase out—by 2021.[397] Other countries around the world are expected to follow suit. But 4G continues to be developed and antennas continue to be erected.

In addition, the onslaught of 5G will mean many more cell towers and small cell antennas being installed in close proximity to people's homes and places of work.

## What's A Safe Distance To Live From A Cell Tower?

You wake up one morning and suddenly realize you've got a cell phone tower looming over your back yard. How safe is that? Common sense tells us that, all other things being equal, power (how strong the radiation is) and proximity (how close the cell tower is) are important.

**Power, the strength of the signal, or how much energy is being radiated by that cell tower is obviously important.** Yes, it is and in the US the FCC limits this to 500 Watts per channel, which is huge (by comparison, newer cell phones operate at two-tenths of a Watt). But what really matters is what you are exposed to—your exposure level.

**Proximity is important, again because common sense tells us that the closer we are to the source of the radiation, the greater our exposure will be.** But all other

393 https://www.ncbi.nlm.nih.gov/pubmed/8982017
394 https://www.ncbi.nlm.nih.gov/pubmed/8985435
395 https://doi.org/10.1080/15368378.2017.1350584
396 http://www.ncbi.nlm.nih.gov/pubmed/27759027
397 https://www.digi.com/blog/how-to-stay-ahead-of-the-3g-network-sunset/

things being equal (I'm saying this because I want to keep things simple), there is another important consideration: the antenna beam.

Cell towers typically have multiple antennas aimed in various directions. Your radiation exposure will be determined by whether or not you are living directly in the main beam of these antennas. Look at the antenna/s to see any of them are pointed in your direction. Next, look to see if there is anything, buildings, hills, and so on, shielding you from this beam.

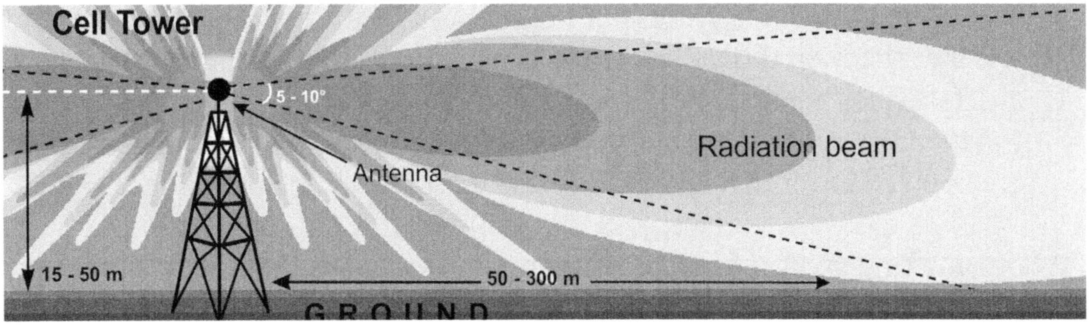


***People who are living in the main beam are exposed to higher radiation levels.***

—*Prof. Girish Kumar, Electrical Engineering Department, IIT Bombay, India*[398]

Saying there is a "safe" distance to live from a cell tower is complete nonsense. Instead of distance, think about and measure your exposure level—that's what's important to know.

## Cell Tower Protection Tips—Free And Easy

If you live in a rural area where the land is flat and there are no trees, then it might be fairly obvious where the nearest cell towers are located because you can see them off in the distance. But if you live in a city, it's a lot more difficult because they are often well hidden.

Here are some tips:

1. **There are various websites which, if you enter your address, list the cell towers in your neighborhood.** The best ones plot this information on a map so you can easily see where they are. These websites also give

398 Image derived from Prof. Kumar *Mobile Tower/Mobile Phone Radiation Hazards Report*, with permission.

information about the frequencies emitted and the number of antennas and the strength of the signal. By entering your zip code, street address and town you can see where the nearest cell towers are situated to your home. For a listing of these websites, see: https://www.electricsenseinterviews101.com/cell-tower-map-by-country/

2. **The second thing you would do is the "line of sight" test.** Is there a cell tower within direct line of sight of your home? If there are buildings between you and the cell tower, this will block the signal to some extent. There are no hard and fast rules here but a cell tower which is in close proximity, say within 100 yards, but is blocked out by another building is less of a concern than another cell tower that is at twice the distance but is in direct line of sight.

Where you find you are in close proximity and you are in direct line of sight of a cell tower, I'd love to give you a free and easy way of dealing with this but there isn't one. The next steps, outlined below, are not necessarily difficult but there are some costs involved.

## Cell Tower Protection Tips—Advanced

As regards cell tower protection, what we've talked about so far is nothing more than guesswork. Educated guesswork, perhaps, but you can't base your EMF protection on assumptions. There are two ways to better inform yourself:

1. Call in an EMF expert
2. Buy an EMF meter, take EMF readings and shield as necessary.

If you call in an EMF consultant, typically they will propose a range of options, including different shielding materials at different prices. You will need to decide with them the best way forward. To see my tips on contacting an EMF expert, see Chapter 19.

If you're doing this yourself, then once you've got your readings you need to:

1. Decide whether to go ahead and shield—refer back to my benchmark EMF levels laid out in Chapter 6 for guidance on this question
2. For detailed instructions on how to shield, refer to Chapter 19.

Sometimes you might buy your own meter and then, realizing your readings are high, you might want to call in an EMF expert anyway to help you with the shielding.

Buying your own EMF meter makes sense in the long run because you can use it over and over again. I do advise taking readings monthly because your EMF exposures change constantly.

Note: if you live in a town or city, even with an EMF meter, sometimes it might not be very easy to know what radiation is coming from the nearest cell tower and what's coming from other sources. Radio towers, TV transmitters, radar, police, fire service communications, your neighbors Wi-Fi, all these are possible sources of radio frequency radiation, right along with wireless devices in your own home, which will complicate things.

## EMF Red Herrings

Cell towers can often be EMF red herrings.

> ***I have people who call me up and say, "I'm worried about the cell tower that's out my kitchen window down the street." And when I get there, I show them that it's not that strong because they are in a rural area... and I show them what the levels are with my Gigahertz Solutions RF meter. Maybe 10–15 µW/m2. But when we go back in the house and it's like 10,000 µW/m2 because of the Wi-Fi router right next to the desk.***
>
> —*Oram Miller, Building Biologist,*
> *EMF Experts Solutions Club interview.*

I've heard this time and again from dozens of Building Biologists and other EMF consultants I've spoken to. They get called out because someone is worried about the radiation coming from the cell tower down the end of the street or from a neighbor's smart meter but when they start doing their testing, it's devices inside the house which are the biggest source of RF radiation.

Confused? This underlines the importance of following the steps laid out in the previous chapters with regards to your cell phone, Wi-Fi, and other home wireless devices. But it also underlines the importance of measuring your exposure with an EMF meter, or getting in a professional to do this for you. This is the best way to clear up any confusion.

What you need to retain from this chapter:

- Cell towers can be visible but sometimes they are hidden—common disguises include silos, cactus plants and church steeples
- Cell towers emit pulsed radio frequency microwave radiation 24/7—it's this cumulative exposure over time that poses a problem
- Studies indicate that the closer you live to a cell tower, the higher your risk of developing cancer and other ailments
- 4G continues to be developed and antennas continue to be erected
- 5G will mean many more small cell towers at higher frequencies in close proximity to people's homes and places of work
- If you are in close proximity to a cell tower and in direct line of sight, this probably means you are in danger—the only way to be sure is to take readings with an EMF meter and/or call in an expert
- Cell towers can be red herrings—again the only way to know is to get some EMF meter readings.

## Chapter 15

# Taming Your Smart Meter

SOME PEOPLE CONFUSE THE TERMS "smart meter" and "EMF meter". An EMF meter is what we use to measure different types of EMFs. It helps us solve the "EMF problem".

Smart meters, on the other hand, are a type of utility meter installed on many homes and businesses that can be used to measure your electric, gas or water usage. The utilities are replacing old mechanical analog meters with smart meters; they argue that it saves money since they no longer have to send an employee out to read the meter.

What's "smart" about them is that they can monitor usage and regularly send your usage data directly back to the utility company.

**The image I've included on the left here is of a digital electric utility meter. This may or may not be a smart meter.** More about this below.

One of the downsides of having a smart meter on your home is the infringement of your privacy.

As activist Jerry Day explains:[399]

> ***[Smart meters] collect time of use data on all of your activities inside your home. They can identify your appliances, when they are being turned off or turned on, whether it's a light or a kitchen appliance or an air conditioner. They know when you're doing everything. They know when you're there, they know what you're doing, they probably know what room you're doing it in.***

399 Jerry Day, EMF Experts Solutions Club interview.

It appears that besides the utility company, this information would be made available to security agencies like the NSA, the CIA and also to banks and other parties who subscribe to it. Ronald M. Powell[400] also suggests that such meters would be vulnerable to hackers who are interested in gaining access to your personal information or shutting down your power.[401]

The question is, is it in your best interest to have intimate data of your personal living habits transmitted out constantly, minute by minute, all day, every day to people who do not have our best interests in mind? Do we want our data being made easily available to other people who want to exploit it? For many, this is a massive issue. But personally, my biggest concern is the health risk.

Smart meters pose a risk to you and your family because they use wireless or other forms of EMF technology to transmit your consumption data.

## Are Smart Meters Dangerous?

Some utilities use the same electrical wiring that runs through them to send the data back to the utility company, otherwise known as broadband over powerline. This can cause dirty electricity in your home (see Chapter 8) and in your entire neighborhood.

**In our testing, we have seen that dirty electricity levels quadruple compared to what you get with an analog meter.[402]**

In Europe, using the electrical wiring for data transmission is quite common. Germany and France both use this method.[403] In the US, wireless is used extensively—which is what I'm going to talk about next.

400 Retired U.S. government scientist, Applied Physics, Harvard University.
401 Ronald M. Powell, Ph.D., *Ranking Electricity Meters for Risk to Health, Privacy, and Cyber Security.*
402 As reported by the Smart Meter Education Network on ElectricSense.
403 The solutions for dealing with these dirty electricity exposures are laid out in Chapter 10.

**Typically, smart meters are part of an overall system that is linked to a series of wireless antennas in a neighborhood through what is known as a mesh network.**

The system collects and transmits wireless information from all the smart meters in your area and sends it back to the utility company. They do so by using radio frequency microwave radiation, just like your cell phone and many other wireless devices.

**These smart meters emit radio frequency microwave radiation that penetrates the walls of your home and into your home 24/7, 365 days.**

Of course, the utility companies trot out the same old arguments that because the radiation being emitted is non-ionizing, that it's safe, that it's low powered and below thermal limits—arguments which are totally flawed, as laid out in Chapter 2.

Daniel Hirsch, a lecturer and expert in nuclear policy at the University of California, Santa Cruz (UCSC), wrote a report[404] revealing that some smart meters emit 160 times more cumulative whole-body exposure than cell phones.

**Some smart meters emit 160 times more cumulative whole-body exposure than cell phones.**

In the case of smart meters that transmit wirelessly, there are often several EMF issues:

1. Radio frequency radiation from the smart meter emitter/receiver
2. Dirty electricity exposures from Switch Mode Power Supplies (SMPSs) that transform the 120 Volt power down to lower voltages for digital circuitry used inside the smart meter.

Typically, these EMFs impact the body in subtle ways over months and years. We don't expect anything to happen overnight. And yet it can. I've heard plenty of

404 https://fr.scribd.com/doc/77657747/letter8hirsch

stories of the very immediate and sometimes devastating effects of smart meters, like when I interviewed EMF consultant Paul Harding and health expert Elizabeth Plourde on this subject.

## Smart Meter Horror Stories

Paul Harding told me the story of how he was sitting on his couch one Saturday morning when the utility company installed a smart meter on the side of his house. He knew because they'd pushed a flyer through his door. That very night he found himself wide-awake at 3:12 am and couldn't get back to sleep. The next night the same thing happened, up until then Paul had always been a good sleeper.

That second night when he awoke, Paul went out to the couch, sat down and scratched his head. Looking down he saw the flyer for the smart meter. "That's the only thing that's changed in my life," he thought. Out of curiosity, he started researching smart meters online. He came across all these other people who were having issues over in California, where smart meters had been previously introduced, and research published by a Navy lieutenant and scientist who had found a link between EMFs and insomnia.[405]

The next Monday morning, Paul called the electric utility to ask them to remove the smart meter. They refused. Paul's health rapidly declined. "I had heart palpitations. I had hair loss. I had memory loss. I had leg cramps in the middle of the night. I had acid reflux. I had diarrhea. I had bloodied colitis. I had eczema, my vision became kind of blurry at times. When I would wake up in the middle of the night when they did their data dump, I was dizzy. I would get sinus infections."

Paul decided to do a neighborhood survey. He went around to the 39 homes nearby.

> ***Out of those 39 homes, 32 of them were waking up at the same time as me. And this was BEFORE I said anything about the smart meters.***
>
> *—Paul Harding, EMF Experts Solutions Club interview.*

Paul's brother, who's an aerospace engineer, said, "You're really going to have to get a meter to figure out what's going on." So, he did, and that's what led to Paul Harding becoming an EMF consultant. He says, "Today, I don't have any of those issues. I don't even need to take a nap to get through the day. I've never been so healthy."

405 https://www.magdahavas.com/wp-content/uploads/2011/06/Glaser_1972_shortened.pdf

**Paul was fortunate enough to realize that a smart meter was causing his symptoms. I've also heard countless stories of cases where people suddenly became symptomatic and they didn't even know a smart meter had been installed on their property.**

For Elizabeth Plourde, it all started when the utility company started installing smart meters in her neighborhood. Elizabeth had opted out and her immediate neighbors had opted out also. So, the smart meters weren't on or very near her property.

Within days of the first smart meters being installed in her neighborhood, Elizabeth developed an itchy rash around her ankle. Two weeks later, she had a solid rash over her arms, legs, stomach and back. The itch from the rash was so ferocious, she couldn't sleep. Her doctor said it was scabies and gave her cortisone cream and pills, which did nothing to stop the spreading or the itching. She went from specialist to specialist, including an allergist, an infectious disease doctor, and another dermatologist. Nothing worked.

Soon she couldn't use a cell phone or a computer without bloody sores breaking out on her arms and legs within minutes.

At a loss as to what might be causing this, she started to do her own research. Looking at the health complaints in Northern California, she was astonished to see how many people had written about problems with skin rashes subsequent to getting a smart meter installed. With the help of an EMF consultant and through her training as a scientist, she was able to help her body recover.[406]

**The surprising aspect of Elizabeth's story is that, even though smart meters were not installed on or near her property, the installation of smart meters in her neighborhood appears to have significantly impacted her health.**

The big difference between smart meter radiation and cell phone radiation is that having a cell phone or not is a matter of personal choice. If you don't want a cell phone, you don't buy one.

406 EMF Freedom, *Solutions for the 21st Century Pollution*, 3rd edition.

**Smart meters, on the other hand, are being forced on people around the globe.**

Also, there are reports of some people saying that they *can* tolerate their cell phone and Wi-Fi but they *cannot* be near a smart meter. The consensus in the EMF community seems to be that smart meters have a different RF pattern due to the microbursts of RF that they emit, which are very short.

> ***Once that thing gets on your house, it's kind of like that Alien movie where the face-hugger gets on you.***
>
> *—Eric Windheim, Building Biologist on the subject of smart meters, EMF Experts Solutions Club interview.*

## Other EMF Dangers From Electric Meters, Whether Smart Or Analog[407]

Let's not forget, whether they be smart or not, there are other types of EMFs emitted from electric meters and from the circuits that run from them to all parts of the house. What I am talking about here are the magnetic and electric fields associated with electric meters.

In addition, in South and Southwestern parts of the US, where there are no basements and electric meters and panels are mounted side-by-side on the outside of the house, the breaker panels that are right beside them also produce large amounts of magnetic and electric fields. This means that especially in warmer climates, where bedrooms in a one-story house are often in the back of the house close to where the electric meter and breaker panel are mounted on the outside wall, RF radiation from a smart meter is not the only reason to avoid having your bed on the inside of that wall.

407 This section and the next section on 'Gas And Water Smart Meters' are contributions from Building Biologist Oram Miller.

**It is not the case that everything was safe before the smart meter was put on the wall.**

What about the huge magnetic field that extends several feet into the bedroom from the back of the analog meter and the breaker panel right beside it? Granted, the magnetic field will be less when most of the lights and other electric appliances are turned off in the house at night, but this magnetic field is one of those overlooked EMFs we talked about in Chapters 2 and 9.

As I mentioned before, distance is your friend when it comes to avoiding point-source magnetic fields, which would include an electric meter and breaker panel.

**No one should EVER have their bed located anywhere close to where an electric meter or breaker panel are located.**

Keep them at least four-to-five feet apart.[408] If you have your breaker panel in the basement, the magnetic field from that should be okay because it is far enough from your bed.

As I mentioned in Chapter 11, if there is a wiring error on one of those electrical circuits that is carrying a load at night while you are sleeping right above or next to that circuit, this can be a problem. Building Biologists have seen examples where a circuit to a freezer in a garage ran right under the bedroom of clients. That circuit had a wiring error and whenever that freezer started running, which it did off and on throughout the night, a large magnetic field was emitted into the bedroom.

Likewise, you can have current flowing on the ground wire that runs in the ceiling of the basement, right under a first floor bedroom from the breaker panel in the back of the basement that runs in the ceiling of the basement, right under a first floor bedroom, as the grounding conductor travels to clamp to the metal water service supply pipe at the front of the house. This will cause a magnetic field under the bedroom throughout the night.[409]

Finally, electric fields emit from plastic Romex circuits in floors and walls coming out of the breaker panel, disturbing the depth and quality of your sleep. For these reasons, you want to have your bed away from the wall with the electric meter (and

408 This can be easily verified with an EMF meter.
409 I explained this in detail in Chapter 9.

breaker panel, if it is outside next to the meter or down in the basement under the bed). Smart meters are not the only reason to avoid having your bed near the meter (and breaker panel). So even if you opt out of having a smart meter, you will still have magnetic fields from the electric meter, and electric fields from plastic circuits. Verify this for yourself with your EMF meter.

## What About Gas And Water Smart Meters?

Electric smart meters are getting the most attention, but utilities are also installing smart water and gas meters. Depending upon where these meters are located in houses in your neighborhood, the RF signals they emit can be a problem.

If the water company has installed smart meters and your water meter is in your basement, you would have known that they had done this because you would have had to let them into your house. That smart water meter in your basement is very probably sending out RF signals on a regular basis up into your living space. How often they do this varies from manufacturer to manufacturer. Some send out RF signals hourly, daily and even weekly. Some municipal water departments have an opt-out program.

**Take advantage of opt-out programs if they exist, or work with your neighbors and fellow city and town citizens to push for one if they don't.**

One electrically hyper-sensitive client of a Building Biologist in Minnesota found out which day of the month the utility company drove by in their truck to take readings. (Normally, the homeowner covered their smart water meter with aluminum foil to protect themselves from the RF radiation being sent out regularly by the meter.) On the day the utility company passed, they would take the foil off their meter so the utility company could get their readings, and then put the foil back when they return home from work.[410]

In those parts of the US that have water meters out at the street, Building Biologists are of the view that the RF signals generally don't reach the homes of their clients strong enough to be a health risk and in these cases are not considered to be a problem.[411] As far as smart gas meters go, gas meters are usually on the side of the house or in the basement.

410 I present shielding solutions for smart meters below.
411 If you are electrically hypersensitive, this may not be the case.

**Some smart gas meters transmit a burst of RF radiation, called a beacon signal, once every six hours, while other brands transmit a beacon signal every 30 seconds.**

It all depends upon the manufacturer and the utility deciding how often they want the beacon signal to transmit. This determines the number of beacon signals per minute and per day to be.

Some gas utilities allow you to opt out. If your utility does not allow this option, petition your state's Public Utilities Commission to mandate that the gas utility provide one. In the meantime, you can cover your smart gas meter with foil or a fabric guard, mentioned below.

## Smart Meter Protection Tips—Precursor

The first questions that have to be answered are, do I have a smart meter? If so, what kind?

There are different types of smart meters out there going under different names. Some report their monitoring of your electricity usage in a wired way, while others use wireless. Some are transmitting a few times a month, while others transmit 190,000 times a day. They do vary.

**The most dangerous smart meter is one fitted with digital electronics, including a switch-mode power supply (SMPS), and wireless connectivity.[412]**

There are only two ways to know with 100% certainty whether your utility meter is a smart meter and the level and type of EMFs it is emitting:

1. Call in an EMF consultant to take readings with an EMF meters
2. Take readings yourself with an RF meter (I guess "calling a friend" counts as a third way).

I know that some of you reading this book will have a hard time taking this step. You're not even sure you have a smart meter, right? So why go to the time, trouble

412 For more detailed information, I recommend reading this report: *Ranking Electricity Meters for Risk to Health, Privacy, and Cyber Security* by Ronald M. Powell, PhD.

and expense of getting readings with an RF meter? Let's get clear on why you can't just give your utility company a call and ask them:

- Your utility company can't or won't give you the information you need. They might refuse to give you the information or you might get an employee who knows nothing about smart meters and EMFs but pretends they know what they are talking about.
- You ask the utility company what kind of meter it is and they reply "an analog" meter but they "forget" to mention that the analog meter has had a transmitting retrofit board installed within it; that's to say, it's actually a smart meter in disguise.
- They will tell you (if they admit you have a smart meter) that it only transmits when the guy drives by in the truck and triggers the meter to read it and all kinds of fabulous tales like this.[413]

**Moral of the story—don't rely on your utility company for reliable information.**

When you do take readings from your smart meter, document the readings with a video camcorder or take pictures as proof of the levels of RF radiation you're being exposed to. This could help later in any dispute with your water, gas or power utility.

## Smart Meter Protection Tips—Nearly Free And Easy

In most cases, before your analog meter is replaced by a smart meter, you will receive notification from the utility company. This is usually a letter telling you that your meter is going to be replaced by a more modern and improved meter. Often, they'll tell you that this will allow you to save money, but rarely will they call it a smart meter or make any reference to EMFs.

If you can opt-out, even if it means paying more to keep your old meter (yes, this is highway robbery, but it is being challenged by activists around the world), I strongly advise you to do so. In some cases, this will simply be a case of sending a registered letter informing them you don't want your meter changed. Problem solved.

413 To be precise, this last kind of electric meter is not a "smart meter", because it does not communicate with a mesh network of other electric meters in the neighborhood. Known as an ERT model, these models do not emit anywhere near the strength of the RF signal that true "smart meters" emit—there is only one big burst of RF once a month when the utility tech comes around to take readings. However, ERT electric meters can still produce dirty electricity (information supplied by Oram Miller).

How exactly to go about this depends upon where you live. If you're lucky, you will find a local activist group that has all this figured out and you will just follow step-by-step instructions on how to do this. To find an activist group in your area, search online for phrases like "(the name of your town) smart meter". Again, if no group exists, start one of your own!

## Smart Meter Protection Tips—Advanced

Once you've established the nature of the beast, then you can decide how to deal with it.

My preferred course of action is removal. That's right, just call in an electrician and get your smart meter replaced by a nice safe analog meter—this is NOT a big job.

There are different types of analog meters out there going under different names, including traditional analog mechanical meters, traditional analog mechanical meters with no wireless communications capability, AMR meters, traditional analog and electromechanical meters.

**The safest solution is to install an analog utility meter with no electronics, no SMPS, and no wireless connectivity—nothing which transmits your data.**

But sometimes replacement is just not possible. Some localities don't allow it, in which case you need to shield.

The easiest way to shield a smart electric meter is to install a smart meter shield. BUT (and I know I might sound like a broken record) the starting point is to take readings with an EMF meter. There is a tendency to think, "OMG, I've got a smart meter. I need to shield the heck out of it," without taking any readings.

**The golden rule of shielding: measure, shield, then measure again.**

Installing a smart meter shield is usually the easiest way of doing this. It's basically a stainless-steel mesh that you wrap around the glass or plastic cover of the smart meter. It's held in place by Velcro® or by tightening down a metal ring around the perimeter of the guard. Typically, this does NOT provide 100% shielding, but the reduction is measurable and pretty substantial. It's all about reducing your exposure to smart meter radiation as much as possible but not eliminating it, so that it still allows the frequency to get through to the utility, so they can still get their reading. Obviously, you would need to check this point before you buy it, but that has been the experience of most customers of smart meter shields.

The second point is that you need to think about the wall where the smart meter is located. What's behind that wall? Is it a bedroom? Which is why, BEFORE buying a smart meter shield, you would measure your radio frequency radiation exposures in your living areas close to the smart meter—this is your main concern. And obviously you would take readings after shielding to make sure it is effective.

> ***I've been very successful in wrapping a smart meter with RF shielding foil and the foil is really cheap. So, what we do is we get an electrician to pull the meter off the wall, just pull it away from the wall, and then slide this foil behind the meter and cut holes wherever if you have to, if there's wires coming out... You pull the whole box and everything, wrap the whole thing in this foil... So, wrap it pretty well and take the aluminum tape and tape it all up. And you cut a hole at the front of the meter so the signals can get out, but they're directional... and so that anybody can look in there and see the numbers and so the utility won't complain about it.***
>
> —*Diana Schultz, Building Biologist, EMF Experts Solutions Club interview.*

Where you need 360-degree mitigation, for instance the smart meter is on a wall which overlooks your garden to the front of the meter and the back radiates into your home, or the smart meter is in your basement, you would install a smart meter guard AND shielding foil. But if your smart meter is on the outside wall of your property overlooking the street or fields, then your only concern would be shielding the back and sides of the meter, which radiate somewhat into your home (most of the energy of the RF signal is directed away from the house, with only a relatively smaller amount of side- and back-scatter). This you can do easily by shielding the wall behind the smart meter with RF shielding foil or a metal plate. The easiest way is to buy a kit with the shielding material, mounting tape and grounding cord.[414] I will talk about the various paints and wall coverings you can use for shielding and grounding your shielding in Chapter 19.

414 Grounding may not be needed for your shielding to be effective, more about this in Chapter 19.

The page www.electricsense.com/bookbonus has information on where you can buy a smart meter shield, shielding kit and where you can buy the RF shielding foil and aluminum tape mentioned above.

This is an advanced solution and not for everybody. There are times when it's better to call in an EMF consultant who has experience dealing with this kind of thing. This might be one of those times.

What if you find yourself living next to a bank of smart meters? Not just your own, but a whole bunch of them. For some people living in apartment buildings and residential blocks, this is an increasingly common reality. In which case you might need to explore a full shielding solution—see Chapter 19.

## Smart Devices In General

Smart meters are only one part of this Internet of Things (IoT) world we are moving into. Unless you live in a cave and cook your dinner on a skewer over an open fire, chances are your home has been getting "smarter" without you even realizing it. Smart appliances have been sold by shops and online retailers for the last 20 years and are now flooding the market.

Many new TVs, washing machines, dishwashers, AC units, alarm systems,[415] and music systems come with RF chips inside. The more high-end and the more you pay, the greater the chance that your new device is a smart one.

Utility companies are touting energy efficiency, cost savings and automation by syncing all your smart devices with your smart meter and your smartphone. You'll be able to lay on a tropical beach and switch things on and off, lights, music, TV to fool the neighbors into thinking you are home. What the utility companies are not saying is that all these devices are also flooding your home with radio frequency microwave radiation.

Even if you don't have a smart meter, typically these devices are still zapping you 24/7. I made this realization a few years ago when we bought a new refrigerator online for our kitchen and I discovered it was emitting RF radiation.

I was fortunate; I had my RF meter on hand and I realized very quickly that the signal was coming from the refrigerator, so we sent it back and bought a non-smart version locally, which I tested before we bought. Without an RF meter it can be

415 Many modern alarm systems, including wired ones, have detectors which emit RF radiation, sometimes beyond the frequency that affordable EMF meters can measure—scrutinize carefully the documentation before installing.

difficult to know if your latest appliance emits RF radiation. Sometimes you can turn that feature off, and sometimes you can't.

What you need to retain from this chapter:

- A smart meter is a type of utility meter that can be used to measure your electric, gas or water usage
- "Smart" refers to their ability to continuously, or semi-continuously, send your usage data directly back to the utility company
- Some smart meters use existing electrical wiring to send their data (and your's) back to the utility company. This can cause high levels of dirty electricity in your home
- More commonly, instead of using the wiring, smart meters emit radio frequency microwave radiation to transmit their data
- According to one study, some smart meters can create 160 times more cumulative whole-body RF exposure than cell phones
- If you can opt-out of having a smart meter installed, this is often the best option, even if it means paying more to keep your old meter
- There are only two ways to know with 100% certainty whether your utility meter is a smart meter: call in an EMF consultant or take RF readings yourself
- If your readings are high and you cannot opt out, then you need to shield the meter. This can be done with a smart meter guard and/or shielding foil.

## Chapter 16

# Earthing

When you think about it, don't we live peculiar lives? We sleep in beds that keep us suspended off the floor. We work in offices that are sometimes several stories off the ground. Even when we do seek to connect with nature, a walk in the park, we wear plastic-soled shoes that prevent any direct physical contact with the ground we walk on.

Most of us have completely lost any physical contact with the earth. Is that healthy? Are there health benefits to be gained by reconnecting with nature? And where do EMFs fit into this? These are the two important questions I'm going to answer in this chapter.

### What Is Earthing?

It goes under two names, earthing and grounding—I prefer the word earthing to avoid confusion with the grounding work that electricians do with electrical circuits to provide a path for lightning to reach the earth in a storm and avoid electrical shocks (see Chapter 9).

**Walking barefoot is the simplest way to "earth" oneself.**

There are also more sophisticated ways of doing it, which I will explain. But however you choose to earth, fundamentally it's about getting back into contact with Mother Earth.

> ***Earthing, putting your bare feet on the ground soaks up lots of electrons because the earth is negatively charged and our bodies are so full of free radicals from anything from heavy metals, to air pollution, to trans fats.***
>
> —*Stephen T. Sinatra, M.D.*[416]

---

416 https://www.youtube.com/watch?v=XumPQLTzPWI

Earthing is believed to work by virtue of the following two processes:

1. Direct contact with the earth replenishes your body with natural, negatively-charged direct current (DC) electrons, which promotes the normalization of your body's systems and rhythms
2. It facilitates the discharge of the accumulated effects of long-term exposure to harmful man-made EMFs from your body.

## Can Earthing Right All the Wrongs That 21st Century Life Throws At Us?

Righting all the wrongs might be a tall order but people have shared some amazing healing stories about earthing on ElectricSense.com. In 2009, Cindy was actively playing tennis, dancing, and able to extend one foot above her head. She had just turned 50 and was enjoying a very active lifestyle.

In March 2010, Cindy visited an ENT for mold allergies, who prescribed Xyzal for allergies. Soon, after taking this, she began to feel pain in her hands and wrists. Her work meant she was constantly on her laptop. She also kept her cell phone within reach at all times since it served as her business phone.

In July 2010, she consulted a rheumatologist who prescribed various treatments over a two-year period, including taking Aleve and Ibuprofen. Her pain continued to worsen with numbness, stabbing pain and major stiffness.

In 2011, despite six months of consultations with a chiropractor, her symptoms were still worsening, and the pain had progressed to all joints except her hips. From May 2012 until February 2013, Cindy trialed an Antibiotic Protocol , which brought her rheumatoid factor down to normal, but her stiffness and pain in joints and muscles continued.

In August 2013, she read about earthing and started to earth using special sheets while sleeping, and earth with special bands on her wrists and ankles when working or watching TV, and also grounding her laptop.

Cindy said, "I feel immediate relief when a painful joint or aching muscle touches any of the products above that are attached to a ground port outlet... I am content to walk without a limp and even dance."

Another story is that of Jacqueline, who says, "I am quite sensitive to energy and my body's responses, and I noticed a while ago that when I lie down on the earth—either the grass or at the beach, my whole body and mind slow down and feel as though they are coming into line with the rhythm of the earth... I go barefoot for at least 30 minutes outside most days, as does my husband".

Gabrielle says, "I practiced walking barefoot for 45 minutes every day for over two years and my health got so much better. For some reason over the last summer, I stopped and I got sick again so I'm now building my time back up with grounding and 30 minute walks three-to-five days a week".

Rebecca and her husband had worked diligently to get their home and office into the "low EMF" range. She began earthing, "[I] must say, it's very, very powerful. Most of the research is well conducted and NOT funded by the Powers-That-Be. I strongly recommend everyone try this simple approach... I have been surprised to hear myself singing again... and laughing".

Body voltage is a way to measure and understand to what degree you are impacted by AC electric fields and to what degree you are physically connected to the earth.

## Advanced Tip—Measuring Your Body Voltage

Measuring the electric fields in your home with your EMF meter is important—I talked about this in Chapter 9. But what if you could quantify the AC electric tension in your body compared to the ground? You can, by measuring your body voltage.

As Dr. Dietrich Klinghardt explains:

> ***The body acts like an antenna for ambient electric fields in the home and builds up electric tension against the ground which interferes with numerous biological and physiological functions... The higher the body voltage, the worse [it is].***[417]

To measure your body voltage, you can buy a "body voltage meter" or, cheaper still, you can use a regular digital multimeter. Here's a picture of the multimeter I bought a few years ago which I use.

You can pick up a digital multimeter online for $20–30. It doesn't need to be anything fancy but it does need to be able to measure AC voltage AND give milli-volt (mV) readings—important because sometimes your readings will be close to zero on the Volts setting so you will need to change the range to millivolts to get a meaningful reading.

417 Dietrich Klinghardt, 2010. *Energy Medicine and Autism.*

When you earth yourself, your objective is to:

- Normalize your AC body voltage, i.e. reduce your exposure that which is man-made and unnatural
- Normalize your DC body voltage, thereby increasing your exposure to the earth's beneficial natural electrons.

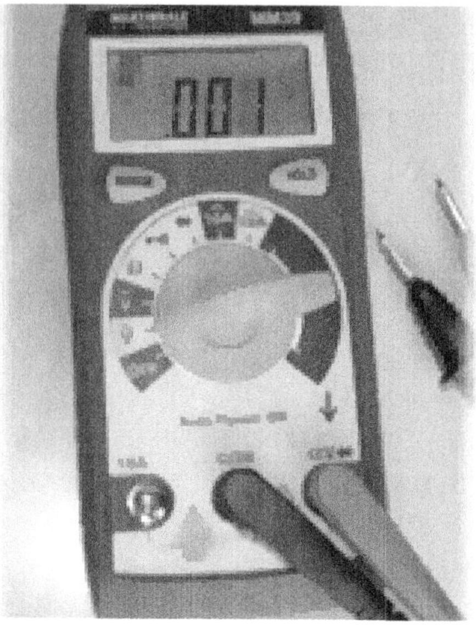


As with the EMF meters, the whole value of this exercise is "seeing is believing". If you see a significant change in body voltage, you'll be a lot more motivated to integrate earthing into your everyday life.

## Measure Your AC Body Voltage Reading Earthed vs. Unearthed

You need to take an AC body voltage reading earthed and compare it with an unearthed reading.

To get an unearthed body voltage reading:

- Put your multimeter on the AC Volts or millivolts setting
- Hold the red probe between your thumb and finger
- Put the black probe to earth, making sure your body is not in any way in contact with the earth—if you're wearing plastic-soled shoes that's fine.
- Make a note of the reading.

To get an earthed AC body voltage reading:

- Do as above, but also put your body in connection with the earth, such as by putting your bare feet on the ground or similar.

When you do this test the "earth" needs to be always the same. It can be your ground connection on your electrical outlet, for instance, but you need to use the same earth for both the earthed body reading and the unearthed body reading.

There are various products that you can buy which allow you to earth indoors, like earthing sheets, mats and straps. If you're using an earthing sheet for your earthing, sit on your sheet making sure your skin is in contact with the sheet while the black probe is on the earthing sheet and the red probe is between your fingers.

**It's not unusual to get readings of 10 Volts (AC) or more unearthed and one or two mV (1 Volt = 1000 mV) when earthed.**

This all depends on the quality of your environment. When I first did this test my environment was already low EMF, I had an unearthed reading of 0.7 Volts AC (700 mV) and an earthed reading of 2 mV AC.

Building Biologist Eric Windheim has measured people with body voltages in their bedroom of 4,000 or 5,000 mV. One time in San Francisco, measured 273 Volts on a boy's pillow—that's 273,000 mV!

The Building Biology guidelines[418] classify AC body voltage readings below 10 mV as "no anomaly", which is considered the safest. But in practice that could be hard to achieve.

**The lower your AC body voltage readings the better. In your bedroom aim to get below 100 mV.**

You may find that your readings change at different times of the day. Your readings will sometimes be higher in the evening because there are more electronics switched on and therefore more man-made electric fields. You should take body voltage readings in any room where you spend a lot of time, but the most important thing is to get low AC body voltage in the bedroom.

## How To Get Your AC Body Voltage Readings Down

Remember, with EMFs there's no such thing as a "safe" exposure level—the same rule applies for body voltage readings. Lower body voltage readings just mean your AC electric field exposure level is lower and your EMF environment resembles more closely that which you could find in nature. Here's how to get your AC body voltage readings down:

1. Take your current AC body voltage reading when lying on your bed. If the reading is above 100 mV, flip the breaker on your bedroom circuit

418 BAUBIOLOGIE MAES/Institut für Baubiologie + Nachhaltigkeit IBN. GUIDELINES. Supplement to the Standard of Building Biology Testing Methods SBM-2015 Building Biology Evaluation Guidelines for Sleeping Areas

2. Test again, if the reading is still above 100 mV, try flipping the breaker on an adjoining room and possibly in the ceiling of the room below the bedroom. Be sure the lights are turned off in the room below the bedroom
3. Keep taking readings and flipping breakers until you get down to an acceptable body voltage reading—ideally below 10 mV but hopefully below 100 mV.

Once you've done this, try adding an earthing sheet into the mix. Do the same procedure, test before earthing and after earthing. Assuming your readings are lower when you are on the earthing sheet—which they always will be unless your earthing sheet is defective—try sleeping for a week earthed. Then decide if you sleep with the earthing sheet or without it.

Two more tips:

1. I don't recommend sleeping on an earthing sheet unless already, prior to earthing, your body voltage reading is low (more about this below)
2. Use a pen and paper to note down your readings between each test and keep a record of your reading and the date you tested so you can refer back to it in six months, or a year or so, when you want to test again I've also included a video here: www.electricsense.com/bookbonus which shows you how to use a multimeter to measure your body voltage.

## What Does The Research Say?

Currently there are about 20 published studies on earthing. This is not a lot, but they are all peer-reviewed—widely regarded as the gold standard in published studies.

One of the biggest benefits of earthing, according to the research,[419] are the anti-inflammatory effects—inflammation is being seen as a common underlying cause of many diseases, including arthritis, cardiovascular disease, diabetes, Alzheimer's and cancer.

**Research shows earthing for as little as half an hour is beneficial.**

419 https://www.ncbi.nlm.nih.gov/pmc/articles/PMC4378297/

Most of the research done on earthing has been carried out by the Earthing Institute, which has conducted testing with hundreds of subjects and found that:[420]

- The autonomic nervous system relaxes within one-to-two seconds
- After about 20 to 25 minutes, stress starts to increase a little bit and there is an increase in respiration rate and heart rate
- This causes an increase in oxygen being absorbed by the blood and going through the body
- After between 20 to 30 minutes of earthing, acute inflammations are improved
- Some people report pain goes away faster.

The research has also found that because earthing can significantly improve blood viscosity (thickness) and flow, earthing also has cardiovascular benefits.[421]

Gaetan Chevalier, PhD, mentions two other benefits:

1. Our body is a bioelectrical system, meaning we have electricity working in us all the time. When we aren't grounded, we create a kind of virtual grounding point, which is often in the bones. After a certain time, the bones provide the missing electrons—which explains why osteoporosis is helped by earthing.[422]
2. Being connected with the earth connects us to the frequencies of the earth. The Schumann resonance is a frequency of 7.8Hz emitted by the earth. "Our brain works best when we are at 7.8Hz. People are calm, that's exactly the alpha state, that's the way we're supposed to function".

## Is Earthing Dangerous?

If you've never heard of earthing before and your only knowledge of it is what you've read in this chapter, then you might be thinking, dangerous? Whaaaaaat is Lloyd talking about?

Well, you might have noticed that as soon as we scratch the surface on any of these EMF topics, we get into controversy. Earthing is no exception. And I have to say that, on balance, it seems far more experts are against the practice of earthing

420 Gaetan Chevalier, EMF Experts Solutions Club interview.
421 https://www.liebertpub.com/doi/pdf/10.1089/acm.2011.0820
422 This is a hypothesis.

than are for it. Not only are they against it, a lot of them are vehemently against it. The logic goes something like this: during the course of their inspection, the EMF consultant meets someone that is earthing and suffering ill-health. The consultant measures high AC body voltage when earthing (which is the opposite of what you want). Subsequent to the inspection the person stops earthing and over time their health improves. Conclusion: earthing does not work and was causing their ill-health. But did their health improve because they ceased earthing or because of the other EMF remediation work that was done?

The opponents to earthing claim it is dangerous because, by connecting yourself with the earth you are unwittingly zapping yourself with high levels of stray current (the AC voltage, in our example) and the dirty electricity that often flows with stray current (or any current, for that matter) in recent decades. Because utility companies have been allowed to use the earth as a return path for household electricity, instead of using neutral wires as in other countries, certain people feel the earth is saturated with dirty electricity. It is true that in North America there is a "stray current" issue (also called stray voltage).

That stray current is present, nobody can deny.

**The bone of contention is whether or not there is a net benefit from earthing—does it do more good than harm? This is harder to assess.**

The person best qualified to assess this is... yourself. But you need to be armed with certain facts. Which is why I included a chapter on earthing in this guide, so you can best decide if and how to earth. Firstly, two observations:

1. There appears to be certain situations where earthing is NOT beneficial
2. There appears to be some situations where earthing MAY be of benefit, in fact it may be of considerable benefit.

I'm going to clarify what these situations are so that hopefully you can benefit from earthing. The truth is, earthing has subtleties which a lot of people are ignoring. Understanding these subtleties can make the difference between earthing having dire consequences on your health or earthing bringing to bear some quite miraculous healing.

## Where Earthing Is Not Beneficial

There is no consensus on this, but I believe earthing in a high EMF may not always be beneficial. Which leads to the question, what's a high EMF environment? I could try and give you readings for RF radiation and magnetic, electric fields and dirty electricity. But because of individual differences, no such precise readings exist and I want to keep this simple. So, I'll just say that, some indoor environments may not be suitable for earthing for some people.

Does that means that all those wonderful ways to earth which have been devised with earthing sheets and wrist straps and pads and so on can be thrown in the trash bin? No, this is only my opinion. The Earthing Institute recommends earthing even with the presence of EMFs in a home and their position is borne out by hundreds of testimonials.[423]

Two more observations:

1. If you're using earthing accessories, then where possible connect these accessories directly to the earth, for instance with a metal ground stake, rather than using the ground terminal on your electrical socket, which may expose you to current on the ground
2. Make sure all your electrical equipment in proximity to where you are earthing is properly grounded and also that your electrical ground has been checked (see Chapter 9).

Can body voltage readings be relied upon to determine where you can earth safely? Not always. Research conducted by Baubiologie[424] shows that there are situations where your AC body voltage can read as low and yet your electric field exposures are high. For instance, if there is a light above your bed, sleeping on an earthing sheet will (should) give you a low body voltage reading but this could also increase the electric field you are exposed to.[425] So ideally you want to ensure that both your body voltage readings and your electric field readings are low.

**The other situation where earthing may not be appropriate is when you are on medication**—such as blood thinners, thyroid medication, or anti-inflammatory medication—in such cases this needs close monitoring as the usual dosages may need revising. Check with your doctor first. [426]

423 https://earthinginstitute.net/an-a-to-z-of-testimonials-by-condition/
424 http://bit.ly/ElectricSense_CautionGroundingPadsandSheets
425 The Earthing Institute, who have conducted important research on this subject, say their research shows that this is not an issue. You can view their research here: https://earthinginstitute.net/
426 In order to render a sound opinion, your doctor would need to be educated as to what earthing does and how it works—you could lend them a copy of this guide!

## Where Earthing Is Beneficial

Following my recommendations above, you may be able to safely and effectively earth in your home. I earth daily. In the summer I walk barefoot in my garden and in the winter, when I can't go out, I use a ground stake and earth strap to earth indoors. I do this in my living room where, just behind my sofa, there is a window where I pass the earthing wire which connects to a ground stake on the other side of the window.

**Walking outside barefoot in nature or swimming in the sea are two of the safest ways to earth.**

If you are walking barefoot then a lawn or a sandy beach is ideal for this. Beware of walking where you might cause yourself injury or where the ground has been sprayed with pesticides or other chemicals. Gardening is also a good way of earthing. Even if you are wearing rubber-soled shoes you will still earth with the contact of your hands on the soil. Another way to earth is to wear special earthing shoes. This is what I like to wear when I'm walking in a rural setting when I can't walk barefoot. For information on where to buy earthing shoes, see: www.electricsense.com/bookbonus

Our environment is becoming more polluted, so safe effective earthing is more challenging now than ever. But the potential benefits are considerable. Try earthing for 30 minutes a day for a week. See how it feels. Above all, listen to your body.

What you need to retain from this chapter:

- At its most basic level, earthing is about getting back into contact with Mother Earth
- Body voltage is a way to measure and understand to what degree you are impacted by AC electric fields and to what degree you are physically connected to the earth
- To measure your body voltage, you can buy a "body voltage meter" or, cheaper still, you can use a regular digital multimeter
- Generally speaking, you want to lower your AC body voltage readings and normalize your DC body voltage readings
- You should be able to lower your AC body voltage in your bedroom by flipping your bedroom breaker switch and nearby circuits as necessary—get below 100 mV.
- Then try adding an earthing sheet into the mix and taking readings and decide if its beneficial to earth

- Studies show there are many health benefits to be gained from earthing, one of the main ones is an anti-inflammatory effect
- Earthing is controversial—the bone of contention is whether it does more good than harm
- I recommend earthing outdoors—earthing indoors may not always be beneficial
- Body voltage readings cannot always be relied on to determine where you can earth safely—ultimately, you need to listen to your body.

## Chapter 17

# What Are We Doing To Our Children?

IF YOU ARE A PARENT, grandparent, aunt, uncle, or maybe just a concerned citizen, just to warn you up-front, you might find what I'm going to share in this chapter deeply disturbing.

What we are doing to our children is my BIGGEST concern. Because everything I've told you so far about the far-reaching effects of EMFs applies to children too.

**The effects of EMFs on our children are even more profound and devastating than they are on adults.**

My concern about what we might be doing to our children is what motivated me to start talking about EMFs online back in 2009. I just felt compelled to speak out.

## Our Children Are Hooked

A 2014 survey by the American Academy of Pediatrics found that up to 75% of four-year olds have their own cell phone.[427]

Elsewhere in the world, it's a similar story:

- In the UK, a quarter of children under six already have their own cell phone[428]
- 51% of German children aged six to 13 have their own cell phone
- Across Europe, 46% of children nine to 16 own a smartphone
- In South Korea, 72% of children own a smartphone by the age of 11 to 12.[429]

---

427 https://pediatrics.aappublications.org/content/136/6/1044
428 http://bit.ly/2n9pGiR
429 https://edition.cnn.com/2017/12/11/health/cell-phones-for-kids-parenting-without-borders-explainer-intl/index.html

Not only have kids around the world got their own cell phones, they are using them a LOT. A 2018 study found that 45% of teenagers are almost constantly online.[430] Other research shows children in the US average seven hours of screen use a day![431]

## Our Children Are Literally Being Killed

In June 2015, 15-year-old British schoolgirl Jenny Fry was found hanged in woodland near her home.

Jenny started experiencing tiredness, headaches and bladder problems in 2012. Seeing that her health was declining, her mother decided to do some research. She discovered how dangerous Wi-Fi could be, so she had it taken out of their home. Jenny was then fine at home, but continued to be ill at school in certain areas.

Jenny's mum shared her research with the head teacher, but he refused to take action. Jenny started receiving lots of detentions, not for misbehaving, but because she would take herself out of the classroom to find another where she was able to work. Her mother said, "As soon as Jenny walked away from a router she felt instantly better so she was almost hunting out areas of the school which weren't covered by Wi-Fi just to do her work".

Speaking after her daughter's inquest, Mrs. Fry said, "Wi-Fi and children do not mix. I believe that Wi-Fi killed my daughter". The teenager's parents are now campaigning to remove this technology from classrooms.[432]

Joe Darnell and his family were just coming off Thanksgiving and they noticed that Kyanna, their seven-year-old daughter, wasn't her usual self. At first, Joe and his wife thought it was a minor illness, perhaps vertigo because that runs in the family. As the days passed, things rapidly deteriorated. They took her to the doctor to run some tests and do an MRI—they found a large tumor in her brain. Neither chemo nor radiation treatment seemed the right choice, but they heard of another child that had been given a similar diagnosis and had followed an alternative treatment which had been successful.

The oncologist found various issues, but he also told them that "She has an issue with electromagnetic fields". That was the first time that Joe and his wife had heard about the health effects of EMFs.

430 https://cbsn.ws/2lv95pv
431 https://cbsn.ws/2lv95pv
432 https://dailym.ai/2mICht4

They set about cleaning the EMFs in their home, dealing with their cell phones, Wi-Fi, general ground current issues, dirty electricity and magnetic fields in her bedroom—a small fan at the base of her bed meant she was often sleeping in a magnetic field all night long. Tragically, Kyanna died less than two months after being diagnosed.

Her father Joe admits that "the EMFs were one issue in many. But that's where the seed gets planted... It's kind of the catalyst that gets everything else going and creates a lot of these other issues". Joe's subsequent research made him realize that this was the work he must do—he now works as an EMF consultant helping people reduce EMF exposures in their lives.

## Children Are More Vulnerable

For more than 20 years, for anyone that's been following the research, it's been blindingly obvious that children are way more vulnerable to EMFs than adults.

In 1996, Prof. Gandhi from Utah University[433] was the first to discover that children are more at risk with radio frequency radiation than adults. His research showed that five-year-old and ten-year-old children have higher absorption rates than adults because their skulls and bones are thinner and their brains and bodies contain more fluid so they naturally absorb more cell phone radiation than adults.

These findings were confirmed in his 2012[434] follow-up study, and then again in 2015.[435]

**A ten-year-old child absorbs 153% more cell phone radiation than an adult.[436]**

As Martin Blank[437] explains:

- Children continuously grow at a rapid pace, so they undergo a faster pace of cell division, making their DNA more vulnerable
- The bone in a child's head is thinner, so the brain's neurons are less protected
- The radiation absorbed by children from cell phones is greater than in adults because children have higher levels of conductivity.

433 https://ieeexplore.ieee.org/document/539947?arnumber=539947
434 http://bit.ly/Researchgate-exposurelimits
435 https://www.tandfonline.com/doi/abs/10.3109/15368378.2011.622827
436 https://www.tandfonline.com/doi/abs/10.3109/15368378.2011.622827
437 *Overpowered: What Science Tells Us About The Dangers of Cell Phones and other Wi-Fi Age Devices.*

Simply put, children are not little adults—their bodies operate differently to those of adults.

Let's not forget, brain cancer is now the leading cause of cancer death in US children.[438]

And this is not just about exposure to the brain either; this radiation has full body impact AND all forms of EMF exposure have full body impact. EMF expert Stephane Belainsky has observed epilepsy issues in children exposed to 150 V/m or more of electric fields in their homes—official ICNIRP guidelines are for 5000 V/m.[439]

**In another study, it was found that a FIVE-YEAR-OLD absorbs up to 60% more radiation PER POUND of body weight than an adult. A one-year-old BABY can absorb around DOUBLE the radiation.[440]**

So, the younger the child, the more profound the effects of these exposures.

Unfortunately, EMFs don't wait for a child to be born to start zapping them. Exposure starts while children are in the womb and can then affect their lives in so many ways, like: obesity,[441] asthma,[442] behavioral and attention problems,[443] and brain function.[444]

Given that the first nine months of our lives are considered the most important period, this does not bode well.

***The fetus is getting its fetal programming and its epigenetic programming that is its way of reacting to the environment in the very first month of its life so if we disturb the fetal programming we can have a lot of consequences.[445]***

EMF consultant and naturopath Dr. Ross Andersen makes the case that EMFs can impact our children even before the nine-month pregnancy period.

---

438 https://www.medscape.com/viewarticle/868864
439 Michael Bevington, 2013. *Electromagnetic Sensitivity and Electromagnetic Hypersensitivity.*
440 http://bit.ly/33mhzPn; http://www.iegmp.org.uk/documents/iegmp_6.pdf
441 https://www.researchgate.net/publication/230586909; https://www.nature.com/articles/srep00540
442 https://jamanetwork.com/journals/jamapediatrics/fullarticle/1107612?resultClick=3
443 Birks L, et al. *Maternal Cell Phone Use During Pregnancy and Child Behavioral Problems in Five Birth Cohorts. Environment International.*
444 https://www.ncbi.nlm.nih.gov/pubmed/16846979
445 Dr. Ernesto Burgio, presentation at the 5th Paris Appeal Congress in Belgium, https://www.youtube.com/watch?v=iPQSotTJORw

***Children are being born with significant challenges, physically and mentally because of the exposure not just during the nine months but prior to conception.***

The term he coined for this is fetal electromagnetic radiation syndrome, which he likened to fetal alcohol syndrome (FAS). It's widely accepted that FAS can cause behavioral issues, and some argue it can cause abnormalities in the face. Which begs the question, are we going to see our future generations literally disfigured by EMF exposures?

## Do EMFs Cause Autism?

Back in the 70s and 80s approximately one in 2,000 children were estimated to have diagnosed with autism spectrum disorder (ASD).[446]

According to a 2018 study, the prevalence of autism in the US is now one in 40.[447] And this phenomenon is not restricted to the US. Other developed nations are experiencing a similar trend.

Are EMFs 100% to blame? Probably not on their own, but there are at least half a dozen good research papers pointing the finger at EMFs.

Dr. Martha Herbert, a pediatric neurologist with Harvard University, studied the biological factors that are linked to autism[448] and found a strong correlation with electromagnetic fields, particularly of the type emitted by Wi-Fi. She found that calcium signaling in the brain, which regulates the flow of information to the cell membrane, is disturbed by EMF exposures.

This ties in with Martin Pall's work, which suggests that the same mechanism I outlined in Chapter 3—with the voltage gated calcium channels—leads to an increased risk of autism.

**EMF exposures disturb calcium signaling in the brain, which can increase the risk of autism.**

Studies[449] tell us that stem cells (important because of their ability to regenerate and repair damaged tissue) are particularly affected by RF microwave radiation.

446 https://www.webmd.com/brain/autism/features/autism-rise#1
447 https://www.verywellhealth.com/is-there-a-real-increase-in-the-incidence-of-autism-260133
448 https://www.ncbi.nlm.nih.gov/pubmed/24095003
449 https://www.youtube.com/watch?v=iPQSotTJORw

**EMFs also cause damage to stem cells which in children can impair brain development in a way that likely contributes to autism.[450]**

The general consensus though is that it's not just EMFs that are to blame. A 2007 study found that EMFs probably work in conjunction with other environmental factors (like chemicals) and genetic factors to cause autism.[451]

In 2001, pioneering Dr. Dietrich Klinghardt noticed a higher rate of autism among the children of parents who worked at Microsoft. He decided to go into the children's homes and do some EMF testing. He found dramatically higher levels of radio frequency radiation in the homes of families with autistic children. He has since incorporated this information into his autism prevention and recovery program, requesting that parents reduce wireless and other electric field exposures. Researcher and father of two autistic children Peter Sullivan says, "Parents who follow [Dr. Klinghardt's] strict guidelines often see their children improve and even recover in about six months".[452]

Autism aside, numerous studies highlight a link between radiofrequency radiation exposures, cerebral cortex modification, and a reduction in the number of neurons. In another study, children and adolescents were found to have a six-to-seven point loss of IQ linked to wireless exposures.[453]

In other words, cell phones are making our children dumber.

## Four Easy Steps To Protect Young Children

In order to help young children, Dr. Toril Jelter and Cindy Sage developed a simple low EMF protocol which involves turning off:

- Baby monitors
- Cordless phones
- Wi-Fi
- Electricity in the bedroom at nighttime.

They found that over 80% of children showing signs of being affected by EMFs had a noticeable improvement, often in as little as two weeks, after this protocol was put in place.

450 Dr. Joseph Mercola, *EMF'D.*
451 http://www.avaate.org/spip.php?article693
452 http://www.clearlightventures.com/blog/2015/9/11/the-emerging-link-between-wireless-and-autism
453 http://www.ilgiornale.it/news/politica/cos-tablet-pc-e-cellulari-ci-cambiano-cervello-1740785.html

## The Triple Whammy

As Dr. Herbert explains, "We are getting a triple or quadruple whammy between the biological effects, the psychological effects and the brain wave effects."

So, there are firstly the general biological effects on the body, secondly the specific effects on the brain as described above, and thirdly the psychological effects—all of which are way worse in children than in adults.

Autism straddles both these last two categories, as does ADD and ADHD. Again, there's sufficient research on the link between ADD/ADHD and EMFs to believe that their effect is not just a coincidence.

And, the link between digital dosing and ADD/ADHD is becoming ever clearer too.

**The more teens check social media and stream video, the more likely they are to develop symptoms of attention disorder.[454]**

## Non-EMF Effects Too

Putting the EMF question to one side for the moment, there's plenty of research to suggest that the more children use cell phones and similar technology, the more likely they will be harmed emotionally, mentally, behaviorally, in fact in just about every imaginable way.[455]

Victoria L. Dunckley, MD, author of the book *Reset Your Child's Brain*,[456] blames a lot of children's mental health woes on the effects of electronic screen media. She uses the term Electronic Screen Syndrome to describe a collection of symptoms relating to mood, anxiety, cognition, behavior, and social interactions that can cause significant impairment in school, at home, or with friends.

**Research suggests that all screen activities provide unnatural simulation to the nervous system and can cause adverse effects.**

In Chapter 11, I mentioned how dangerous blue light at night can be. Well, it would seem that this is even more the case for children.

454 https://apsard.org/wp-content/uploads/2018/07/ADHD-digital-media-jama_Ra_2018_oi_180072.pdf
455 https://jamanetwork.com/journals/jamapediatrics/article-abstract/2722666
456 Victoria L. Dunckley - *Reset Your Child's Brain: A Four-Week Plan to End Meltdowns, Raise Grades, and Boost Social Skills by Reversing the Effects of Electronic Screen-Time*

**Because light from screen devices mimics daytime, it suppresses melatonin, a sleep signal released by darkness. Just minutes of screen stimulation can delay melatonin release by several hours and desynchronize the body clock. Once the body clock is disrupted, all sorts of other unhealthy reactions occur, such as hormone imbalance and brain inflammation.[457]**

## EMFs On Wiring

While the effects of wireless radiation on our children become ever clearer, let's not forget that the science is also very clear about the dangers of EMFs from wired sources, and has been for a very long time. A 1979 study clearly identified a link between levels of magnetic fields commonly found on electrical wiring, and childhood leukemia.[458]

Epidemiological studies (research on populations) done by Dr. Samuel Milham support these findings.[459]

**The trend of childhood leukemia developing at a certain age is a modern one, which followed the introduction of the power grid, and this peak does not exist in unelectrified regions.[460]**

Added to this are the effects of dirty electricity exposures on children. The La Quinta Middle School incident I mentioned in Chapter 10, where dirty electricity readings were so high they overloaded the meter, is an indication of the kind of havoc these exposures may be wreaking. To date, 49 former pupils have developed cancer in their 20s and six students have now died. This begs the question, in how many other schools are our children being silently zapped?

457 http://bit.ly/psychologytoday-Screentime-kids
458 https://www.ncbi.nlm.nih.gov/pubmed/453167
459 Samuel Milham, 2012. *Dirty Electricity: Electrification and the Diseases of Civilization.*
460 Martin Blank, *Overpowered: What Science Tells Us About The Dangers of Cell Phones and other Wi-Fi Age Devices.*

## How To Protect Your Children

Let me make three observations:

1. The younger your children are, the more they need protection.
2. Just like for yourself, when taking steps to protect your children you need to look at ALL four types of EMF exposure. Don't make assumptions. Either take readings yourself or get an expert in to take readings for you.
3. If you're preaching to your kids about safe cell phone use and you spend half your life with your cell phone stuck to your ear, they're not going to listen. Start by walking the talk.

## The Thorny Cell Phone Question

There's no doubt in my mind, cell phones are very bad news for kids. But kids love them. Kids want social acceptance, having the latest smartphone helps them "fit in". The peer pressure is enormous. They can follow the news on social media, and they can interact with their friends in real time using Facebook, Instagram, WhatsApp and all the rest of it.

Are you ready to deprive your children of all this? Or is it only going to be partial deprivation you are going to inflict on them?

**At what age is it safe to give your child a cell phone?**

For parents that are EMF aware, this is probably the number one question on their minds. The answer:

**It's not safe to give your child a cell phone at any age.**

Of course, this is not really the right question to ask because there is no black and white. Nevertheless, I asked this question to researcher Lloyd Morgan, who's particularly well qualified to answer it given his own personal experience with EMFs (Chapter 11) and the research he's carried out.

**I would say wait until 13, which is kind of an arbitrary age... I would then still have some rules.[461]**

461 Lloyd Morgan, senior researcher Environmental Health Trust.

A good resource is www.waituntil8th.org which helps empower parents to delay giving children a smartphone until at least 8th grade (US).

Hold out as long as you can before giving them a cellphone. Then the key is the rules that you set—that's to say how you allow them to use their cell phone.

## The Rules (Free And Easy Protection)

**Rule #1 is to make airplane mode the default setting with Wi-Fi and Bluetooth off.** If you can make them understand this, you will be doing them a BIG favor. I recommend the following rules as a minimum:

1. No cell phones in their bedrooms at nighttime. Create a habit where everyone puts their cell phone in the Kill Tin (Chapter 7) two hours before bedtime
2. The cell phone should only be used against the head for talking in emergencies
3. Maximum two hours of wireless use per week.

Two hours a week is not much, I know, so if your kids have been given free reign this might take some negotiating and might take time to achieve. Why two hours a week? Frankly, zero is best but we are looking for a happy medium.

Again, this is not just about cell phones. The above recommendations apply to ALL wireless devices, including laptops and computers.

## Safe Cell Phone Use For Kids

Rules are all well and good, but if your kids are anything like mine imposing any kind of rule can be highly challenging. Here are two strategies you can use to help them swallow the seemingly bitter pill of going low EMF:

1. Lead by example. If you've already applied most of the cell phone radiation tips outlined in Chapter 7 to yourself, or at least the most important one (obsessive airplane mode use), then you'll only be asking your kids to do what you already do.
2. Get your kids interested in the topic. If you start being careful with how you use your own cell phone and personal devices, at some point they are

> going to notice and start asking questions. That would be an ideal way of starting the EMF conversation. You can further this dialogue by leaving a copy of this guide on your living room table, or perhaps buy a copy of the movie Generation Zapped and have a family screening.

Be "smart" about this; this could very easily turn into a hot potato. Be patient, educate them bit by bit, avoid conflict.

## EMFs In Schools

When you have dealt with ALL aspects of the EMF question in your home as best you can—wireless and wired, as explained in the previous chapters—then you can tackle what's going on in your kid's school.

Again, think wireless and wired. That there is so much Wi-Fi in schools around the world is tragic. Not only that, but the Wi-Fi used in schools is a lot more powerful than that used in homes.

**The Wi-Fi systems in schools are typically hundreds of times more powerful than the home consumer systems you may be familiar with.**[462]

Righting this wrong is not going to be easy, but it is possible. People are succeeding, like mother-turned-EMF activist Cece Doucette.

Cece had been busy fundraising to get her local school equipped with iPads, Chromebooks, Smart TVs, Smart Boards and so on, which she'd been told the school badly needed. Then one night, she was at a book group and one of her friends, who is an electrical engineer, mentioned that she was reading a book called *Zapped.*[463] Cece's curiosity was piqued, and she started doing her own research, which she shared with the school. Initially it fell on deaf ears but after quite a few meetings with the school board and bringing in experts to speak on the topic, her school eventually became the first public school district in the United States to adopt a "best practices for mobile devices" policy.

As for wired exposures in your child's school, I suggest the best way of dealing with this is to go in with your EMF meter and dirty electricity meter and discreetly

---

462 American Academy of Environmental Medicine https://www.emfacts.com/2013/03/aaem-on-wifi-in-schools/
463 Ann Louise Gittleman, *Zapped*

take some readings—I know of no law which prevents you measuring EMFs on school grounds. Then, if you find the readings are of a concern, you need to start talking to other parents and teachers, invite expert speakers, and speak to the school board.

For a list of organizations that can help you remove Wi-Fi and lower the EMFs in your school, go to: www.electricsense.com/bookbonus. I've also included an MP3 of my interview with Cece Doucette so you can better understand what she did.

Here's a summary of what you need to retain from this chapter:

- The effects of EMFs on our children are even more profound and devastating than they are on adults
- A five-year-old absorbs up to 60% MORE RADIATION per pound of body weight than an adult.
- Exposure starts while children are in the womb and can affect their lives, causing many health issues like obesity, asthma and behavioral problems
- There's sufficient research to believe the more children are exposed to EMFs the greater their risk of autism, ADD/ADHD and the more likely they will be harmed emotionally, mentally, behaviorally
- EMFs from electrical wiring are particularly dangerous for children
- The most powerful way of helping your children go low EMF is by leading by example, by YOU going low EMF first
- It's not safe to give your child a cell phone at any age but at least wait until they are 13 and then have some rules
- Once you have dealt with the EMFs impacting your children in your home you should take steps to protect them at school.

Remember, the safety standards do NOTHING to protect our children—there aren't even any safety standards to protect our children! If you've got kids, grandkids, or friends with children, I can't stress enough how important it is to take on board the information in this chapter and act on it!

# Chapter 18

# EMFs And Women

BY NOW YOU'VE GOT A pretty good idea of the many ways EMFs can zap you. In this chapter, I want to talk about the *particular* risks for women. It's not that nobody's talking about this, some experts are. But nobody seems to have realized what a MAJOR issue this is. Plus, I'm going to share some female-oriented solutions.

## EMFs And Breast Cancer

Here are a couple of things you should know up front:

1. Breast cancer is the most common cancer for women worldwide[464]
2. Only about one in ten breast cancers are hereditary.[465]

That's to say breast cancers are increasingly common and in 90% of cases they are NOT due to "bad genes". So, what are they due to?

The Mayo Clinic cites hormonal, lifestyle and environmental factors.[466] We don't know exactly what causes breast cancer, but we do know that different kinds of EMFs have a role to play.

### Nearly 70 research studies show how EMFs can promote breast cancer.[467]

High levels of estrogen (a hormone that regulates the female reproductive system) have been shown to be a risk factor for breast cancer.[468] Melatonin plays a vital role in preventing high levels of estrogen in the body.

464 https://www.wcrf.org/dietandcancer/cancer-trends/breast-cancer-statistics
465 https://www.ncbi.nlm.nih.gov/pmc/articles/PMC3618918/
466 https://www.mayoclinic.org/diseases-conditions/breast-cancer/symptoms-causes/syc-20352470
467 https://www.emfresearch.com/emfs-breast-cancer/
468 https://www.maurerfoundation.org/estrogen-and-breast-cancer/

In Chapter 11, I spoke about melatonin at some length. It's something of a super-hormone and it's important for several reasons: reinforcing your immune system, anti-cancer and anti-ageing. The problem is, EMF exposures at nighttime reduce your melatonin production—this is the important link between EMFs and breast cancer.

**Reduced levels of melatonin can lead to higher levels of estrogen, which increases the risk of breast cancer.**

This is only one way EMFs may cause breast cancer. There are many others.[469]

## Bras Are NOT Suitable For Carrying Cell Phones

A survey of women aged 15–40 years old found that "pocket and near-the-breast storage were significant by age".[470] We don't have any firm data on this, but in younger women, walking around with your cell phone in your bra has become a cool and trendy thing to do. Cool, hip and trendy perhaps, but also stupid.

A research team studied four young women—aged 21 to 39 years old—with multifocal invasive breast cancer. The researchers observed that all of the women developed tumors in areas of their breasts right next to where they carried their cell phones in their bras—often up to ten hours a day for several years. None of the young women had a family history of breast cancer. They all tested negative for breast cancer genes (linked to about one-half of breast cancer cases) and they had no other known breast cancer risks.[471]

Other studies on human breast cancer cells in test tubes show that cell phone radiation exposure within 10 cm of cells can cause significant adverse biological effects.[472] [473]

**Carrying your cell phone in your bra is a risk factor for breast cancer.**

There's a tendency to think of breast cancer as a "woman problem" but if you're a guy and you carry your cell phone in your breast pocket, then you should know that plenty of studies show that you too are at risk.[474]

469 https://www.emfresearch.com/emfs-breast-cancer/
470 https://journals.plos.org/plosone/article?id=10.1371/journal.pone.0167996
471 https://www.hindawi.com/journals/crim/2013/354682/
472 https://www.ncbi.nlm.nih.gov/pubmed/25703814
473 http://bit.ly/ncbi-breastcancer
474 https://www.emf-portal.org/en/article/21996

## EMFs Can Make You Infertile

It's estimated that there are over 48 million infertile couples worldwide.[475]

Approximately 35% of women and 45% of men worldwide are considered to have reduced fertility and about 7% of women and men are effectively infertile.[476] [477]

**Male fertility problems are considered central in about 40% of couples experiencing child-bearing hurdles, which means a staggering 60% is due to female infertility.[478]**

How big a role do EMFs play in these fertility issues? I believe they play a very BIG role—read on and you'll see why.

Naturopath David Getoff told me about his patient and her husband who'd been desperately trying to get pregnant for two years. Using kinesiology (a form of muscle testing), David investigated her response to various toxins in the environment and nutrients. There didn't seem to be any problem—until he got to EMFs. David's testing indicated that EMFs were impacting her health. Her husband was in IT and very attached to his electronic gadgets, so going low EMF was going to be tough. But she managed to convince her husband to make some concessions. They replaced their Wi-Fi with a hardwired connection, replaced their cordless phone with a corded landline, and told friends to call the landline number instead of the cell phone.

David's patient got pregnant in 30 days! She still comes to see David, and now she has a healthy baby.

## What Does The Science Say?

Most of the studies done on infertility have looked at how EMFs impact male fertility—I reviewed the science in Chapter 4. There's a reason for this; to study women requires fairly invasive techniques—given that the female reproductive apparatus is located deep inside the body—so less studies have been done. Nevertheless, there are some studies so let's look at those.

In a 2014 US study,[479] researchers looked at women trying to get pregnant, measuring their enzyme levels (alpha-amylase, an enzyme with a known association to

475 http://www.pubmedcentral.nih.gov/articlerender.fcgi?artid=PMC3525527
476 http://www.ncbi.nlm.nih.gov/pubmed/15049583
477 http://www.ncbi.nlm.nih.gov/pubmed/14500443
478 https://fr.scribd.com/document/241338809/The-Adverse-Effects-of-Electromagnetic-Fields-on-Reproduction
479 https://www.ncbi.nlm.nih.gov/pmc/articles/PMC3984126/

stress) in their saliva. They found that women with the highest levels of this enzyme in their saliva had a 29% reduced probability of getting pregnant compared to those with the lowest levels.

Other studies by Austrian researchers[480] [481] have shown that people living within a 100-meter radius of cell phone towers have higher levels of biochemical stress markers, notably, salivary enzyme, alpha-amylase.

**The implication is that women who are trying to get pregnant who are exposed to EMFs from cell towers, cell phones, and so on, are likely to have increased levels of salivary alpha-amylase enzyme—causing them to have a reduced chance of getting pregnant.**

A 2017 study[482] carried out on mice to investigate the long-term effects of mobile phone radiation concluded that these exposures impair the female reproductive system and probably cause oxidative stress (a strong inducer of tissue damage). Other research has similar findings[483] and has also found that this oxidative stress may damage the oocytes (cells in the ovaries), impair their fertilization capacity, and lead to embryo fragmentation and developmental abnormalities.[484]

**These studies indicate that cell phone radiation can cause significant damage to the tissues of the female reproductive system, thereby making it harder to get pregnant.**

Other studies have found that exposure to mobile phone radiation can reduce hormone secretion[485] and impair fertilization and embryo development.[486]

More recent studies are showing that where mothers are able to get pregnant that cell phone use increases the risk of premature birth[487] and miscarriage.

480 https://www.ncbi.nlm.nih.gov/pubmed/20442833
481 https://www.ncbi.nlm.nih.gov/pubmed/20708499
482 http://www.ncbi.nlm.nih.gov/pubmed/28780396
483 http://www.ncbi.nlm.nih.gov/pubmed/24105626
484 https://www.ncbi.nlm.nih.gov/pubmed/28513460
485 https://www.ncbi.nlm.nih.gov/pubmed/28780396
486 http://www.ncbi.nlm.nih.gov/pubmed/27983879
487 https://www.ncbi.nlm.nih.gov/pubmed/30995291

**Magnetic field exposures can increase the risk of miscarriage THREE-FOLD.**[488]

This study by Kaiser Permanente examined 913 women in the San Francisco Bay Area as they went about their typical day. They routinely came into contact with magnetic fields from electrical wiring, power lines, transformers and other everyday exposures. These Kaiser Permanente findings sound shocking—and are—but they confirm the findings of previous studies.[489] [490]

The ramifications of the studies I've shared here are even greater and more profound when you take into account that women are born with all the eggs they will ever have. This finite number of eggs begins to decline at birth.[491]

**When a woman's eggs are zapped by EMFs, the eggs that are lost are gone forever.**

This is why infertility caused through EMF exposures is a major concern for women, for society and, dare I say, for humanity.

When I interviewed Professor Kumar on this question, he commented that "a pregnant woman and the fetus both are vulnerable because of the fact that these RF radiations continuously react with the developing embryo and increasing cells. Microwave radiation can damage the placental barrier; the membrane which prevents the passage of some materials between the maternal and fetal blood, protecting the fetus... it is believed that the eggs, which form the embryo, are affected and the damage will become apparent after the child reaches puberty".

## The Dangers Of Ultrasound

In Canada in 2009, 99.8% of pregnant women were reported as having had at least one ultrasound.[492] There's no reason to believe that these percentages are much different for the US and other developed countries.

Ultrasound is universally accepted as being part and parcel of having a baby—ultrasound is considered safe. And why wouldn't it be safe, it's "just sound waves", right?

488 https://www.nature.com/articles/s41598-017-16623-8
489 http://www.ncbi.nlm.nih.gov/pubmed/11805581
490 http://www.ncbi.nlm.nih.gov/pubmed/11805582
491 https://www.yalemedicine.org/stories/fertility-test/
492 http://bit.ly/Canada-pregnacy

When my wife was pregnant, I remember for both her pregnancies, the excitement of seeing our children on the ultrasound monitor for the first time at the local clinic. It really was a magical moment.

Unfortunately, I didn't know then what I know now.

What I know now is that, despite medical assurances of safety, ultrasound is NOT just sound waves. It uses non-ionizing radiation.

### The US Food and Drug Administration's (FDA) admits that ultrasound uses non-ionizing radiation.[493]

I don't think I need to remind you of the dangers of even low levels of non-ionizing radiation.

According to Dr. Kelly Brogan, today's ultrasound machines have significantly higher peak exposure levels and intensity (from 46 to 720 mW/cm2) than earlier versions. And these "newer versions remain largely unstudied, frequently defective, and without federal requirements for operator training".[494]

Research conducted by author Jeanice Barcelo[495] points to a string of potential dangers for fetuses exposed to ultrasound scans:

- Similar biological damage to that caused by X-rays[496]
- DNA single and double strand breaks[497 498]
- Deformities and mutations in offspring[499]
- Growth restriction[500]

Not to mention the harm that ultrasound can inflict on the pregnant mother, including decreased ovulation rates and damage to the menstrual cycle.

Am I saying, don't use ultrasound under any circumstances? Absolutely not. But understand the dangers and then decide what's right for you. If you're not clear on the risks involved with ultrasound, I recommend you read Jeanice Barcelo's

493 https://www.fda.gov/radiation-emitting-products/medical-imaging/ultrasound-imaging
494 https://kellybroganmd.com/human-studies-condemn-ultrasound/
495 https://www.electricsense.com/ultrasound-pregnancy-risks/
496 https://www.ncbi.nlm.nih.gov/pubmed/7455124
497 http://bit.ly/academia-ultrasound
498 https://ncbi.nlm.nih.gov/pmc/articles/PMC5413823/
499 J. Thacker, 1973. "The Possibility of Genetic Hazard from Ultrasonic Radiation", *Current Topics in Radiation Research Quarterly*, 8, pp 235–258.
500 D.B. Rivers, et al., 1972. Changes in the rate of development of chick embryos subject to diagnostic pulsed ultrasound, Proc 17thAnn Meeting of Am Inst Ultrasound in Med, , p 20; R.M. Moore, 1982. "Effects of sonic radiation on growth and development", Am J Epidemiology, 116, p. 571.

book, *The Dark Side of Prenatal Ultrasound and the Dangers of Non-Ionizing Radiation – Part 1.*

Difficulty getting pregnant, increased risk of miscarriage, birth defects and other health complications in later life, not to mention behavioral problems further down the line for exposed fetuses (Chapter 17), all this makes for a very rocky road. How about we talk about solutions?

## Tips For Pregnant Women

If you are a pregnant mother, you are in the category which I consider to be most at risk. It's a question of protecting yourself AND your future baby. I could just say apply every single recommendation I make in this guide as best as you possibly can. But I guess that would be a bit daunting. Let me make it easier by giving you my top five tips for pregnant mothers:

1. Only use cell phones in absolute dire emergencies
2. As far as possible, banish ALL forms of wireless (Wi-Fi, Bluetooth devices, etc.) from your home
3. Do not use personal wireless devices of any kind (fitness trackers, etc.) and avoid spending time around people that use these devices
4. Either call in an EMF consultant to get your home checked for wired and wireless EMF hotspots and/or invest in EMF meters and follow the steps laid out in this guide to do it yourself
5. Go through Chapter 11 again on creating a low EMF sleep sanctuary and apply as many tips as you possibly can.

If you have a job that requires working in an office where there are a lot of wireless devices or your job requires that you regularly use your cell phone, then I would seriously consider taking a nine-month sabbatical. This might sound extreme but it's your future baby's survival and life-long health that's potentially at risk here.

What about shielding your tummy? You can buy protective clothing specially designed to shield your pregnant tummy but there are risks which few people are aware of.

My biggest concern is that any kind of shielding, unless it's done properly—meaning applying the golden rule of measure/shield/measure—can increase your exposures.

Obviously, measuring from inside the bump is impossible. Meaning we are totally in the dark as to the effectiveness of this kind of shielding. I'd love to be able to share some studies as to the effectiveness of this kind of shielding, but I don't know of any. Companies selling tummy shields have a moral duty to speak openly about the limitations of their product.

**Beware of misleading advertising regarding tummy shields for pregnant women—it's possible that partial shielding of this type could significantly increase your future baby's EMF exposures.**

Apply the five tips above. That is the BEST form of EMF protection for your future baby. I talk in detail about the downsides of protective clothing in Chapter 19, I strongly recommend you read that chapter before you rush out and buy anything like this.

## Recommendations For Women Of Childbearing Age

If you are pregnant, applying the five tips I shared above as fully as you can is an absolute NO-BRAINER. It might fly in the face of convention, but it doesn't matter. If you are pregnant and you've bought this guide, just let your maternal instincts do the rest.

If you're not pregnant and you'd like to get pregnant in the near or distant future, my recommendations are essentially the same as above. What changes as you get closer to actually getting pregnant is your level of commitment in applying these protection tips.

| Your Personal Situation | Your Degree of Commitment |
|---|---|
| You're trying to get pregnant | High |
| You might want to get pregnant one day | Lower |
| You're not interested in getting pregnant | Lower still |

I'm not saying that your degree of commitment should be lower if you're not interested in getting pregnant, I'm just making the observation that it probably will be.

If you're not of childbearing age, then my recommendations are the same as for everybody else. Just to be clear, I recommend a low-EMF lifestyle for EVERYONE, but pregnant women and women of childbearing age have a particular responsibility to go low EMF.

What you need to retain from this chapter:

- Nearly 70 research studies show how EMFs can promote breast cancer
- Reduced levels of melatonin can lead to higher levels of estrogen, which increases the risk of breast cancer—this may be the principal "EMF cause"
- Carrying your cell phone in your bra is a risk factor for breast cancer
- Studies indicate that women who are trying to get pregnant who are exposed to EMFs from cell towers etc., have a reduced chance of getting pregnant
- Magnetic field exposures can increase the risk of miscarriage THREE-fold
- Infertility caused through EMF exposures is a major concern for women because when a woman's eggs are zapped by EMFs, the eggs that are lost are gone forever
- If you are a pregnant mother, you need to be particularly vigilant about protecting yourself from EMFs
- Women of child-bearing age generally need to take extra care to protect themselves from EMFs.

# Chapter 19

# Advanced EMF Solutions

When I first started reacting to my cell phone in 2002, I really didn't understand much about EMFs. Truth be told, I didn't want to understand. I just wanted whatever was happening to me to stop happening and to be able to get on with my life.

I didn't have an overall strategy either. I was just haphazardly trying and buying everything and anything. That's what I'm going to talk about in this chapter.

Perhaps you are electrically hypersensitive, reacting to very minute exposure level. Perhaps you just want to take EMF protection to the next level, to know what to do and what not to do. Either way, this chapters for you. Let's first get clear on what not to do.

## EMF Gadgets

By EMF gadgets, I mean things like cell phone chips, diodes, holographic stickers, harmonizers, resonators, neutralizers and similar. The companies selling these EMF gadgets have some very clever marketing with strong claims. Sometimes these claims are backed up by research. That's why many of these products look so convincing.

**The common denominator with all these gadgets is that it's impossible to achieve a measurable reduction in your exposure using these devices—by measurable I mean lower readings on an EMF meter.**

In 2002–2004, when I was struggling to deal with my symptoms, I kept getting convinced. I kept buying EMF gadgets. This might sound frivolous of me, but when you're in pain every day and someone offers you what seems like a magic pill that will make it go away, it's hard to refuse.

This was 15+ years ago. Today the Internet is awash with these devices. And their marketing is yet more sophisticated. It's often laced with research and testimonials from satisfied customers and even money-back guarantees.

## Buyer Beware

I need to warn you about unscrupulous companies. For legal reasons, I can't name names, but research and testimonials can easily be bought and paid for.

Yes, even research can be bought and paid for. This should come as no surprise to you because, as I laid out in Chapter 3, the telecom industry has been doing this on a large scale for decades.

These companies pay to have research done but, in reality, they pay for a desired result. And they put testimonials on their website from friends or family members or they just make them up.

There are companies that do appear to have created a product that offers some beneficial effect.[501] For instance, these can include reduction of heating effects from cell phone use, reduction of DNA damage in laboratory animals, and reduction of Rouleaux Formation (blood cells sticking together).

But from Chapters 4 and 5 you know that EMFs can impact you biologically in a myriad of ways. What use is an EMF gadget if it reduces Rouleaux Formation but does not protect you from DNA damage? What use is an EMF gadget that protects your DNA but not your mitochondria?

**No EMF gadget I am aware of can protect you from ALL the adverse biological effects of EMFs.**

All this might sound as though I'm telling you not to buy any of these products. I am NOT. What I'm saying is that cell phone chips, diodes, holographic stickers, harmonizers, resonators, neutralizers and similar devices should NOT form the basis of your approach to dealing with EMFs.

501 https://www.createhealthyhomes.com/cellphone_chips.php

## The Dangers Of EMF Gadgets

1. Studies say the effects of EMF exposures are cumulative. Given that no EMF gadget protects you from ALL the adverse biological effects of EMFs, what sense does it make to continue exposing yourself to a potentially catastrophic build-up of exposures?
2. An EMF protection gadget that makes it so you can't feel these exposures might sound attractive. But if you continue to be biologically affected, how can this be a good thing?
3. Most of these gadgets are about making these EMFs safe somehow. But should EMF protection be about artificially devising ways of enabling your body to endure higher and higher doses of EMF exposure? This doesn't sit well with my philosophy, which is one of respecting and being in harmony with nature.
4. The risk is, your EMF gadget only masks your symptoms, similar to how a lot of prescription medication works. It's much better to deal with the root cause of your symptoms. Reducing your EMF exposures in a way that can be easily measured sits well with this approach.
5. These devices can lull you into a false sense of security—they make you feel protected when in fact your mind has fooled you into thinking the device is protecting you in some way.

This "fooling" can be likened to the placebo effect. The mind is very powerful. So powerful that if you truly believe something will heal you, then it almost certainly will. There is a good deal of science behind this. This happened to me time and time again.

**I spent the best part of two years and $25,000 buying and trying everything I could get my hands on that offered hope in any shape or form to make my symptoms go away.**

Sometimes I wouldn't feel any relief at all. Sometimes I would feel better for a few weeks, then my symptoms would come back, sometimes with a vengeance. Unfortunately, long-term, none of these devices worked for me. I'm not the only one saying this. If you look at my website, it's littered with testimonials from people saying the same thing.

That's not to say there isn't a place for these devices. Some people do appear to benefit from using EMF gadgets. Is there a genuine healing effect? Or is it placebo? Does it matter?

If there is a genuine healing effect, then obviously there is every reason to buy. Unfortunately, this is very difficult to determine because most, if not all, of these devices claim to work at a subtle energy or quantum level, where it's hard to perceive any measurable benefit.

If there is a placebo effect—healing caused because you believe in the EMF gadget—then that leads to other questions. Why spend money on a device where there is no inherent benefit? What happens when you realize there is no real benefit and stop believing? If it is about placebo, then why not use brain retraining, meditation and similar protocols to create a healing effect, which would put you in control rather than relying on a gadget? Annie Hopper's neural retraining system has helped many people overcome electrical hypersensitivity.[502]

Building Biologists and most EMF consultants advise that you focus on finding and reducing sources of EMFs, particularly in your home and office, rather than just trying to neutralize their effects.

To summarize:

1. Be aware of the limitations of any device that offers EMF protection that can't be easily measured.
2. Only use such devices as an adjunct, something you add for good measure. Don't rely on them as your sole means of protection. Call upon a Building Biologist or other EMF expert to identify and reduce the presence of EMFs, rather than rely on subtle energy devices to neutralize the effects of EMFs on your body.
3. Some of these devices can become "negatively charged" and start working against you. If you are symptomatic, have occasional abstinence periods where you stop using the device to see if you feel better without it.
4. Only buy from a reputable company where they offer at least a 30-day money back guarantee.
5. Work with an experienced kinesiologist who can muscle test to find precisely the EMF gadget that works best for you.

---

502 As discussed in an EMF Experts Solutions Club interview with Annie Hopper. If you are electrically hypersensitive, I strongly encourage you to explore learning how to break/reprogram the pattern of disease—this is an essential part of the healing process for most people.

The primary place where "EMF gadgets" could be of use is when you are out of your home, away from the environment that you can control and protect.

## The Fundamentals

The reason my initial approach wasn't working, and the reason it doesn't work for many people, is because I was overlooking the fundamentals. The reason I overlooked the fundamentals is because I didn't realize there were any fundamentals!

I just thought I needed to deal with the EMF I was reacting to. In my case, it was my cell phone. So that became my focus. Which is why I went down the "chips, diodes and harmonizers" route.

Big mistake. You shouldn't only deal with cell phone radiation if the only EMFs you can feel are those emitted by your cell phone.

On the contrary, our bodies are impacted by many different EMFs at a range of different frequencies on a 24-hour basis. This is a scientific fact.

Here are the fundamentals you need to always keep in mind, or UMM as I like to call it:

1. Understand your exposures. That means looking at ALL four categories of EMFs: magnetic fields, electric fields, radio frequency radiation, and dirty electricity
2. Measure—use good quality EMF meters to identify hotspots and obtain readings
3. Mitigate.

The third step, mitigation, means doing one or more of the following:

1. Turn off and eliminate the source of the EMFs
2. Increase distance—move the source further away from you or you move further away from the source
3. Shield yourself from the source.

So, there are three fundamentals, **UMM**, and three ways to mitigate. All this should come as no surprise—it's what I've been saying throughout this guide! If you are electrically hypersensitive, that means you need to rigorously apply these fundamentals. And you've probably noticed there is one aspect that I haven't talked about yet, which is shielding.

## Getting Rigorous In The Bedroom

Yes, we're back to the bedroom again because, as you learned in Chapter 11, your bedroom needs to be your healing haven. Creating a low EMF bedroom is your ABSOLUTE priority.

The only way to get rigorous in the bedroom is to first know what you are dealing with. That means getting readings for ALL four categories of EMFs, which you can do with just two EMF meters and a multimeter in under an hour. See my cheat sheet with step-by-step guidance on measuring EMFs in the bedroom at www.electricsense.com/bookbonus

Here's a reminder of the benchmark readings I shared in Chapter 6:[503]

| Benchmark Levels | | | |
|---|---|---|---|
| Radio Frequency Radiation | Electric Fields | Magnetic Fields | Dirty Electricity |
| 0.02 V/m | 1 V/m* or 100 mV** | 0.5 mG | 50 GS units |

*This is using an ungrounded electric field meter.[504] **mV is the body voltage reading.

By comparing your readings with the benchmark readings, you then determine where you need to focus your efforts.

A really effective way of dealing with electric fields in the bedroom is to get an electrician to install an automated or remote control cut-off switch. I've been sleeping with an automated cut-off switch in my bedroom for +10 years. Power is automatically cut off when there is nothing switched on in my bedroom—thereby eliminating associated electric fields, magnetic fields, and dirty electricity. When I switch a light on, the circuit is powered up. See www.electricsense.com/bookbonus for more details.

Let's say you're getting high readings for RF radiation. Assuming you're not able to sleep in a better location and you're not able to eliminate the source of the

503 Remember, I'm not saying these are safe levels, but if for instance you can get RF radiation levels down to 0.02 Volts/meter (V/m), then these are what I consider low levels.

504 Most electric field meters are ungrounded, which introduces a greater margin of error.

radiation because it's coming in from outside, that means you need to consider shielding options.

Three things I want to say upfront:

1. It can be complicated to effectively shield, so shielding should only be undertaken as an absolute LAST RESORT
2. Shielding should ONLY be done using an EMF meter, following the simple protocol: measure your exposures/shield/measure your exposures
3. Running headlong into shielding without following this simple protocol can not only be disappointing, it can also be dangerous because you can make matters WORSE—you can increase your exposures.

**First measure. Then shield. Then measure again.**

If you take readings with your EMF meter, then you shield, then you measure again and your readings after shielding are higher than before you shielded, that means you need to work on your shielding again. Keep refining your shielding until your readings improve—if they don't improve, then remove the shielding.

**When you shield from outdoor RF sources, that means that RF signals from indoor wireless devices will continue to be present, and worse yet, those signals will reflect off the inside of your shielding and amplify in your living space.**

The solution is to switch over to hardwired options for anything that is wireless in your home, including telephone, Internet, streaming TV, music speakers, thermostats, surveillance cameras, baby monitors, and so on.

There are two ways to go about shielding in the bedroom:

1. Shielding just the bed
2. Shielding the entire room.

Let's talk about the shielding just your bed first.

## Shielding Your Bed

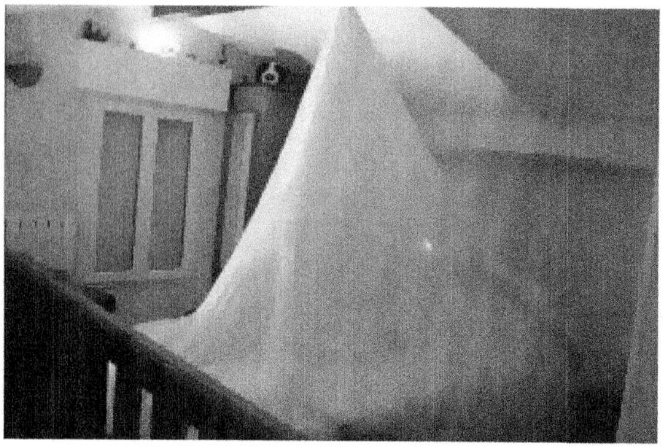

What I like about this approach is that it's simple and effective to do, using a faraday canopy.

This is what a faraday canopy looks like (picture on left). It looks like a mosquito net but instead of keeping out mosquitoes, its job is to keep RF microwave radiation out.

**The objective is to create a sealed enclosure—similar to a Faraday cage.** This can be a VERY effective way of shielding yourself from RF radiation. And it's very easy to apply. But there are some cons.

The cons:

1. You need to budget around $1000 or more for a double bed-sized canopy
2. Not everyone is comfortable sleeping under a big net
3. If the fabric is not groundable, you can *increase* electric field EMFs while you protect yourself from RF—see below.

How to choose your faraday bed canopy:

1. **Only buy from a reputable company.** Some companies don't offer refunds for faraday canopies. Check that before you order.
2. **Look for good shielding performance.** This is a key point. There's usually a trade-off between shielding performance and density of the netting. High shielding performance can mean the netting is heavy and thick and doesn't allow for much air circulation. That can make it very difficult for you to sleep under it. If, on the other hand, the material is lightweight, it may not offer such good shielding performance. You can check for this with your RF meter.

## What Is Good Shielding Performance?

Shielding performance is usually given in decibels (dB) for a certain frequency, or percentage of shielding, known as attenuation or weakening of the signal. For instance, if the shielding performance of the canopy you are interested in is rated at

20 dB, that equates to about a 99% reduction in field strength.[505] So, if the shielding performance is shown as 90% up to 6 GHz, you know that only 10% of cell phone radiation, Wi-Fi and other frequencies up to 6 GHz will penetrate your canopy.[506]

Is this sufficient? Probably, yes. But there is no definitive answer. A lot depends on how extreme your symptoms are.

> ***Anything over 20 dB is generally starting to get fairly good. Often, the difference between the shielding material is not the material itself but how well it's placed. Are you surrounding the source enough, are you surrounding yourself enough?***
>
> *—MICHAEL R NEUERT, MA, BSME, EMF EXPERTS SOLUTIONS CLUB INTERVIEW.*

Two other things to bear in mind regarding shielding performance:

1. **Check the technical specifications for the shielding performance BEFORE you buy.** If these specs are not shown, that is a red flag. Only buy when you are clear as to the shielding performance.
2. **Take care when washing your canopy.** Some canopies are fragile and washing them can break the threads and severely reduce the shielding performance. Follow the manufacturer's instructions for washing and test with your EMF meter after a wash to make sure it's still shielding properly.

Other important points:

1. Even if you buy a faraday canopy, you still need to apply the shielding protocol (measure/shield/measure). DO NOT just assume the shielding works.
2. If you are not on the ground floor, remember to ensure you create a sealed enclosure. That will usually mean you need a floor mat under your bed to shield from radiation coming up from below with shielding on the sides reaching town to contact the mat on the floor.

505 A 10 dB reduction is equal to 90%, 20 dB to 99%, 30 dB to 99.9% reduction, and so on.

506 Oram Miller comments that the dB rating of RF-shielding fabrics listed on various EMF-related catalogues and websites is determined under laboratory conditions. You may measure somewhat less reduction with your own RF meter due to reflections and other factors, so use these dB numbers as a general, not absolute, guide and anticipate that your shielding will probably be less.

3. If you live in an apartment or condo wired with regular plastic jacketed wiring and your bed is against a shared wall containing circuits for the neighbor that you cannot shut off, you should move the bed across the room or sleep in another room that does not share a wall with a neighbor.[507]
4. Be mindful of electric fields. All canopies are very conductive (that is how they block RF signals) and can create an electric field issue when electrical circuits are in walls next to the bed and/or you have plastic lamp cords laying close to, or worse yet, inside the bed canopy. That is to say, the canopy may solve your RF radiation problem but amplify an existing electric field at the bed. Always measure with your electric field meter (or multimeter meter) to see if you have high electric fields when you are in your canopy.[508] [509]

This story, shared by EMF consultant Joe Darnell,[510] highlights this last point:

> ***We have a bed canopy to shield from some of the radio tower issues and the cell tower issues that we had, and I was doing it wrong for quite a while. If you touch something that's blocking—and a lot of these materials are really good at shielding or blocking wireless frequencies—as soon as you touch that, you become a part of that. So instead of all the electricity [from the plastic circuits in walls and floor] being blocked and travelling into the blanket or into the canopy, it then travels through you, which raises your contact current. If I touch my canopy, mine raises up to 150 microamps, which is well above 18 microamps. If you do that all night long...***[511]

Research conducted by the Electrical Power Research Institute shows that contact currents over 18 microamps are associated with cancer.[512]

One last thing. Sleeping in a faraday canopy is not "normal". Remember, we are surrounded by countless different frequencies, both beneficial and non-beneficial.

507 You could also shield the shared wall with grounded shielding paint—see next section.

508 Typically you would compare your body voltage meter reading without the canopy and then inside the canopy (make sure the reading does not go up when you touch the canopy—it should go way down when it is properly grounded). At the very least shut off the breaker(s) of circuits in walls and under the floor of that bedroom at night to reduce electric fields where you sleep, whether you use a grounded bed canopy or not.

509 You can purchase a bed canopy with groundable fabric. SwissShield makes a canopy fabric that can be grounded. The preferred method of grounding is with a stake in the garden—see Chapter 9. ALWAYS follow the manufacturer's recommendations on grounding your canopy.

510 Joe Darnell, EMF consultant, EMF Experts Solutions Club interview.

511 Grounding a canopy made with shieldable fabric should avoid this problem.

512 https://www.ncbi.nlm.nih.gov/pubmed/11015118

Sleeping under a faraday canopy might do a good job of blocking out harmful man-made exposures but it also shields you from the earth's natural (and mostly very subtle) beneficial frequencies. It can also reflect back to you your own frequencies, as physicist Guy Hudson[513] explains.

> ***Faraday cages, the standard ones, are made purely of reflective materials. So, if you've got an overactive electrical immune system, when you go into the purely reflective thing, it's like going into a hall of mirrors. So, what you're doing is you're getting back your own signals far more powerfully than you're used to.***
>
> *—GUY HUDSON, PHYSICIST AND EMF CONSULTANT, EMF EXPERTS SOLUTION CLUB INTERVIEW.*

**For this reason, sleeping under a faraday canopy should be a temporary measure—this is my personal opinion. Some experts disagree with this.**

If you are electrically hypersensitive, a faraday canopy is a good way of buying some time for six months or a year or so. During which time you can concentrate on mitigating ALL the EMF exposures in your life and also address your health holistically—see the next chapter—to heal your hypersensitivity so you can eventually phase out the canopy.

## Shielding Your Bedroom

This IS more complicated than installing a faraday canopy. And if you shield incorrectly, you could make matters worse.

**For this reason, my number one recommendation if you want to shield your bedroom, is to work with an EMF consultant.**

Ideally, the EMF consultant would do the shielding themselves or they would supervise the work of a painter and electrician. The supervision can be done

513 Guy Hudson, physicist and EMF consultant, EMF Experts Solution Club interview.

"on-site", so they come to your home or it can be done via telephone (preferably a landline or VOIP!). To find an EMF expert locally, contact:

1. The Building Biology Institute[514]
2. Geovital International[515]

There are other competent EMF consultants that don't formally belong to either of these organizations.[516] Also, word of mouth is often the best way of finding someone locally.

## How To Shield Your Bedroom

I strongly recommend shielding your bedroom with the assistance/supervision of an EMF consultant. But I know that no matter what I say, some of you will want to do this yourself—the main reason being to save money. I can't deny that doing it yourself will be cheaper BUT it will be difficult to achieve the same level of mitigation that a professional can give, particularly when it comes to which materials to choose, where to put them, and how to avoid missteps. Another often-overlooked pitfall is that you may well solve one EMF problem and create another.

That said, here are some pointers for DIY shielding from RF radiation:

1. Follow the simple protocol: measure/shield/measure
2. First, try and determine the sources of the RF exposure and reduce them
3. If they are coming from inside your home, try to find hardwired alternatives so you can turn off those sources
4. If they are coming from outside your home, shielding may be your only solution.

There are two ways to go about shielding your bedroom from RF radiation:

1. Using special shielding paints and materials to create a Faraday cage effect. This will mean shielding windows, doors, floor and ceiling. Special

514 If you are in the US or Canada, see: https://buildingbiologyinstitute.org/ if you live in another country see https://buildingbiology.com/

515 See https://en.geovital.com/

516 Some of these consultants have taken Building Biology training and become certified, for instance, but have not yet joined the Building Biology Institute, and therefore do not yet appear in the Institute's website directory.

shielding film can be used for the windows. Non-metallic window frames need to be painted.

2. Partial shielding. This solution works when most of the radiation is coming from one direction. You would first determine with your EMF meter which the radiation is coming from. Then you would shield that wall or perhaps two walls.

This latter partial shielding option is favored by several EMF consultants I've interviewed. The advantage of partial shielding is it's a lot easier and less expensive than full Faraday cage-style shielding. Sometimes you might start out with the partial shielding option, which morphs into full shielding as you realize that that is the best way to get the lowest readings.

There are many shielding products on the market. Let me talk about what I've used:

1. Y-shield paint for shielding RF—easy to apply. Can be used indoors or outdoors. Usually requires several coats to shield effectively. It's black, so you will need several coats of paint or paper to cover over it. Gives 30+ dB of RF shielding up to 18 GHz.[517]
2. Giron—this is for magnetic field shielding, which is a whole different ball game. But this is good stuff (see below).[518]
3. Special netting, also for RF—I bought it years ago. I'm not sure of the performance but my EMF meter tells me it still shields.
4. Mylar, also for RF (see below).

## Low Cost Shielding

Are you looking for an inexpensive way to shield RF that comes in from outside? Here are some suggestions for shielding a room for under $100:

| Product name | Comment | Price |
|---|---|---|
| Mylar film | Sold as a thermal blanket | < $5 |
| Aluminum foil | Sold as cooking foil | < $5 |
| Aluminum or steel window screen | Sold as insect screen | < $10 |

517 Effective shielding with RF-shielding paint probably extends beyond 18 GHz into the mmW super-20 GHz high band that everyone is talking about with 5G—see Chapter 12.

518 Y-Shield, mesh and fabric/netting does not block magnetic fields.

All these products have their pros and cons. Very low-grade aluminum foil can be fragile and tear easily, it can also create humidity. Mylar tends to be more robust, but humidity can also be a problem. Depending on what you are trying to shield, an aluminum or steel window screen can be a better choice.

With regard to the aluminum/steel window screen, EMF expert Michael Neuert explains:

> ***I believe most of the screen that's out there we call 16 mesh, where in an inch there would be 16 wires. You can probably go as wide as 12 wires in an inch but 16 is good, 24 is better. The finer the mesh, the better*** **[for RF shielding].**

In both instances you would need to measure/shield/measure. And also ground. Usually.

> ***In some cases, we unground some surfaces which normally should be grounded but the end result is better ungrounded.***
>
> —*Stephane Belainsky, electromagnetic hygiene technician, EMF Experts Solutions Club interview.*

A few final points:

1. Your RF and electric field/body voltage meter/s will tell you if the shielding works better grounded or not grounded—in other words, go with the option that gives you the lowest RF and electric field reading. If electric fields are high, you must ground the material.
2. You will only shield as a last resort—I know I've said that before, but I can't overstate how important this is.

## Extreme RF Shielding

An increasingly common problem is in apartment buildings where there are multiple smart meters for different apartments situated in close proximity to bedrooms.

"You don't want to live in the unit next to the place where the electricity comes in for the entire building", comments Oram Miller. Not only will there likely be high RF levels from the smart meters, you will likely also have high magnetic fields. This is because of proximity to the back of the meters and main shut off switches for each apartment. You can also have magnetic fields due to wiring errors and current on grounding wires and metal conduits running under or over the unit closest to these meters and shut off switches. It is usually an EMF nightmare in the room adjacent to these meters and switches. Avoid them altogether.

When I interviewed Building Biologist Diana Schultz, she told me about a gentleman who was living in a one-story condo building in San Antonio, Texas. On the outside of his master bedroom, there were nine smart meters! Twenty feet away on the next building, there were another nine smart meters aimed right at his building, at his window.

Diana shielded all the windows in his condo with a film. Then, on that one wall nearest the smart meters, not the rest of the bedroom, she put up two layers of foil and staple-gunned them right to the drywall. She then installed another layer of drywall on top of that so that the client could hang pictures and have use of a regular wall. She says, "you couldn't tell it was there. And it knocked it all completely out".

Again, this is an extreme case that shows it is possible to effectively shield but, in cases like this, calling in an EMF consultant is often the best option.

## Magnetic Field Shielding

A quick word about advanced ways to shield from magnetic fields (I covered magnetic fields in Chapters 2 and 9). These are by far the hardest type of EMF to shield from. The problem is magnetic fields go through just about everything. That's to say, regular building materials, even metal, offer no protection at all. So, what can be done?

It all depends upon what's causing your magnetic field. Fortunately, you can easily figure that out with your EMF meter. If it's something in your home, like being too close to your electrical breaker panel or your refrigerator, then a specialized shielding material like Giron can be used successfully in some cases.

Magnetic fields coming from electric meters and breaker panels are only related to how much electric current is running through them at any given time.[519] The more lights and other devices you have turned on in the house, the higher the magnetic field will be and the farther it will extend out from the meter and panel. The magnetic field around meters and panels is purely due to the fact that the hot and neutral wires

519 The Building Biology profession has recommendations for electricians to help them choose breaker panel models and ways to wire them up to minimize magnetic fields.

inside of it are separated by up to several inches (and farther apart inside a breaker panel), unlike circuits where the hot and neutral wire are side-by-side.

We also want to keep as much return current flowing as possible on the neutral wire of the electric services wires going out of the house back to the electric utility transformer as is coming in on the hot wires. This means minimizing current on parallel metallic paths that current can take to get off the property and flow back to the neighborhood transformer (these parallel paths can include the metal water service pipe and TV cable sheathing—see Chapter 9).

**Magnetic field shielding works differently to other types of shielding, as it is only capable of compressing and redirecting magnetic field flux lines, NEVER eliminating them.**

You have to angle the shielding so that it redirects the flux lines away from where you want to provide shielding. If you overcompensate and angle the shielding so that it is directly perpendicular to the flux lines, they will simply pass right through the material as if it wasn't there.

Also, you cannot have any sharp edges. You must curve the shielding material around corners because you want the flux lines to follow the contours of the material.

Successful shielding of magnetic fields is a very tricky business, one that confounds the experts. Many Building Biologists are of the opinion that it is generally not a successful undertaking in many cases. You have to have enough room to extend your shielding in all directions on a flat surface, such as a wall when trying to shield a point source, such as a breaker panel. If the source is large, as with a large electric service panel cabinet, the magnetic fields will pass through the earth underneath and circle right up through the floor of the adjoining room that you may be trying to protect. How are you going to shield against that?

You will have the best luck shielding relatively small point sources,[520] such as a breaker panel mounted on a wall, and much less success with a large source, such as a large stand-alone electric panel cabinet in an apartment or a transformer. Also, floors are difficult to shield from current on metal water pipes in the ceiling of the underground garage of an apartment building.[521]

520 Point source magnetic fields are emitted by devices such as refrigerators, stoves, fans, transformers, etc. See Chapter 9.

521 Building Biologists recommend not living in an apartment or condo unit on the first floor.

Emil de Toffel, founder of LessEMF, explains how to shield the magnetic fields from an electric meter:

> *If you're standing inside the building and you're looking at the wall where the electric meters are located [whether they are smart or analog], imagine that you could put a little "x" on the wall where each of them is mounted. If it's possible, if there's enough wall space surrounding that area, then you can put magnetic shielding up on that wall and get a very good result. If you're starting out with 6 mG at the wall, then you can reduce that easily by a factor of three or four getting to say 2 milligauss or so. And then, as you move away from the wall, naturally the levels decrease even further than that.*
>
> *The answer is yes, you can do it. You're going to use a material called Giron, which is a flexible material. In other words, it can be rolled out or it can be laid flat on the wall or attached to the wall... the way you approach this is you take your Gaussmeter and you make a grid on your wall. An imaginary one-foot grid and get a piece of paper and draw that grid. And then you're going to make readings in each of those one-foot squares. What you're looking for here is the pattern on the wall of the hot zone, we call it. That is all that area of the wall that reads above your desired level. So, let's say your target level is 2 mG, you're going to map up how much of that wall reads at 2 mG or higher. And that's how much of that wall you're going to cover with the magnetic shielding.*

Whatever magnetic field reading you measure just beyond the edge of the shielding you put up, that is how much you will have in the room you are measuring just on the other side of the object producing the field (such as a breaker panel). The further you extend Giron or other magnetic field shielding out to the sides and above and below the source, the lower the reading will be just on the other side of the shielding from where the source is located. Hopefully this makes sense. Remember, magnetic fields are going to go around the edge of any shield you put up on the wall, so extend your shielding out far enough in all four directions that the strength of the field that does go around the edge is minimal, as close to 1 mG as possible.[522]

522 Information supplied by Oram Miller, Building Biologist.

Two more tips:

1. Make sure you measure at different times of the day and even on different days to get reliable readings. This is because electric currents can vary at different times of the day and from one day (or even moment) to the next.
2. There are other materials that can be used for magnetic field shielding, but Giron is widely regarded as being a very cost-effective solution.

However, if the source of magnetic fields is an overhead powerline, for instance, these magnetic fields are too large to be successfully shielded with any material. The technical solution would be to make an enclosure, that is to say, a complete box around your home with magnetic shielding, but that's just not practical. Moving to another house might be the only realistic solution.

## The Double-Edged Sword

RF shielding can have favorable consequences. But it can also have some VERY unfavorable consequences if you neglect to eliminate cell phone, Wi-Fi, and any form of wireless radiation from within your shielded area.

A common mistake is shielding your bedroom but then bringing your cell phone in your bedroom. This will have a "microwave oven effect" on whatever is inside the shielded area (you). The email below indicates how this "microwave oven effect" can also be an issue when using personal shielding solutions.

> ***I am on call for heart surgery 24/7. I sleep with my phone next to me, but in a Faraday bag with the opening facing away from me. Obviously, I can't seal the bag, or I couldn't be reached... is this helping at all?***
>
> —*Marion (received by email)*

I replied to Marion saying that she should absolutely NOT sleep with her phone under any circumstances. If she needed to be reached by phone during the night, she should put her phone as far away as possible but have it sufficiently close that she can still hear it when it rings.

## Other Bedroom/Nighttime Tips

I'll assume you've already actioned ALL the recommendations I laid out in Chapter 11 for the bedroom. If not, go back there now and do whatever else you can do.

Here are some tips to take things to the next level in your bedroom and at nighttime:

1. **Replace your mattress**. When was the last time you replaced your mattress? My recommendation is to buy a chemical-free, organic mattress that does not contain metal springs and use a wood frame and headboard for the bed.
2. **Get rid of anything with metal in it**. Mattresses with metal springs can worsen the effects of EMFs.[523] There is also the issue of residual geomagnetism found in metal bed springs. Metal objects generally can make EMFs bounce around your bedroom in unpredictable ways. However, Building Biologists point out that metal objects do not in and of themselves cause EMFs. They reflect and amplify electric and magnetic fields that are in the room from other sources.
3. **Eliminate harsh modern lighting from your bedroom.** Candle-light and traditional incandescent light bulbs are preferred. Think about the kind of light you see at sunset. This is what you want to mimic, with low levels of blue light.
4. **Use blackout curtains.** With so much street lighting everywhere, darkness is becoming a rarity. I've been sleeping in total darkness for years via a combination of French shutters and thick curtains. It's an easy way to boost your body's ability to produce the wonderful hormone, melatonin! Also, melatonin is enhanced by carefully figuring out which circuits to shut off in and around your bedroom at night, as I covered in Chapter 11.
5. **Use a battery-powered alarm clock.** I'm just throwing this one in here but if the power is off in your bedroom at night, you'll already have figured this one out.

So, what about using shielded clothing to protect yourself from EMFs?

523 https://pdfs.semanticscholar.org/5e39/a4cf96c56ef7f5678ea6baf7109a5bb8f10d.pdf

## Shielded Clothing

There are so many personal shielding products on the market:

- Hats
- Head nets
- Gloves
- Scarves
- Hoodies
- Jeans
- Sleeveless blouses
- Pants
- Boxer shorts
- Aprons
- Sleeping Bags
- Body Nets

Sleeping bags are not clothes. I included them because I wanted to give them a mention. People have reported getting relief from shielded sleeping bags which cover you head to toe. Apply the same selection criteria when choosing your shielded sleeping bag as for the faraday canopy above.

Unfortunately, shielding clothing, as in shielded garments that you wear every day, is another controversial subject. Some people swear by them. Like Ian:[524]

> *I wear a small Silverell t-shirt to protect my heart as I get afib [abnormal heartbeat]... this shirt alone reduces the incidence of my afib attacks by 90% or more... when I don't wear the shirt, I am in afib all the time... so it works.*

Others, like Thomas, say they make their symptoms worse:

> *I made a hood out of EMF blocking fabric and wore it under my hats and when I slept. It made my insomnia worse, not better! The best solution for me is to avoid places where there is known Wi-Fi cordless phones, etc.*

Experts are also divided:

> *Appropriate garments can reduce microwave exposures in genital organs and breasts, but do not necessarily reduce EHS symptoms as the pulsing signals are still getting into your body's nervous system via arms, legs and head. I suggest that if you want to try screening clothing then you try just one or two items and see if you find them helpful.*
>
> —ALASDAIR PHILIPS, ELECTRICAL ENGINEER, RESEARCHER AND FOUNDER OF POWERWATCH.[525]

524 From ElectricSense.com comments.
525 Alasdair Philips is founder of https://www.powerwatch.org.uk

***Protective clothing works, we have proof, and the people that do it, I would like to say here that people with ALS or MS or Parkinson's, with these serious neurological diseases tremendously benefit from this.***

—DR. DIETRICH KLINGHARDT, EMF HEALTH SUMMIT INTERVIEW.

***People who are EMR sensitive have gotten relief of their symptoms and there can be a measurable verification by reputable EMR specialists using top-of-the-line meters.***

—BILL CADWALLADER, MBA, EMRS, CERTIFIED ELECTROMAGNETIC RADIATION SPECIALIST

So, let me try and bring some clarity to this issue. Below are the pros and cons as I see them.

## The Pros

There are some situations where shielded clothing is an absolute no-brainer:

1. When your symptoms are so extreme you literally can't go out the door without getting zapped so severely that you have difficulty functioning.
2. In specific situations, for instance, when travelling. Planes, trains, automobiles are all cases where shielded clothing can bring necessary relief.

## The Cons

1. Shielded clothing is made from man-made, non-natural materials. Some people can develop a skin rash or other reaction when in contact with these materials.[526]
2. Walking around in a "bee suit" can draw unwanted attention![527]

526 A solution may be to use natural materials, such as cotton and silk, with silver and other metallic threads woven into them to provide RF shielding. Sensitivity is so individualized that you need to just see what works for you, regardless of what anyone else says does or doesn't work for them.

527 A bee suit won't protect you from EMFs. But the kind of full body protection you would need would look like a bee suit made out of special materials.

**Shielded clothing should only be a temporary measure.**

If your symptoms are so extreme that the only way you can go outside and go about your daily business is by wearing shielded clothing, then that's what you must do. But your focus should be on dealing with the root cause of your symptoms. I will talk more about this later. Shielded clothing will at least buy you some time to do this.

## How To Choose Your Shielded Clothing

Here are some tips:

1. Buy from a reputable retailer so you can send your clothing back if you are not happy with it
2. Test your shielded clothing with your EMF meter—you should see a noticeable/measurable reduction in exposure when you take readings with your RF meter "inside" the shielded clothing
3. Fully body shielded clothing offers the best protection. The bee suit is effective but not easy to wear. A combination of shielded hoodie, socks, trousers and head net will give you less conspicuous full body protection
4. Remember that shielded clothing only protects you from radio frequency EMFs. It does NOT stop magnetic nor electric fields. LessEMF does sell a heavy metal-mesh hood that does protect the head from magnetic fields. It resembles chainmail worn by jousters in England during Medieval times.

One last tip: avoid wearing metal-framed glasses. I started wearing plastic-framed glasses some 15 years ago when I discovered research[528] that shows that metal frames can cause a significant increase in EMF.

Here's what you need to retain from this chapter:

- EMF gadgets like cell phone chips, diodes, holographic stickers, harmonizers, resonators and neutralizers might sound enticing but no EMF gadget I am aware of can protect you from ALL the adverse biological effects of EMFs
- It's very difficult to know if there is a genuine healing effect with these EMF gadgets because most of them claim to work at a subtle energy level, where it's hard to perceive any measurable benefit

528 https://link.springer.com/article/10.1007/BF02446229

- Your focus should be on the fundamentals of EMF protection, meaning you need to understand/measure/mitigate using conventional means—only add EMF gadgets into the mix once you've done all this
- With regards to RF radiation, remember to reduce your usage, increase distance and favor hardwired options whenever and wherever possible
- Ultimately, mitigation may mean you have to shield, but you should only shield as an absolute last resort
- The most important room to shield is your bedroom and the easiest way to do this is with a Faraday bed canopy
- Full room shielding is a more comprehensive solution—but it can be difficult to achieve and if you get it wrong, you can make matters worse.
- Partial room shielding can be a better option—you might start out with the partial shielding option which could morph into full shielding if you realize that that is the best way to get your readings the lowest
- It's possible to effectively shield a room for under $100 provided you follow the golden rule of measure/shield/measure
- Magnetic fields are the hardest type of EMF to shield—whole-house solutions are not practical, but localized magnetic fields can be shielded with special materials
- Shielded clothing can offer much needed relief if your symptoms are extreme or if you are travelling, but should only be used as a temporary measure.

Chapter 20

# Natural Solutions To EMFs And Other Toxins

EVERYTHING I'VE TALKED ABOUT SO far in this guide goes under the banner of *direct EMF protection*. In this chapter, I'm going to take things a step further, to what I call *indirect EMF protection*. This information will be invaluable to anybody who wants to take their health to the next level. If you are symptomatic around EMFs, pay particular attention because no matter how rigorously you apply direct EMF protection, chances are you will make little progress with your symptoms without following through on some, if not most, of the steps laid out in this chapter.

Firstly, nutrition. There have been so many books written on this subject, I couldn't hope to do it justice here or be so presumptuous as to tell you what the best diet is for you. Nutrition is super important in a general sense but if you're being bombarded with EMFs and your nutrition is poor, then just think of the damage that can wreak on your cells. This whole cycle of excess calcium, peroxynitrite production and oxidative stress (Chapter 3) is going to be cranked up a notch. What can we do to nutritionally to repair the EMF damage?

There is no one-size fits all. But let me share some broad guidance and resources:

1. **Hydrate.** Optimum hydration is absolutely VITAL. EMFs are contributing to dehydration issues that many of us are experiencing. Just because you're not thirsty, doesn't mean you're not dehydrated. Quantity and quality of water is important but "eight glasses of water a day is not the way". New research has revealed the importance of structured water. For an excellent resource on how to optimally hydrate and incorporate structured water into your diet, read *Quench* by Dr. Dana Cohen and Gina Bria.
2. **Eat whole, natural, and organic foods.** Processed foods are to be avoided. You don't have to go 100% organic and there is no guarantee that organic

produce doesn't contain pesticides and other chemicals but, generally, it will be less polluted and more nutritious.

3. **Eat locally grown produce.** Locally grown food has a better chance of getting on your plate quicker (which means it's fresher) and it avoids the need for excessive refrigeration. It will almost certainly be nutritionally superior to food brought in from the other side of the world.
4. **Eat seasonal.** Seasonal foods tend to be fresher and more nutritionally dense, but it's also about respecting the cycles of nature. Nature has a way of producing certain foods at times when our body needs them, and you should eat them when nature intended.
5. **Include good quality fats in your diet.** Extra-virgin olive oil, coconut oil, palm fruit oil, grass-fed butter and ghee, sesame seed oil, argon oil... Your diet should contain small quantities of a wide variety of organic oils. Getting your omega-3 and omega-6s is important, but there is a lot more to it than that. Notably, consuming good quality fats bolsters hydration. Read *Cellular Awakening* by nutritionist Barbara Wren. Also read *The Big Fat Surprise* by Nina Teicholz.
6. **Establish regular mealtimes.** Also, spicy or acidic foods in the evening can cause stomach trouble and heartburn for sensitive individuals. Avoid difficult to digest foods (cooked meats and raw vegetables) within two hours of bed.
7. **Eat fermented food.** Fermented milk, turnips, eggplant, cucumbers, onions, cabbage, all these foods are chock-full of good bacteria. Research has shown how important the ideal balance of good and bad bacteria in your gut is. Read *Fermented Foods for Health* by Deirdre Rawlings, PhD, ND.

## The Importance of Supplements

In our twenty-first century EMF world, is it really possible to satisfy all your nutritional needs without the need for nutritional supplements? Yes, I believe it is in the long-term. I only take one supplement and I'm going to share below what that is.[529]

But first I want to share with you some supplements that can help your body repair some of the damage caused by EMFs. Again, we don't fully understand all the ways EMFs damage our bodies, but we do know that they create free radicals and, in particular, peroxynitrite.

529 Board Certified Clinical Nutritionist David Getoff, whom I consulted to write this chapter and whose expertise I value, does not believe this is possible.

Antioxidants are known to be a powerful antidote to this cellular damage. They help ward off cellular damage by removing excess free radicals before they can do harm. The good news is, these antioxidants are naturally found in many foods, especially organic vegetables. So, again, with the right diet you may not need supplements.

But if you are symptomatic around EMFs or because of work/time constraints you eat processed foods or your diet is less than optimum, then supplements are very probably going to be beneficial, at least for a time.

## Antioxidants

Oxidation gets a bad rap, but our bodies require oxidation to function. However, we need to regulate this process, which we can do by taking antioxidants:

**Vitamin C**. High doses of vitamin C can strengthen your immune system and are anti-inflammatory—your body does not produce vitamin C. Naturopath David Getoff[530] recommends up to 1000 mg of Vitamin C three times a day and sometimes even more.

**Vitamin E**. Needed to help make the vitamin C work better. The softgels with all four tocopherols are a good choice.

**Astaxanthin**. A type of algae makes astaxanthin, which is used as a source for the astaxanthin used in supplements. It's important because it's known to be 550 times stronger than vitamin E and 6,000 times more potent than vitamin C.[531]

**Glutathione**. An important antioxidant that promotes the detox function of the liver. Your body produces it naturally, but less so as you age. Only the better liposomal products work well.

**Iodine tablets**. Helps the brain function properly. Can be taken in tablet or liquid form, sold as Lugol's Solution.[532]

**Vitamin D3**. Is important for so many bodily functions and risk factors that everyone needs to look into it.[533]

The best way, by far, to increase your vitamin D3 levels is exposing yourself to sunlight. According to the Vitamin D Research Council, 98% of the public are deficient in vitamin D3.[534]

530 David Getoff, EMF Experts Solutions Club interview. https://naturopath4you.com/
531 https://articles.mercola.com/vitamins-supplements/astaxanthin.aspx
532 David Getoff says he never uses more than 1-1/2 mg per day with any patient
533 David Getoff recommends a 25 (OH) vitamin D blood test and has his patients work to stay in a US lab value range of approximately 60-80ng/ml.
534 David Getoff, EMF Experts Solutions Club interview.

Here are some tips for safely boosting your vitamin D3 levels through sun exposure:

- Build up your tolerance regularly and gradually if you're not used to taking the sun
- Prefer the early morning sun, particularly if you live in hotter climes
- Aim for regular daily sunbathing—depending on where you live and the time of year, even ten minutes a day can give you the vitamin D3 you need.[535]

**The antioxidant which I take daily is olive leaf extract.** One study found that olive leaf extract can offer protection from Wi-Fi radiation.[536] Note: don't confuse this with olive oil; olive leaf extract is made from the leaves, whereas olive oil is made from the fruit.

A hundred capsules retails for about $12, Nature's Way brand. I take four tablets a day (in total), taken before breakfast and lunch.

## Other Important Supplements

**Magnesium.** Calcium and magnesium go hand in hand. EMF exposures cause a loss of calcium, which also means a loss of magnesium. You become unglued. "Magnesium will only be properly absorbed if there's a significant amount of oil and vitamin Bs in the body".[537] Magnesium is a very calming and soothing mineral, it can also be very effective to take in the evenings to help you sleep. If you don't respond well to magnesium and you feel revved up, that indicates vitamin A toxicity.[538] The suggested dosage is: 300–600 mg of magnesium citrate.[539]

**B-complex.** A combination of B vitamins that helps support the nervous system and many other bodily functions. If there is sensitivity to EMFs, then it's usually a B vitamin deficiency.[540]

**Whey protein powder.** More protein is often required to repair the damage being done by EMFs.[541]

535 http://bit.ly/vitamincouncil-vitaminD
536 https://www.ncbi.nlm.nih.gov/pubmed/23994945
537 Ann Louise Gittleman, EMF Experts Solutions Club interview.
538 Garrett Smith, EMF Experts Solutions Club interview.
539 Emma Jones, naturopath, EMF Experts Solutions Club interview.
540 Emma Jones, naturopath, EMF Experts Solutions Club interview.
541 Paul Doyon, Building Biologist, EMF Experts Solutions Club interview.

**Zinc.** Also helps reduce the damage caused by free radicals. If you are zinc-deficient, you can't utilize vitamin B6 properly. "Zinc is very much lacking in people's diets".[542]

**Melatonin**. Should only be taken for sleep issues. Take a half milligram dose of melatonin about 45 minutes before you go to bed and progressively increase your dosage until you sleep better.[543] It can also act as a powerful antioxidant—see Chapter 11.

**L-lysine**. A dose of 100–200 mg taken at night can curtail the production of nitrate oxide (free radical).[544]

Dr. Klinghardt also recommends RayWave and E shield powder from Kiscience.

These aren't necessarily the most important supplements for *you*. To know that, you would need to undergo testing. But the above list is derived from experts I've interviewed who had success treating people with these supplements or using them themselves.

## Detoxification

We live in an increasingly toxic world. Not just EMFs, but toxins are all around us in the air we breathe, the foods we eat, the soaps, shampoos and creams we put on our skin. Your body is detoxing all the time but sometimes your detox systems, like your liver, your skin, and your kidneys become overwhelmed.

Think of your toxic load like a barrel that fills up over your life. Many of us get to a point where our body gets overloaded, the barrel is full and starts to overflow. When this happens, you start to experience symptoms and eventually dis-ease if you don't do anything.

> ***Some of us are less able to detoxify than others. This is what appears to be part of the picture of why some people become EMF-sensitive and some don't.***
>
> *—Dr. Lyn Patrick, EMF Experts Solutions Club interview.*

How this toxic overload is experienced will vary from person to person. If you are symptomatic around EMFs, then unless you undertake a rigorous detox program you will most probably stay electrically sensitive. This has been my experience, and this is the overwhelming consensus from the many experts I've interviewed on this subject.

542 Andrew Tressider, EMF Experts Solutions Club interview.
543 David Getoff, EMF Experts Solutions Club interview.
544 Paul Doyon, EMF Experts Solutions Club interview.

When I became EMF sensitive, I thought the problem was all about EMFs and that I just needed to deal with the EMFs. How wrong I was. What I was experiencing was the result of a general toxin overload. The EMFs were triggering symptoms, but I had lots of toxin issues.

> ***I think it's possible to have EMF exposure that leads to EHS, but I think in most of the cases I ever talked to, have had mold exposure or pesticide exposure, something concrete that they don't realize. And that is making the cells sick, the membrane's impaired, and then yielding sensitivity to EMF.***
>
> *—DR. LISA NAGY, EMF EXPERTS SOLUTIONS CLUB INTERVIEW.*

Which kind of brings us full circle. Remember when I went to my doctor and he said it was stress? In a way he was right. It just wasn't the kind of stress he was meaning.

> ***If you think of the EMFs as a stress, there's a lot of evidence to show that EMFs tend to cause the same stress chemical reaction in the body as emotional stress, physical stress from heat, heat shock proteins, all the different chemical stress... I see it is a total stress load.***
>
> *—MICHAEL SCHWAEBE, EMF EXPERTS SOLUTIONS CLUB INTERVIEW.*

Unfortunately, most EMF sufferers just focus on the EMFs. Sometimes they become obsessive about EMFs and lose sight of this general toxin problem. The way to deal with this general toxin issue is detox. In most cases it's a long process. It took me years to detox. In some cases, it's quite complicated because as much as we detox we need to replenish, so it can be a balancing act.

An excellent resource on dealing with EMFs through nutrition is the book *Zapped* by Ann Louise Gittleman, which goes into more detail on a lot of what I've talked about here and even offers meal plans.

## Getting Help

Nutrition and detox can be a minefield. Ideally, this is best done with a professional who has experience with detox protocols who can run some tests and help you with a personally tailored detox regime.

This might be:

- A functional medicine doctor
- A nutritional balancing practitioner
- A naturopath
- A Board Certified Clinical Nutritionist (CCN).

Many of these practitioners now consult online, so you don't need to live near one of these specialists to benefit from their services.

There are various on-line courses that can help you. Naturopath David Getoff has some excellent resources on his website.[545]

Heavy metal toxicity deserves a special mention here.

## Metal Toxicity

Dr. Lyn Patrick and many physicians, like Dr. Belpomme, who treat electrical hyper-sensitivity confirm that people with high levels of metals in their body are the most sensitive to EMFs.

**Experts are also talking about the antenna effect of metals, whereby metals can work literally as an antenna and trigger your immune system.**[546]

Many people's immune systems are already severely challenged, it doesn't take much to take them over the edge and lead them on a path of dis-ease. Metal toxicity can be diagnosed with some inexpensive tests and metal chelation protocols used to detoxify metals.

Oral health is a big issue here. Most metal amalgams contain mercury. Although they appear solid, these amalgams release mercury vapor pretty much constantly.[547] Worse still, Wi-Fi (and most probably cell phones also) cause more mercury vapor to be released.[548] Mercury, one of the most potent neurotoxins known to man, can then work its way into your brain causing untold damage.

545 https://naturopath4you.com/
546 Peter Sullivan, EMF Experts Solutions Club interview.
547 https://www.fda.gov/medical-devices/dental-amalgam/about-dental-amalgam-fillings
548 https://www.fda.gov/medical-devices/dental-amalgam/about-dental-amalgam-fillings

***People with metal amalgams literally have a conductive battery effect in their mouths between different metal amalgams and their saliva—which can be measured.***[549]

Even if you have gold or nickel fillings, it makes a lot of sense to replace them with ceramic or zirconia fillings, preferably by a holistic dentist. To find a practitioner near you, contact the International Academy of Oral Medicine and Toxicology[550] or the Holistic Dental Association.[551]

For metal detox, Dr. Klinghardt[552] recommends:

- Ionic footbath: 30 minutes three times per week
- Sauna therapy: at least five minutes daily sweating
- KiScience Detox powder: one teaspoon twice a day
- Coriandolo Plus: two dropperfuls three times daily, before meals (Kiscience)
- Polmolo: two dropperfuls three times per day (Kiscience).

For binders (used to speed up the process of elimination) alternate between:

- Zeolite: half a teaspoon three times a day away from meals (Biopure)
- Chlorella: (15–20 tablespoons three times per day) between meals (Biopure).

Other avenues to explore when considering toxicity levels are chemicals, pesticides, mold, lyme, food allergies and pathogens (viruses, bacteria, fungi, protozoa, and worms).

## Less Obvious Forms Of EMF Protection

**Deep breathing.** I spoke before (Chapter 3) about how important sufficient oxygen is to your cells. The only natural way to increase the oxygen levels in the body is through breathing. There's loads of great videos on YouTube which show simple but effective breathing exercises.

**Exercise.** You don't have to run a marathon. A daily 30-minute vigorous walk will stimulate your body in so many ways and naturally oxygenate your cells. If you

549 Dr. Carey O'Rielly, EMF Experts Solutions Club interview.
550 https://iaomt.org/
551 https://holisticdental.org/
552 As recommended by Dr. Dietrich Klinghardt on the 5G Crisis Summit.

can manage something a bit more aerobic, like jogging or swimming, better still. The important thing is regularity—I exercise every day.

**Meditation.** A lot of people think meditation is not for them or they haven't got time. Make time. EMFs stresses our bodies in so many ways, meditation is an incredibly powerful way of de-stressing and bringing your mind and body into more of a healing state. There are so many great resources on meditation (the Dr. Joe Dispenza books and the Dr. Wayne Dyer books are both very good) or perhaps you can work with someone locally. I meditate daily.

**Joy.** If we all set our minds and our hearts to experience joy and share joy, the world would be a better place. If you are struggling to deal with the effects of EMFs on your health, then it might seem as though there is not much to be joyful about. But there is, don't forget, you are in control of what you think and feel and what you focus on. Make sure you keep focusing on joy and what brings joy into your life.

**Spend time in nature.** Think disconnect-reconnect. The more you can disconnect, get away from EMFs and connect with nature, the better. Forests, beaches, lakes are all ideal places to reconnect with nature, even if wireless is present there too. If you live in a city, make regular use of the local park.

You might be thinking, how can all this mind-body stuff possibly protect me from EMFs? I assure you it can because mind-body work directly affects your cells,[553] remember that's where EMFs are impacting you.

A few last words about sleep because it is sooo important.

## More Sleep Tips

Help your body establish a natural healthy sleep pattern by doing the following:

1. **Keep a regular sleep schedule.** Try to go to bed and get up at approximately the same time each day to stimulate your circadian rhythm. If you need to change these times, help your body adjust by making the change in small daily increments, such as 15 minutes earlier or later each day.
2. **Take a siesta to make up for lost sleep.** If you need to make up for lost sleep, instead of sleeping late, take a daytime nap. I find a five- or ten-minute nap can really recharge my batteries.

553 Joe Dispenza, 2014. *You Are The Placebo.*

3. **Create a relaxing bedtime routine.** In the hour before bedtime, do things that cause minimal mental and emotional turmoil, and avoid excessive noise.
4. **Avoid drinking too much liquid in the evening.** Avoid caffeinated drinks, tea, coffee, and soda in the two or three hours before bedtime. Strong coffee can take more than six hours to work through your system.

My preference is for natural solutions. But if your symptoms are extreme, then studies show that you can get effective relief by taking calcium channel blockers.[554] These are prescription drugs so you would need to see a doctor for this. Keep in mind, this is a Band-Aid solution; it doesn't treat the root cause of the problem. If you are symptomatic around EMFs, you need to focus on identifying and dealing with the root cause of your symptoms, which is best done with a medical professional.

Here's what you need to retain from this chapter:

- There are lots of things we can do nutritionally to repair EMF damage on our bodies, top of the list is optimal hydration
- Antioxidants are a powerful antidote to the cellular damage caused by EMFs, organic vegetables are a good natural source
- Vitamin D3 is one of the most powerful antioxidants—just ten minutes sunbathing a day can give you all you need
- If you are symptomatic around EMFs, this suggests your body is overloaded with toxins and you need to detox—in parallel with EMF mitigation
- Nutrition and detox can be a minefield—this is best done with a medical professional who can give you a personally tailored detox regime
- Physicians who treat electrical hypersensitivity confirm that people with high levels of metals are the most sensitive to EMFs—this can be easily tested and treated
- Less obvious forms of EMF protection are deep breathing and meditation—both can be used in different ways to greatly improve your cellular health.

554 https://www.ncbi.nlm.nih.gov/pmc/articles/PMC3780531/

## Chapter 21

# Enjoying The Ride

You've probably realized, if you didn't know already, that what we call health is directly related to the health of your cells and the ability of your cells to communicate effectively.

Mainstream science views this as a biochemical process. Which is true, in part. But first and foremost, it's an electrical process because all these chemical changes derive from the movement of electrons in your cells at the molecular level.

What has the power to disrupt and distort this movement of electrons? Yes, EMFs. Be they wired or wireless, whether emitted by your cell phone, Wi-Fi router, smart meter or electrical wiring, be they electric fields, magnetic fields or dirty electricity.

This disruption and distortion lead to biological effects, many of which are adverse. There are thousands of studies that support this. Then, downstream of these bio affects, are the myriad of chronic diseases and conditions that I've talked about, like cancer, that are linked to these exposures.

At one time it seemed hardly a day went by when I didn't discover that EMFs could impact our health in some new, never discovered before, way. And there is more to discover, particularly with respect to the synergy between EMF exposures and other toxins. Between EMFs and glyphosate[555] , and between and EMFs and air pollution, a lot remains to be said and, yes, more studies need to be done.

But more studies do NOT need to be done to start taking action to protect yourself. And this is my sincere hope that you take action to protect yourself because as I've laid out there are so many ways you can do this.

EMFs have got a grip on our lives, our economies, and our societies like nothing else. This is coming to a head with the roll-out of 5G. For those only listening to the propaganda from the telecom industry, it would seem stupid not to fully embrace

555 Glyphosate, commonly found in Roundup, also triggers the body to make peroxynitrite

this amazing new technology. But with the information I've laid out in this guide, I hope you will be able to make a more informed choice.

Ultimately, this is about more than just creating a healthy home and work environment. It's about creating a better world for all of us, a sort of enlightenment.

Taking the path of EMF enlightenment means understanding AND acting on the information I've laid out on these pages, which comes down to the choices you make. Some of these choices are going to be tough. Telling your boss about the dangers of Wi-Fi, telling your kids they can only use a cell phone for a few minutes a day, telling your partner you want to sleep with the power off to the bedroom. Also, choices about what you spend your money on. Our lives are being hijacked by corporations that do not have our best interests at heart, that are, in some cases, ruthlessly seeking profits at any cost. Are you supporting and feeding this system? Do you have the latest cell phone, do you have a fancy car, are you constantly replacing things that work perfectly well and don't need replacing?

That's not to say you can't have the latest cell phone or home entertainment system, but spend your money responsibly. Use these technologies safely, don't let them take over your life and define who you are. Be mindful of the consequences.

Unfortunately, I've noticed most people don't get it until they've got it. That's to say they don't understand the consequences until they experience it themselves. If you're not symptomatic, the challenge for you is to take action NOW to prevent yourself from becoming electrically hypersensitive (EHS), to prevent EMFs from impacting your quality of life, or causing some other dis-ease. I've shared solutions in the format of easy/intermediate/advanced. Focus first on applying the easy solutions in each chapter and stay mindful of the fact that even if you can't feel anything that EMFs are still harming you.

If you are EHS, the challenge is to NOT stop believing in your body's ability to heal and your own personal power. Despite once being electrically hypersensitive and not being able to use computers and electronics, not being able to go out and about and travel without experiencing debilitating symptoms, I can now do all of this.

My journey back to health was achieved by doing most, but not all, of what I've laid out in this guide.

I was (am) lucky. One day I was suddenly able to feel what EMFs were doing to my body. When this happened, it felt like a burden, an unbearable one. Gradually, I started to accept what was happening to me and listen to my body. Over time I came to realize what a blessing this "sensitivity" was (is).

I've shared a lot of science because I know for a lot of you reading this, particularly those of you who are not symptomatic around EMFs, this is important. Reading and learning the science helped me to understand why I was experiencing symptoms. But dwelling on this too much can work against you as well and put you in a state of overwhelm.

Here are some pointers if you are EHS:

- Keep working on the EMF mitigation
- Keep believing that you can heal
- Keep a supportive network of family/close friends around you
- Keep enjoying life
- Keep bouncing back from apparent setbacks.

Also, perhaps most importantly, keep listening to your intuition, because this is where your personal power lies.

We're in a culture where we are encouraged to be in our heads a lot, thinking and analyzing. But, particularly if your health is challenged, this can cause a lot of stress. What you need to do is just the opposite, follow and trust your intuition. How can you do this?

**Learn to trust yourself and learn to feel when something feels right.**

This feeling part is key. I don't mean physically touching, I mean feeling a situation or a course of action. It's following this intuition, cultivating this natural intelligence, which is the fastest path to healing.

This is a process. It takes time. You can nurture this process by being more observant. Are there things you do in your day that leave you feeling drained and others that leave you feeling full of energy? Pursue interests that inspire you and energize you. Yoga and meditation for instance (see the resources I shared in Chapter 20).

We've covered a lot of ground here. Be kind to yourself because you won't be able to do everything straight away. So just keep ticking as many boxes as possible. Keep moving forward. Keep enjoying the ride.

# About The Author

One day in 2002 Lloyd Burrell answered his cell phone and soon after developed highly debilitating symptoms from all types of electromagnetic devices in his home and workplace. He went to multiple medical professionals who couldn't help him. For two years he lived in a state of doubt, fear, and denial. He tried to carry on a normal life and pretend his symptoms didn't exist.

Lloyd wasted thousands on solutions that didn't work. It took him nearly 10 years to recover his health.  Going through all those years of pain...tens of thousands of dollars in expenses...and the heartache of feeling alone and that no one understood... has given him a unique approach to dealing with EMFs.

He has now made it his life's mission to raise awareness about the dangers of electromagnetic fields (EMF) and share the remarkable discoveries he's made on his journey.

Lloyd is a regular speaker at on-line events, podcasts, radio shows and hosts his own bi-monthly EMF-Health podcast. He is the author of two eBooks on EMFs, creator of the EMF Health Summit and founder of the website ElectricSense.com.

Lloyd is married with 2 grown up children and lives in sunny South West France.